The Bounds of Cognition

The Bounds of Cognition

Frederick Adams and
Kenneth Aizawa

BLACKWELL PUBLISHING
350 Main Street, Malden, MA 02148-5020, USA
9600 Garsington Road, Oxford OX4 2DQ, UK
550 Swanston Street, Carlton, Victoria 3053, Australia

First published 2008 by Blackwell Publishing Ltd

1   2008

Library of Congress Cataloging-in-Publication Data

Adams, Frederick.
    The bounds of cognition / Frederick Adams and Kenneth Aizawa.
        p. cm.
    Includes bibliographical references and index.
    ISBN 978-1-4051-4914-3 (hardcover : alk. paper)   1. Cognition—Philosophy.   2. Philosophy
and cognitive science.   I. Aizawa, Kenneth, 1961–   II. Title.

    BF311.A297 2008
    121—dc22

                                                2007024734

A catalogue record for this title is available from the British Library.

Set in 10.5 on 13 pt Minion
by SNP Best-set Typesetter Ltd., Hong Kong
Printed and bound in Singapore
by Utopia Press Pte Ltd

For further information on
Blackwell Publishing, visit our website:
www.blackwellpublishing.com

Contents

Preface   vii
Acknowledgments   xii

1   Introduction   1

2   Refining the Issues   16
   2.1 What are the Boundaries?   16
   2.2 What is Cognition?   22
   2.3 The Possibility of Extended Cognition   25
   2.4 Conclusion   29

3   Original Content   31
   3.1 Part of the Mark of the Cognitive:
        Non-Derived Content   32
   3.2 The Basics on Derived and Underived Content   35
   3.3 Dennett's Critique of Original Content   39
   3.4 Clark's Critique of Original Content   46
   3.5 Anti-Representationalism in Dynamical Systems
        and Mobile Robotics   51
   3.6 Conclusion   55

4   Cognitive Processes   57
   4.1 Individuating Process Types in Science   58
   4.2 Individuating Processes in Cognitive Psychology   60
   4.3 A Broader Category of Cognition   70
   4.4 Conclusion   74

5   The Mark of the Cognitive, Extended
    Cognition Style   76
    5.1 Cognition as Information Processing, as Computation,
         and as Abiding in the Meaningful   76
    5.2 Operationalism   79
    5.3 Is This Merely a Terminological Issue?   83
    5.4 Conclusion   85

6   The Coupling-Constitution Fallacy   88
    6.1 Some Examples of the Coupling-Constitution Fallacy   93
    6.2 Replies to the Coupling-Constitution Fallacy   99
    6.3 Conclusion   105

7   Extended Cognitive Systems and Extended
    Cognitive Processes   106
    7.1 Dynamical Systems Theory and Coupling   107
    7.2 Haugeland's Theory of Systems and the Coupling of
         Components   112
    7.3 Clark's Theories of Systems and Coupling   119
    7.4 Conclusion   130

8   Cognitive Equivalence, Complementarity,
    and Evolution   133
    8.1 Cognitive Equivalence   133
    8.2 The Complementarity Argument   143
    8.3 Evolutionary Arguments   147
    8.4 Conclusion: The Importance of the Mark
         of the Cognitive   150

9   Inference to the Best Explanation and
    Extended Cognition   152
    9.1 What is the Theory of Enactive Perception?   153
    9.2 Noë's Evidence for Enactive Perception   156
    9.3 The Case against Enactive Perception: Paralysis   166
    9.4 Conclusion   172

10 Future Directions   174

Bibliography   180
Index   187

Preface

This book came about adventitiously. Some time in the early summer of 1998 or so, Fred came across a paper by Andy Clark and David Chalmers, advancing what seemed to us to be the outrageous hypothesis that, at least at times, cognitive processes extend into the tools people use. Fred thought we should jump on this right away, because it was definitely a new idea. Ken thought the idea was preposterous and not so very convincingly argued, so that there must be something better to write about. But, as both of us continued to read a bit more on the topic, we were surprised to discover that the idea was gaining some momentum. We were amazed to find how many other philosophers and psychologists seemed to support the idea that cognitive processing is not brain bound. These included Dan Dennett, Merlin Donald, John Haugeland, Edwin Hutchins, Robert Port, and Tim van Gelder. This persuaded both of us that the topic of extended cognition deserved our critical attention.

Within a few weeks our first paper on the topic, "The bounds of cognition," was completed and under review. Eventually, it appeared in 2001. By June of 2001, the idea of extended cognition had grown large enough to inspire Richard Menary to organize the first Extended Mind conference at the University of Hertfordshire. Having by then read our paper, Andy Clark took us to task for our views on intrinsic content and the nature of science, among other things. That critique supports the old saying that there is no such thing as bad press. Andy's criticism got our paper noticed in the extended cognition literature. Indeed, we became two of the representatives of the benighted cognitive science orthodoxy.

Richard was among those Andy got interested in our paper – not that Richard believed a word of what we said, however. By the summer of 2003,

Richard was assembling a collection of essays on extended cognition based on the papers presented at that first Extended Mind conference. Since Andy's paper included some replies to our "Bounds" paper, Richard proposed to have us to reply to Andy's paper, and in turn have Andy reply to us. A critical exchange seemed to us to be a great idea and we enthusiastically accepted Richard's invitation. So, some time in the fall of 2003, we managed to finish our reply to Clark and braced ourselves for the return salvo.

In a separate development, by the summer of 2003 Phil Robbins and Murat Aydede managed to get wind of our "Bounds" paper. They were assembling a collection of essays on situated cognition and invited us to contribute a paper on extended cognition. This also sounded good to us, so that by the fall of 2003 we had actually completed a draft of a third paper on extended cognition.

The following year and a half seemed to show only an increase in the interest in, and support for, this crazy hypothesis of extended cognition. There were, of course, the collections of papers being assembled by Menary and by Robbins and Aydede, but there were also papers that responded critically to "Bounds," either in passing or in detail. The latter included a paper by Tarja Susi, Jessica Lindblom, and Tom Ziemke, two more papers by Andy (!), and another forthcoming paper by Richard. Then there were new books defending some version of extended cognition. Rob Wilson's book *The Boundaries of the Mind* appeared in 2004, as did Alva Noë's *Action in Perception* and Larry Shapiro's *The Mind Incarnate*. We also found out that Teed Rockwell had a forthcoming book supporting his version of extended cognition. Raymond Gibbs also had a forthcoming book on embodied cognition. Richard himself was then circulating a book proposal on the topic as well. Since, as far as we could tell, the craziness was still gathering steam, the natural thing to do was for us to write a book of our own.

To begin with, we believed we needed to put forth a positive picture of what cognition is and why one should believe that it is typically brain bound. Our view should seem quite familiar, since it seems to articulate some of the most basic presuppositions of contemporary cognitive psychology. Although we do not want to attach any philosophical or scientific weight to the matter, we think the view expresses orthodoxy in cognitive psychology. We maintain that cognitive processes use particular kinds of mechanisms that operate on specific kinds of mental representations. This is more of an outline for distinguishing between cognitive processes and non-cognitive processes than it is a full-blown theory of cognition. What we want, for present purposes, is not a theory of cognition *per se* but a proposal that is sufficiently detailed that it enables us to explain why the cognitive processes we encounter on a daily basis are typically brain bound, rather than spread over brain, body, and environment. Though we may eventually offer more detailed theory of what we believe cognitive processes are like, for now such a more detailed theory runs the risk of inviting challenges to the positive theory of cognition rather than facilitating the recognition of what we take to be the real bounds of cognition. In other words, we develop only about as much of our positive view of cognition as we think we need in order to keep cognitive psychology on track.

In addition to a positive view of what cognition is, we found that we needed to synthesize and organize many of the leading ideas in the rapidly growing extended cognition literature. We had to develop a critical view of what extended cognition was all about, the kinds of reasons that have been given in its support, and why one should be skeptical of these reasons. Here is a thumbnail sketch of the view.

The hypothesis of extended cognition maintains that cognitive processing spans the boundaries of brain, body, and environment. The most frequently encountered kind of argument for this view begins with observations about the causal roles that bodily and environmental processes play in human behavior, and then tacitly infers from these observations that the bodily and environmental processes are themselves cognitive processes. One familiar example draws attention to the extensive interaction one has with pencil and paper when using them to compute the sums of large numbers. Don't these interactions give us good reason to think that the use of pencil and paper is an instance in which cognitive processing extends into the tools we use? We think not – and this is the primary shortcoming in the extended cognition literature. Just because a process Y interacts with a cognitive process does not mean that Y is itself also a (part of a) cognitive process. We argue that this kind of reasoning is fallacious; it is what we have called the "coupling-constitution fallacy."

Abetting this fallacious inference is a second shortcoming of the extended cognition literature: insufficient attention to what makes a process cognitive. By largely ignoring what it means for something to be cognitive, or by advancing a loose conception of the cognitive, one can make the hypothesis of extended cognition seem more plausible. To take an example we will repeat later, if you think that cognitive processing is simply any old kind of information processing, then it should not be a surprise that you can adopt the hypothesis of extended cognition. After all, information is practically ubiquitous and human interaction through the body and with the environment brings about the uptake and transformation of that information. Right away, such uptake and transformation get to be extended cognition. The point is not so much to take anyone to task for endorsing such a simplistic theory of cognition; it is to draw attention to the need for a more sophisticated theory. That is one way in which inattention to what we frequently call "the mark of the cognitive" leads to confusion. This same inattention abets another leading argument for extended cognition. In the literature, it is frequently observed that the information processing capacities of tools augment or complement the information processing capacities of the brain, as when using pencil and paper helps us in computing the sums of large numbers. This is, of course, correct. This complementary relationship between brains and tools, however, is supposed to support the view that cognitive processing extends into these complementary devices. There is a move from complementarity to extended cognition. But, of course, a compressor and an expansion coil have complementary roles to play in air conditioners, although this provides no reason to think that a compressor is an expansion coil or vice versa. Nor does it provide any reason to think that the kind of process that occurs in a compressor is the same kind of process that takes place in an evaporation coil, or vice versa. Here again, without attending to the mark of the cognitive, it is much easier to overlook this problem.

A third shortcoming is insufficient attention to the difference between an extended cognitive system hypothesis that says that the human brain, body, and environment form a cognitive system and the extended cognition hypothesis that says that cognitive processing extends from the brain into the body and environment. While causal connections among objects might suffice for configuring those objects into a system, it is not at all clear that one can get from the truth of a cognitive system hypothesis to the extended cognition hypothesis. After all, there are many X systems in which X processing does not pervade the whole of the system. Not all the parts of a computing system compute. Computing takes place in the central processing unit, but probably not in the fan or cathode ray tube.

We would be perfectly happy if the advocates of extended cognition were to see the wisdom of our ways and either abandon the view or move on to others. But, of course, that won't happen. We are sure that advocates of extended cognition will press on. So, we hope that our criticism will at least be constructive criticism for them. We hope that they will take our criticisms as genuine challenges that need to be addressed. We have tried to be as careful and sympathetic as possible in interpreting what the hypothesis of extended cognition is supposed to be and what arguments are being offered on its behalf. We have also provided a large number of detailed references and quotations to bolster our analyses. Finally, we have tried to be as explicit as possible about what we assume and why we assume it. Of course, in giving arguments in a finite text, we will have to use some premises that are not themselves explicitly justified by arguments in the text. By and large, however, we have tried to use only premises that we think are shared by those in the extended cognition camp.

Frederick Adams and Kenneth Aizawa

Acknowledgments

In trying to find some common argumentative ground with the fans of extended cognition, we have benefited from the numerous comments and replies to our work. Our philosophical friends include Colin Allen, Murat Aydede, John Barker, John Bickle, Dave Chalmers, Jeff Dean, Fred Dretske, Ray Elugardo, Carl Gillett, Sanford Goldberg, Tom Polger, Joel Pust, Phil Robbins, Mark Rowlands, Rob Rupert, Larry Shapiro, and Rob Wilson. We are especially grateful for Andy's critical responses to our papers and for Richard's invitation to participate in the second Extended Mind conference at the University of Hertfordshire in July 2006. We always love traveling to England, but it is even better when we get to talk about the philosophical issues that are on our front burner. We might also interject that, without bold thinkers – such as Andy, Richard, and others – willing to venture crazy and outrageous hypotheses, we natural-born critics would not have had the opportunity to advance the issues in the debate and in this book. Regardless of who turns out to be correct, we think we are all getting clearer on the nature of cognition, and on what it takes to demonstrate when processes and systems are cognitive and why.

On a more formal note, we are grateful for permission to reuse some material that has appeared, or will appear, in other writings: to the Journal of Philosophy, Incorporated, for permission to use material from Aizawa's "Understanding the embodiment of perception," *Journal of Philosophy*, 104, 5–25; to Taylor and Francis for permission to use material from our collaborative papers, "The bounds of cognition," *Philosophical Psychology*, 14, 43–64, and "Defending non-derived content," *Philosophical Psychology*, 118, 661–9 (accessible online through http://www.informaworld.com); to Cambridge University Press for permission to reprint material from our

"Why the mind is still in the head," to appear in P. Robbins and M. Aydede (eds.), *Cambridge Handbook of Situated Cognition*; and to Ashgate Publishing for permission to reprint material from our "Defending the bounds of cognition," to appear in R. Menary (ed), *The Extended Mind*, Aldershot, Hants: Ashgate.

Finally, we would like to thank our editor, Jeff Dean, our copy editor, Geoffrey Palmer, and the cover design team at Blackwell for their excellent support in the production of this text. We hope our philosophical views live up to their standards.

F.A. and K.A.

Chapter 1

Introduction

In the *Monadology*, Wilhelm Gottfried Leibniz claimed that

> 7. Further, there is no way of explaining how a Monad can be altered or changed in its inner being by any other created thing, since there is no possibility of transposition within it, nor can we conceive of any internal movement which can be produced, directed, increased, or diminished there within the substance, such as can take place in the case of composites where a chance can occur among the parts. The Monads have no windows through which anything may come in or go out. The attributes are not liable to detach themselves and make an excursion outside the substance, as could *sensible species* of the Schoolmen. In the same way neither substance nor attribute can enter from without into a Monad. (Leibniz, 1979, pp. 251–2)

The Leibnizian idea is that monads, or minds, do not causally interact with things outside of themselves. They are, as we might say, closed causal systems. Instead, the apparent causal relations between one monad and the rest of creation are simply due to the infinite power of God to pre-establish a harmony among the internal workings of individual monads so that they *appear* to causally interact.

It is an understatement, however, to say that few philosophers or psychologists these days take seriously the idea that human or animal minds work as do Leibnizian monads.[1] The orthodox view in cognitive science

---

[1] Rockwell (2005), however, suggests that this claim is somehow surprising or controversial: "But – and here is the punchline – the causal nexus that is responsible for the experiences of a conscious being is *not* contained entirely within the brain of that being" (Rockwell, 2005, p. 58).

maintains that minds do interact with their bodies and their environments. Cognitive processes within brains are not causally isolated from the rest of the world. Cognitive processing depends on the environment in ways too numerous to mention. The developing fetal brain can be poisoned by maternal alcohol consumption. Dense congenital cataracts can impair the development of normal visual processing, especially during a critical or sensitive period of child development. Years of practicing the violin can shape the amount of cortical material dedicated to representation of the fingers of the left hand. Humans and other animals causally interact with the world in order to perceive it by vision, olfaction, and audition. Cognitive processes are influenced by low oxygen concentrations at high altitudes and high nitrogen concentrations at great underwater depths. Cognitive processes are also influenced by any number of psychoactive drugs from alcohol to nicotine to Δ^9-tetrahydrocannabinol. Cognitive processes clearly depend on the body and environment. In short, contemporary cognitive psychology is anti-Leibnizian: cognitive processes do causally depend on bodily and environmental processes.

Under the influence of the phenomenological tradition in philosophy, dynamical systems theory, and mobile robotics, the extended cognition movement has sought to move beyond mere anti-Leibnizianism. The extended cognition movement maintains that cognitive processes depend on bodily and environmental processes, but not merely causally. It is not just that bodily and environmental processes causally influence cognitive processes; they literally constitute or realize cognitive processes. Cognitive processes do not occur exclusively within brains; they span brains, bodies, and environments. Cognitive processes extend from brains into their surrounding bodies and physical environs. A handful of examples will illustrate the kinds of cases used to challenge orthodoxy.

A common method for finding the product of 347 and 957 is to write the problem down on a piece of paper, aligning the "3" in the hundreds place of the first numeral with the "9" in the hundreds place in the second numeral, aligning the "4" in the tens place of the first numeral with the "5" in the tens place of the second numeral, and so on.[2] This facilitates the application of the partial products algorithm in several ways. Since the numbers are written one above the other, one can rely on vision to keep

---

[2]   This kind of example appears in Clark and Chalmers (1998, p. 8) and Gibbs (2001, pp. 117–18).

the ones, tens, and hundreds places coordinated. One does not have to devote special attention or burden memory in order to accomplish this coordination. In addition, since one can write down a number that has to be carried above the column to which it will be carried, this removes the burden of remembering the number to be carried. Further, by recording one's work on paper at each step, one is spared the task of remembering where one is in the calculation and the results of past bits of computation. It is because the use of pencil and paper generally provides a faster and more reliable method of computing the products of large numbers that one so frequently turns to it.

Surely the best known example in the extended cognition literature is the Inga–Otto thought experiment, developed by Clark and Chalmers (1998). In this story, Inga is a normal human subject who hears from a friend that there is an interesting exhibit at the Museum of Modern Art and decides to go see it. She thinks for a moment before recalling that MOMA is on 53rd Street, and then sets off for 53rd Street. In contrast to Inga, Otto suffers from Alzheimer's disease and has numerous memory lapses. To help him compensate, he must rely upon cues in his environment. In order to handle addresses, Otto relies on a notebook in which he writes this kind of information. Thus, when he hears his friends talking about the interesting exhibit at the Museum of Modern Art, he reaches for his notebook to look up the address. Finding that the museum is on 53rd Street, he sets off.

Other examples involve the role of the body and movement in cognitive life.[3] During the course of normal human activity, the head and eyes typically move through space. This happens any time a person walks, drives a car, or turns her head. During these activities, the light entering the eye carries information about the relative distances of objects. The light projected from more distant objects changes differently than does the light projected from less distant objects. In a simple case, there is what occurs when one fixates on objects on the distant horizon. Here, nearer objects appear to be displaced farther in the direction opposite to the motion than do more distant objects. Humans are extraordinarily good at using this motion parallax as a guide to the relative distances of objects. As vision scientists often put it, motion parallax is a powerful monocular cue for relative depth.

---

[3] These are the kinds of examples that appear in Noë (2004), Rowlands (1999), and Hurley (1998, forthcoming).

One hypothesis concerning these cases is that they are all instances in which human cognitive processes in the brain take advantage of non-cognitive tools found in the body and environment. On this orthodox construal of tool use, humans have a more or less stable set of cognitive capacities for learning, remembering, perceiving, and attending. Learning and training make for greater or lesser degrees of stability. Learning and training can yield dramatic changes in the cognitive processes involved in such abilities as playing a violin, tasting fine wine, and speaking natural languages. In many situations, however, humans do not seek to modify their cognitive apparatus. Instead, they live with the cognitive mechanisms they have and complement them with tools that enable them to compensate for their cognitive shortcomings. It is because of limitations on human short-term memory that humans use pencil and paper for computing the products of large numbers. Because the information about whether or not to carry a one is on the paper, it need not be kept in memory. Because of the alignment of the columns of numerals on the page, one need pay less attention to being sure that tens are added to tens and hundreds are added to hundreds. In the Inga–Otto case, the reason Otto uses the notebook to store information is obviously that his long-term memory is failing him. He lacks the normal memory resources that Inga possesses. The notebook enables him to compensate for this lack. Otto's use of the notebook is not exactly like Inga's use of normal long-term memory. The notebook is a tool that he uses, in conjunction with his spared cognitive capacities of seeing, reading, and writing, in order to achieve some tolerable level of functionality. The different ways in which bodily motions influence the play of light from objects near and far is a potentially useful tool for determining relative distance. Humans use this tool, among many others, because they cannot directly perceive the relative distance of objects.[4]

Recent work advancing the hypothesis of extended cognition offers radically new and different analyses of these cases. Advocates of extended cognition complain that orthodox cognitive science is in the grip of a picture of the locus of cognition. Orthodoxy maintains, without justification, so the story goes, that cognitive processing occurs within the brain. Advocates of extended cognition take the foregoing cases to show, or make

---

[4]   Gibson (1979) maintained that humans can directly perceive the things that their environments provided for them. Humans can directly perceive affordances. Not to beg the question against Gibson, who has inspired many in the extended cognition camp, we might assume that the relative distance of objects in the environment is not an affordance.

plausible, the view that cognitive processing literally extends from the brain into the bodily and environmental tools that humans exploit. The manipulation of pencil and paper in the computation of large products becomes a literal part of one's cognitive processing. The notes in the notebook that Otto keeps with him constantly constitute part of Otto's memory and the physical basis of part of his stock of beliefs. The use many animals make of bodily motions to induce motion parallax constitute part of their perceptual processing. In short, according to the hypothesis of extended cognition, the tools many organisms use (often) become part of their cognitive processors. This view is so radical that one might well be skeptical that anyone really means to assert such a thing. Yet there are many clear and simple assertions of it:

> Cognitive processes span the brain, the body, and the environment. (van Gelder and Port, 1995b, p. ix)

> Cognitive processes are not located exclusively inside the skin of cognizing organisms. (Rowlands, 1999, p. 22)

> What I am claiming is that not only thoughts, *but also feelings and sensations*, must be seen as supervening on the entire brain–body–world nexus. (Rockwell, 2005, p. 71)

> Cognitive processes are partly constituted by physical and bodily movements and manipulations of objects in real-world environments. (Gibbs, 2006, p. 12)[5]

Not satisfied with noting the causal dependencies between cognition and bodily and worldly processes – not satisfied with simply rejecting Leibnizian monadology – the advocates of extended cognition champion a constitutive dependency.

What motivates this bold new hypothesis? In our reading of the literature, we have come across essentially five distinct types of arguments for the hypothesis of extended cognition. The most pervasive type focuses attention on the way in which structures outside of the brain causally interact with parts of the body and external world. We group these arguments under a broad category of "coupling arguments." They invoke one or another type of causal connection or coupling relation between the brain and the body/external world in order to make the case that the non-brain

---

[5]   See also Rowlands (2003, ch. 9) and Wilson (2004, p. 195).

components should be understood as realizing cognitive processes. According to Mark Rowlands,

> cognitive processes are not located exclusively inside the skin of cognizing organisms because such processes are, in part, made up of physical or bodily *manipulation* of structures in the environments of such organisms. (Rowlands, 1999, p. 23)

The psychologist Raymond Gibbs, discussing intentions rather than cognitive processing *per se*, reasons in essentially the same way:

> The windsurfer continually affects and is affected by the set of the rig, so the behavioral intention to successfully windsurf emerges as a result of the interaction between the person and environment. Focusing on the agent alone, or on how the agent responds to the environment, fails to capture the complex nuances of windsurfing behavior. Just as it is important to understand the significance of paper and pencil when one does long division, where the cognition of doing long division is in part "offloaded" into the environment, the intentionality in windsurfing is best understood as a distributed cognitive behavior involving a person, a device, and the environment. (Gibbs, 2001, pp. 117–18)

These examples are among the more succinct presentations of this argument.[6]

Another type of argument might be thought of as a version of a coupling argument. These arguments begin by drawing attention to causal connections between the brain and parts of the body or environment, but then, rather than concluding that cognition extends into these parts of the body or environment, they conclude that the brain and the body, and perhaps the environment, constitute a cognitive system. They conclude that there is an extended cognitive system. From this conclusion, there is a tacit shift to the conclusion that cognitive processing extends from the brain into the body and the environment. Part of Haugeland's articulation of embodied and embedded cognition involves this two-step argumentation.[7] Clark and Chalmers may also have some version of this in mind.

---

[6]   Cf., in addition, Clark (2001, p. 132), Clark (2002, pp. 23–4), Wilson (2004, p. 194), Noë (2004, pp. 220 and 221), Rockwell (2005, p. 46), and Menary (2006, p. 331).
[7]   Haugeland (1998, pp. 208–9).

After describing some examples where they believe there is extended cognition, they write

> In these cases, the human organism is linked with an external entity in a two-way interaction, creating a *coupled system* that can be seen as a cognitive system in its own right. All the components in the system play an active causal role, and they jointly govern behavior in the same sort of way that cognition usually does. If we remove the external component the system's behavioral competence will drop, just as it would if we removed part of its brain. Our thesis is that this sort of coupled process counts equally well as a cognitive process, whether or not it is wholly in the head. (Clark and Chalmers, 1998, pp. 8–9)

Notice that Clark and Chalmers move from a claim about a brain and an external object constituting a cognitive system – the cognitive system hypothesis – to the claim that cognitive processing is not wholly in the head – the extended cognition hypothesis. That is, the argument has the implicit two-step structure we mentioned above: first infer from the existence of certain causal interactions that there is a cognitive system involving brain, body, and environment; and then infer from the cognitive system hypothesis that there is extended cognition.

A third pattern of argument supposes that there are cases in which processes that span the brain and body, or brain, body, and environment, are in all relevant respects just like cognitive processes that occur within the brain. Add to this the tacit premise that if there is this equivalence, then the processing spanning the brain and body, or brain, body, and environment, is cognitive processing. This yields a simple *modus ponens* argument for extended cognition.[8]

The fourth type of argument sits uneasily with the third. These are "complementarity arguments." The cognitive equivalence arguments rely on putative equivalences between cognitive processes thought to occur in the brain and processes occurring in the brain, body, and environment. This is the kind of thinking one finds underlying the claim that Inga is, in all important and relevant respects, exactly like Otto. By contrast, the complementarity arguments rely on the fact that, because brain processes

---

[8] One way of reading the so-called "parity principle" from Clark and Chalmers (1998) invokes this kind of reasoning. Hurley (forthcoming) also invokes this kind of reasoning about acallosal subjects to suggest that they may be cases of extended cognition.

are of one character and bodily and environmental processes are of another, brain processes and bodily and environmental processes work well together. The combination of intracranial and extracranial processes achieves results that are in some sense superior to those achieved by just the brain alone. It is the fact that the brain alone figures out large products relatively slowly and with relatively low reliability, where the brain – in conjunction with sensory and motor skills and pencil and paper – more quickly and more reliably computes large products, that argues for the view that cognition extends into the arms, hands, pencil, and paper. What makes for a tension between these two lines of thought is – to put matters crudely – that, in the first line, one is making the case that Otto and Inga are cognitively the same, but in the second that Otto and Inga are not cognitively the same.

The fifth, and most distinctive, of all the arguments contends that the theory of evolution by natural selection supports the view that cognition extends into the environment. The major premise of the argument is that, if some cognitive feature is adapted to work in conjunction with some feature of the environment, then that feature of the environment is really part of the cognitive apparatus of the mind. This is an argument developed in considerable detail in Rowlands (1999) and briefly reviewed in Rowlands (2003).

Given that there is so much to be said in favor of the hypothesis of extended cognition, one might wonder what could possibly sustain the old-fashioned hypothesis of brain-bound cognition. The advocates of extended cognition have a short answer: mere prejudice. Haugeland begins his discussion of embodied and embedded cognition by paying homage to René Descartes's enduring influence on contemporary cognitive science orthodoxy.[9] Descartes, of course, did not maintain that the mind is causally isolated from the material world. He was a two-way interactionist, famously believing that mind and body interacted by way of the pineal gland. What Descartes did maintain was that reason is constituted by a distinct thinking substance that survives bodily death. One way to be anti-Cartesian would, thus, be to endorse some form of physicalism and maintain that reason, or the mind, or cognition, is realized or constituted by the brain. Something like this is cognitive psychological orthodoxy. Haugeland, however, champions a more radical course. He proposes that the mind is constituted not just by the brain, but by the brain, body, and environment. The mind

[9] Haugeland (1998, pp. 207–9).

is embodied in flesh and blood and the larger causal nexus of the world. Rowlands (1999, 2003) and Rockwell (2005), in their own ways, also conjecture that the current demarcation of the boundaries of cognition is a remnant of a largely discredited Cartesian view of cognition.[10] The charge appears again in a plainer form in Clark and Chalmers (1998), Clark (2003), and Clark (2005). There, the idea is simply that the hypothesis that cognition is brain-based is merely an unjustified prejudice. Rockwell (2005), for his part, provides a somewhat different diagnosis of the prejudice: "But I also maintain that to say a mind must be embodied only by the brain of an organism is a hangover from a justly discredited epistemology that builds its foundation on atomism and sense-datum theory" (Rockwell, 2005, p. 49).

Despite the growing popularity of the hypothesis of extended cognition, we remain defenders of orthodoxy. We argue that there are principled reasons for believing that the kind of cognitive processing cognitive psychologists care about is, essentially without real-world exception, intracranial. Two principal hypotheses about the nature of cognitive processes support this. In the first place, we maintain that cognitive processes involve non-derived mental representations; that is, cognitive processes involve representations that mean what they do in virtue of naturalistic conditions that do not include the content-bearing states, properties, or processes of other entities. Because these representations are typically found inside, but not outside, the brain, cognitive psychologists have one principled reason to think that cognition is typically intracranial. Second, cognitive psychologists attempt to distinguish the cognitive in terms of its underlying mechanisms. Cognitive processes are those that take place in virtue of certain mechanisms. Although these mechanisms could (conceptually, metaphysically, and physically) occur outside of the brain, they typically do not. In general, these mechanisms are often poorly understood, but they have features that are familiar to any serious student of cognitive psychology. For example, there is Miller's (1956) discovery that short-term memory has some sort of "size capacity." Consider a task such as listening to a string of distinct letters of the alphabet presented one per second, and then repeating the sequence. Normal human subjects are generally quite capable of performing this task for strings of five, six, and seven letters. But for eight-, nine-, and ten-letter strings, recall falls off dramatically. The standard hypothesis is that short-term memory has a fixed capacity of seven,

---

[10]   Rowlands (1999, pp. 1–7), Rowlands (2003, p. 7), Rockwell (2005, pp. xi–xxii).

give or take two, items. Seven items fit comfortably in memory, where more tend to "fall out" and be forgotten. We do not mean to propose that in order to be short-term memory, something must respect Miller's rule. Rather, we propose that findings such as this should guide us in determining what memory is like and what really differentiates cognitive processes and mechanisms from non-cognitive processes and mechanisms. Our empirical hypothesis, the one we think is embraced by the majority of cognitive psychologists, is that there are many, many mechanisms that underlie these sorts of phenomena, and that they are found in human brains, but not in the bodily or extracorporeal environment. Although one might build a mechanical or electronic device that has the capacities of a normal human brain, those found in the mundane use of pencil and paper to compute large products and to keep track of addresses are not like this. These sorts of observations, and they are truly legion, provide a second principled basis for thinking that cognitive processing is typically intracranial.[11] So, the way we see it, there are two principal features of intracranial processes – their use of non-derived representations governed by idiosyncratic kinds of processes – that serve to distinguish cognitive from non-cognitive processes. These features constitute a "mark of the cognitive" and they provide some non-question-begging reason to think that cognition is intracranial.

As for the case supporting extended cognition – namely, the five kinds of arguments briefly introduced above – we believe that they are based on insufficient attention to three plausible distinctions. First and foremost, not enough attention is paid to the difference between the claim that a process is causally connected to some cognitive process Y and the claim that the process constitutes part of some cognitive process Y. Time and again in the literature, one finds a more or less detailed narrative of some sequence of events or some putative psychological phenomenon that emphasizes one or another type of causal interaction between the brain, the body, and the environment. There then follows a quick move from the observation of these causal connections to the constitution claim of extended cognition. The circulatory system causally supports cognition. Many humans (especially yogi) can causally affect their heart rate by thought alone. So there is two-way causal coupling between cognitive

---

[11]   Both of these considerations in favor of brain-bound cognition were broached in Adams and Aizawa (2001). The concern for the nature of cognitive processing also appears in Wilson (2002) and Rupert (2004).

processes and circulatory processes, but it is false that cognition extends into the circulatory system. Thought is not circulation. We dub this fallacious general pattern of reasoning "the coupling-constitution fallacy." Second, there is inattention to the difference between the claim that Y constitutes part of a cognitive system and the claim that Y constitutes part of a cognitive process. This is the distinction between the extended cognitive system hypothesis that asserts that Otto and his notebook form an extended cognitive system and the extended cognition hypothesis that asserts that cognitive processing extends from Otto's brain into his notebook. Where one should certainly allow for stylistic variations in the expression of philosophical ideas, it turns out that the extended cognitive system hypothesis is much weaker than the extended cognition hypothesis. Third, there is insufficient attention to the development of a plausible theory of the cognitive or a plausible approach to a theory of the cognitive. If one is to maintain that cognition extends beyond the boundaries of the brain, one needs a theory of the difference between the cognitive and the non-cognitive. One at least needs a plausible sketch of how to find such a difference. Nevertheless, the few accounts of the mark of the cognitive one finds in the extended cognition literature are clearly inadequate. In fact, these few accounts employ a transparent strategy in trying to support the hypothesis of extended cognition. They invoke a promiscuous standard for the cognitive or a promiscuous method for finding what is cognitive. So, if one wants to find cognition in new and unexpected places, such as the body and the physical and chemical environment, it turns out to be convenient to have easily satisfied conditions in a theory of the cognitive. The theory that any sort of information processing constitutes cognitive processing is just such a theory. If just any sort of information processing is cognitive processing, then it is not hard to find cognitive processing in notebooks, computers, and other tools. The problem is that this theory of the cognitive is wildly implausible and evidently not what cognitive psychologists intend. A wristwatch is an information processor, but not a cognitive agent. While it is plausible that information processing is necessary for cognition, it is outlandish to suppose that such a notion of the cognitive is sufficient to describe the kinds of processing that cognitive psychologists typically care about. What the advocates of extended cognition need, but, we argue, do not have, is a plausible theory of the difference between the cognitive and the non-cognitive that does justice to the subject matter of cognitive psychology. Further, they lack even a plausible strategy for finding an adequate theory. This, of course, brings us back to our observation that what provides the principled basis for saying that the cognitive is intracranial is what we take to be a plausible theory of the cognitive embodied in orthodox cognitive psychology.

We think that recognition of these three principal weaknesses in the extended cognition literature will illuminate much of what is problematic there, and we hope that it will go a long way to dispelling any rational appeal that the hypothesis of extended cognition might enjoy. In the most optimistic case, it will direct attention to some of the more subtle and useful ideas that appear elsewhere in the extended and embodied cognition literature. However, these three recurring problems do not exhaust the difficulties with the case for extended cognition. There are also problems with the more idiosyncratic arguments for extended cognition, namely, those based on the complementarity of intracranial and transcranial processes and the use of evolutionary theory. Regarding the complementarity arguments, we have to wonder why the combination of cognitive processes in the brain with apparently non-cognitive processes found in tools should lead us to conclude that they make up a process that is wholly cognitive. Regarding the evolutionary argument, we must wonder why the theory of evolution, a theory of biology, should be expected to tell us anything about where in the world cognitive processes are found. Shouldn't a theory of cognition be invoked in the service of determining this?

Those familiar with our paper "The bounds of cognition" will recognize much of what we have just set out. This book is an elaboration and clarification of many of the views first broached there. It takes into account comments and criticism we have received since its publication. In addition, however, it extends this earlier work by covering some of the more recent developments in the literature. Our hope is that a more careful articulation and defense of some of our assumptions will bolster the case we have already made against extended cognition. Further, we hope that our attempts to address the more recent arguments for extended cognition can be developed in compelling detail on our first run through them in this book. At the very least, we hope our account will articulate what critics of the hypothesis of extended cognition would like to see better supported.

Our plan for redirecting the extended cognition agenda will begin in earnest in Chapter 2, where we will further clarify the issues. In Chapters 3 and 4, we develop and defend in more detail our positive approach to the mark of the cognitive, namely, that cognitive processes differ from non-cognitive processes in terms of the kinds of mechanisms that operate on non-derived representations. We offer this as part of a theory of the cognitive, rather than as (part of) a definition of the term "cognitive." We do not mean to stipulate that this is just what we mean by "cognition."[12] Nor do we mean to be offering an account of what "folk psychology" or common sense maintains about what cognition is. One consequence of offering a partial theory of the cognitive, rather than any of these other things, is that we can refine it only as far as (we take) the current evidence in cognitive psychology to warrant. Chapter 3 will explain what we intend by non-derived content in contrast to derived content and explain what commitments we think we have in virtue of it. It will also defend the hypothesis of non-derived content against objections. Chapter 4 will describe in more detail what we mean when we claim that cognitive processing is to be identified in terms of underlying mechanisms and principles.[13] We will use some textbook examples from the theory of memory, attention, and visual processing to substantiate our claim that cognitive psychology proceeds in this manner. We will also describe cases from other sciences indicating how they too use a scientific methodology in which kinds are individuated in terms of their causal principles. Together, Chapters 3 and 4 will describe a generic form of what we take to be the orthodox view of the cognitive in cognitive psychology. This is not to say that the view is universally accepted. Nor do we mean to imply that it is the only kind of theory that can provide a principled reason to think that cognitive processing is typically intracranial. Instead, we take it to provide one modest, empirically motivated means for rebutting the charge that nothing more than mere prejudice favors the view that cognition is by and large intracranial.

Chapters 5 through 9 constitute our critique of the arguments for extended cognition. Chapter 5 examines some of the extended cognition attempts to say what cognition is or how we might discover what it is. What we find is that these attempts fail to do justice to the subject matter of cognitive psychology. In fact, were these conditions taken seriously by advocates of extended cognition, the argumentation given in the literature would be much different. Given just the implausible theories of what

---

[12] This comment is meant to distance us from the view described by Menary (2006, p. 334).

[13] We think that Rupert (2004) does a fine job of presenting this kind of argument for memory.

cognition is, one would have no need to exotic coupling-constitution arguments, complementarity argument, evolutionary arguments, and so forth. Chapters 6 and 7 review the sundry forms of the coupling-constitution fallacy. These include the rather simple examples, such as the ones by Rowlands and Gibbs presented above, and more complicated "systems" versions given by van Gelder, Haugeland, and Clark. These chapters will also review some attempts that have been made to dismiss, sidestep, or rebut the fallacy. Chapter 8 will return to the observation that there is a cognitive parity or equivalence between transcranial processes and familiar intracranial cognitive processes. Relying on the examples of cognitive processes developed in Chapter 4, we will indicate how a cognitive individuation of processes recognizes dramatic differences between the intracranial and the transcranial. In other words, we will directly challenge the empirical claims about cognitive equivalence. Chapter 8 will also review the complementarity arguments. In an attempt to turn the evident cognitive differences between intracranial and extracranial processes to their advantage, some advocates of extended cognition try to use this as evidence in support of extended cognition. Additionally, Chapter 8 will critique Rowland's evolutionary argument for extended cognition (cf., Rowlands, 1999, ch. 4; 2003, ch. 9). Chapter 9 will examine one specific theory of extended cognition, Alva Noë's (2004) theory of enactive perception. The arguments Noë gives are naturally construed as a species of inference to the best explanation, a kind of argumentation unlike much of what is found in the extended cognition literature. Here we will argue that, Noë's suggestions notwithstanding, the orthodox view of the locus of cognition provides a better explanation of the available data than does his theory of enactive perception.

By this point, one may have noticed that the primary targets for our criticism will be philosophers. This is not to imply that the extended cognition movement is only embraced and advanced by philosophers. There are obviously clear statements of the hypothesis of extended cognition in the work of developmental psychologists, roboticists, dynamical systems theorists, and cognitive psychologists. And, of course, many philosophers draw some measure of their intellectual inspiration for the hypothesis of extended cognition from the work of scientists. We will note examples of this from time to time in the course of the book. Nevertheless, we find that it is the philosophers who have most consistently, explicitly, and elaborately defended the radical extended cognition hypothesis according to which cognitive processes span the brain, body, and environment.[14] So, while we believe that asking where in the world cognitive processes are to be found is an empirical question ultimately to be settled by scientific investigation, we also believe that at this point in time, while the extended cognition movement is still in its early stages of development, there are some basic conceptual or theoretical issues that can be profitably dealt with by philosophers.

Chapter 10 will briefly review our overall position and indicate topics that we think merit further exploration, directions in which much of the extended cognition energies might be better directed. Part of this discussion will review some of the more interesting and plausible features of the extended cognition literature that have perhaps been eclipsed by the hypothesis of extended cognition.

[14] For a discussion of some of the scientific literature in the extended cognition movement, see Adams and Aizawa (forthcoming c).

Chapter 2

Refining the Issues

In this chapter, we wish to focus attention on the bounds of cognition and refine what this means. This involves justifying an account of what cognition is and where it is found. To these ends, we begin with the relatively easier question concerning the hypotheses one might entertain about the location of cognitive processing. An additional goal will be to explain how we can accept the *possibility* of extended cognition into the overall framework we present in this book.

2.1 What are the Boundaries?

To ask about the bounds of cognition is to ask what portions of spacetime contain cognitive processing. It is to ask about what physical, chemical, or biological processes realize, constitute, or embody cognitive processes. It is to ask about the supervenience base for cognition. It is to ask about the physical substrate of cognition.[1] Although these ways of formulating the issue may not be absolutely identical, all of them have been used in the literature as ways of describing the hypothesis that concerns us. For the present, we will not explore any possible differences among them.

---

[1] These ways of formulating the issue presuppose some form of physicalism, which we shall continue to assume throughout this book. In principle, though, one can imagine a substantival dualist taking an interest in the issue by asking what parts of the mind interface with what parts of the world. So, René Descartes thought that human reason interacted with the world via the pineal gland, which is perhaps a reason to think that Descartes did *not* maintain that cognition is localized in the brain.

To date, most discussions of the bounds of cognition have centered on a stark contrast. Either cognition is all in the brain or it extends into the body, or into the body and external environment. It is, however, possible to provide a rough arrangement of theories of the bounds of cognition along a spectrum of increasingly broad boundaries, from a core of neurons within the brain at one end of the spectrum to all sorts of extracorporeal tools with which we interact at the other end. Setting out such a spectrum provides a helpful first step in better appreciating the issues.

The standard view in cognitive science is that cognitive processes do not necessarily pervade the whole of the brain. For one thing, glial cells constitute part of the brain. In fact, glial cells outnumber neurons many times over. Yet they may not support the specific kinds of information processing that are commonly supposed to constitute cognitive processing. Instead, glial cells may perform a range of support functions for neurons, such as insulating neuronal groups and synaptic connections, producing the myelin that insulates cell axons, and removing debris after nerve injury or death.[2] So, strictly speaking, we maintain that the orthodox view in cognitive science is not that cognitive processes necessarily take place within the whole of the brain, but perhaps only within a subset of the neurons constituting the brain.

As we just hinted, we also think it is possible that cognitive processing does not take place even in all of the nerve cells of the brain. For example, it might be that some neuronal pathways in the brain merely transmit or communicate information from one region of the brain to another, without in any way transforming it in ways that count as cognitive. Such neuronal pathways would be mere buses in the electronic digital computer sense of the term. Perhaps the corpus callosum is a mere bus. Perhaps the neuronal pathways connecting the cortical visual areas V1, V2, and V4 are mere information buses. Be this logical and nomological possibility what it may, our guess is that there are few, if any, neuronal pathways that are dedicated only to information transfer. This, however, is an empirical question that we leave open for present purposes. The present point is merely that we do not make, and indeed we do not really need to make, any commitments about just how completely neurons are given over to cognitive processing. Even if only a subset of the brain's neurons is involved in cognitive processing, it will still be the case that cognitive processing is entirely intracranial.

---

[2]   See Kandel et al. (2000, p. 20).

One version of the hypothesis of extended cognition maintains that cognition and cognitive processing involves, or must involve, biological components of the body outside of the brain. This version admits of more or less radical versions depending on the components one wishes to implicate in cognition. At the most conservative end of this spectrum, only other components of the central nervous system are implicated. In this vein, one might maintain that the spinal cord is involved in cognitive processing.[3] This idea was vigorously debated in the nineteenth century as experimental techniques for studying spinal reflexes emerged. Perhaps the kind of information processing that goes on in the neurons of the brain is sufficiently similar to the kind of information processing that goes on in the neurons of the spinal cord to warrant the claim that the spine cognizes or that spinal information processing is cognitive processing. It could also be that there are limited regions of the brain that process information in just the same way as do spinal neurons. One could then maintain that, since the neurons in the brain do cognitive processing, so must the spinal neurons. This is a kind of extended cognition that, while controversial, might not be entirely heterodox cognitive psychology.

We think that orthodoxy is also quite willing to countenance cognitive processing in sensory nerves as far out as perhaps the sensory transducers.[4] Transducers, as typically understood, merely transform information from one medium to another. Photoreceptors transform light entering the retina into graded synaptic potentials. Inner hair cells in the ear transform disturbances in the fluids of the cochlea into graded potentials. Cognition begins somewhere after transduction. Exactly where, we suppose, is up for grabs. Various considerations, however, suggest that cognitive processing could begin quite soon after transduction. There can be little doubt that the neurons connecting the rods and cones in the retina to the occipital lobe of the brain transform information from the photoreceptors in dramatic ways. This feature of the visual system was quickly surmised once it had been found that the human retina contains on the order of 100 million

---

[3]   Rockwell (2005, pp. 26–31) examines the role of the spinal cord in the perception of pain. This is exactly the kind of issue we take to be controversial psychology, but still within the sphere of orthodoxy. Rockwell's point in drawing attention to this information is, of course, to "soften up" the reader for the radical hypothesis that pain is realized in the body.

[4]   We set aside questions about whether the retina is "in the head." It is clearly not within the skull, but it is in the concave structure of the ocular orbit, so perhaps ordinary language allows us to say that the retina is "in" the head. We also set aside any debate about whether the retina is really part of the central nervous system.

photoreceptors, but that the ganglion cells leaving the eye number only about 1.25 million. A wealth of vision science research since that time has been dedicated to discovering just what sorts of information processing takes place between the photoreceptors and cortex. The more the processing in the pathway from receptor cells to the brain resembles the cognitive information processing in the cortex, the stronger the case one might make for there being cognition in this sensory nerve.[5]

Still farther out on the extended cognition spectrum, one might also think that muscles, skin, and bone are cognitive processors and that cognitive processing takes place within the muscles.[6] As best we can tell, this is where orthodox cognitive psychology is likely to become unreceptive. It is certainly where we think things have gone too far. The orthodox might listen to an argument for the view that cognition extends beyond the neurons of the brain into the spinal cord and sensory nerves, but muscular cognition is beyond the pale. The standard assumption is that the kinds of cognitive information processing that take place in nerves are dramatically unlike those that occur in muscles. There could, of course, be biological processes common to nerves and muscles; for example, mitosis, ion transport, cellular respiration, and metabolism. There could also be common chemical and physical processes, such as ionization, hydrogen bonding, catalysis, and polarization. But surely, says orthodoxy, cognizing must end at the neuromuscular junction. When considered in terms of the nature of the biological processes involved, it is outlandish to suppose that neuronal processes and muscular processes equally support cognitive processes.

We speculate that it is because comparing neuronal processes and muscular processes in this way makes this more radical form of extended cognition look so implausible that so few advocates of extended cognition make such comparisons. Instead, the advocates of extended cognition draw attention to the fact that cognitive processes causally interact with muscular processes, that they are intimately connected to them, and that they are coupled to them in a special way. Instead, they describe the nerves and muscles as a system, not noticing that the cognitive system hypothesis is not equivalent to the extended cognition hypothesis. It is this implausibility, we speculate, that has encouraged the advocates of extended cognition,

---

[5]   Rockwell (2005, pp. 21–6) makes this kind of case. Again, for Rockwell, this is part of a "softening up" of the opposition.

[6]   Here, we ignore the possibility that anyone will want to entertain the idea that cognitive processing takes place in the autonomic nervous system.

in general, to move away from claims of similarity of processing of the sort discussed in the Inga–Otto thought experiment to arguments based on causal connections and complementarity.

All of the foregoing views of the locus of cognition might be labeled versions of the hypothesis of the *embodiment* of cognition in the sense that a cognitive process occurs within an organism's body. As Wilson states the view,

> many cognitive capacities in symbol-using creatures, far from being purely internal, are either *enactive bodily* capacities, or *world-involving* capacities. These capacities are not realized by some internal arrangement of the brain or central nervous system, but by embodied states of the whole person, or by the wide system that includes (parts of) the brain as a proper part. (Wilson, 2004, p. 188)

Speaking only of the embodiment of perception, Noë writes, "What perception is, however, is not a process in the brain, but a kind of skillful activity on the part of the animal as a whole" (Noë, 2004, p. 2).[7] The view that cognition sometimes extends from the brain and body into the environment, however, can only naturally be described as the hypothesis of *extended* cognition. This is the thesis that cognitive processing literally extends outside the boundaries of the flesh into the external chemical and physical world. On this theory, cognitive processes are supposed to extend, at least sometimes, into the tools that a cognizer uses.

Is this a thesis anyone seriously endorses? We think so. The view is pretty clearly to be found in the passages we cited earlier in Chapter 1.[8] This is not to say that everyone who is associated with the hypothesis of extended cognition is so clear on what is supposed to be at stake. For example, Daniel Dennett is often taken to be supportive of work on extended cognition, but we think such commitment as he might have to the hypothesis does not come through very clearly in his writing. For example, he tells us that

---

[7]   It is unclear how literally we are to take the claim that cognition or perception involves the whole body. While some perception, such as proprioception and touch, might involve the whole body, neither Wilson nor Noë provide any reason to believe that cognition or perception in general involves, say, the knees or toes.

[8]   Those were van Gelder and Port (1995, p. viii), Rowlands (1999, p. 22), and Gibbs (2006, p. 12).

The primary source, I want to suggest, is our habit of *off-loading* as much as possible of our cognitive tasks into the environment itself – extruding our minds (that is our mental projects and activities) into the surrounding world, where a host of peripheral devices we construct can store, process, and re-present our meanings, streamlining, enhancing, and protecting the processes of transformation that *are* our thinking. This widespread practice of off-loading releases us from the limitations of our animal brains. (Dennett, 1996, p. 134)

Dennett's text can be read as endorsing the radical hypothesis that cognitive processes are found in the tools we use, but also as endorsing the weaker notion that tools help us in performing certain information-processing tasks. To say that we "extrude our minds" does sound like saying that cognitive processing extends into the physical environment constituted by our tools. Offloading portions of our cognitive tasks might also be read this way. Then again, offloading might mean that we give up performing a task using cognitive processes in order to rely on non-cognitive mechanisms and processes to store, process, and represent our meanings. This makes sense of Dennett's talk of "protecting the processes of transformation that are our thinking." In a recent reply to Adams and Aizawa (2001), Menary (2006) also urges a view he calls "cognitive integration" that, like Dennett's, strikes us as ambiguous at many points. Part of Menary's view is that

> To explain how [cognitive] integration works we need to place the cognizer within an environment, where various vehicles are manipulated. On this account we must recognize that the agent often completes a "cognitive task" by manipulating vehicles in the environment . . . The agent sometimes completes cognitive tasks individually by manipulating external classical vehicles . . . and sometimes by co-operating with other cognitive agents in the shared environment. (Menary, 2006, p. 330)

Perhaps this is an endorsement of the idea that cognitive processing takes place in tools, but it might also be an endorsement that we use tools to get some things done. There is nothing controversial in the latter claim. These kinds of potentially ambiguous passages invite the charge that in taking the radical reading of extended cognition we are attacking a straw man. Susi et al. (2003) charge us with doing this. Our reply, obviously, is that while some texts are ambiguous between the radical extended cognition hypothesis and orthodox causal hypotheses, such as that humans use tools to accomplish certain tasks or that humans causally interact with items in their environment, there are others that are not. We have cited several instances where these radical claims have been advanced and we are out to challenge them.

2.2   What is Cognition?

It is tautologous to say that any complete theory of the bounds of cognition must include a theory of cognition; having a theory of cognition will simply be part of what one means by a complete theory. But we want to say more than this bare tautology. It seems to us reasonable to expect that a theory of the bounds of cognition should provide at least some plausible working account of what cognition is. If we have no idea what cognition is, then there is little substance in the claim that cognitive processing extends beyond the boundaries of the brain into the body and environment. It is not helpful at all to be told that cognition extends without some idea of what cognition is.[9]

A second reason to have a theory of the mark of the cognitive is that it helps show the principled basis there is for thinking that cognition is intra-cranial. A common suggestion in the extended cognition literature is that it is some accident of intellectual history that common sense and orthodox cognitive psychologists speak as they do. As we mentioned in Chapter 1, it is commonly suggested that cognitive psychology is mired in Cartesian prejudice, that there is no principled reason for thinking that cognitive processes take place only within the brain or central nervous system. The way to respond to these charges is to provide a principled basis for thinking that the processes that are plausibly construed as cognitive occur, almost exclusively, in the brain. Part of doing this involves providing a theory of

---

[9]   Notice that when Richard Dawkins introduced his theory of extended phenotypes, he offered a theory of what a phenotype is. According to Dawkins, a phenotype is "The manifested attributes of an organism, the joint product of its genes and their environment during ontogeny" (Dawkins, 1999, p. 299; cf., Dawkins, 2004, p. 377). Perhaps there are reasons to object to this theory, but at least it is on the books. In pointing this out, we are deliberately standing on its head an objection raised by Larry Shapiro in personal communication. Where Shapiro claims that Dawkins does not need a "mark of the phenotype" in order to advance his theory of the extended phenotype, we think that Dawkins does and that Dawkins does in fact provide one. We expect the comparable work from advocates of extended cognition.

the mark of the cognitive, a theory of the difference between cognitive processes and non-cognitive processes.

Yet a third reason to pay attention to the theory of cognition being invoked is that claims about the bounds of cognition are intimately connected to that theory in both subtle and not so subtle ways. As we noted in Chapter 1, if one thinks that cognition is simply any sort of information processing, then – so understood – cognitive processing is likely to be found crossing the brain, body, and environment. Information is everywhere and is transformed as it propagates through media. Indeed, cognition understood as any old type of information processing would be found in compact disk players, televisions, telephones, gas gauges, and on and on. Processing information is plausibly construed as a necessary condition on cognition, but not plausibly construed as sufficient for cognition. Similarly, if one thinks that cognitive processing is simply any sort of dynamical system process, then – so understood – cognitive processing is again likely to be found spanning the brain, body, and environment. But, so understood, cognitive processing will also be found in the swinging of a pendulum of a grandfather clock or the oscillations of the atoms of a hydrogen molecule. Being a dynamical system is pretty clearly insufficient for cognition or even a cognitive system. These seem to be obvious interactions between the theory of what cognitive processing is and the theory of where cognitive processing is to be found. One might object that no advocate of extended cognition ever claimed that cognition is simply any old form of information processing or that cognitive processing is state change in just any dynamical system. Perhaps so, but the point is, first, that one needs to attend to the mark of the cognitive, and, second, one needs to be sensitive to the interactions between hypotheses concerning the bounds of cognition and the mark of the cognitive. Consider now some of the more subtle interactions between theories of what cognition is and where it is to be found, using examples familiar from the extended cognition literature.

In the Inga–Otto thought experiment, Inga and her normal internal memory are supposed to be in some important sense *cognitively* equivalent to the combination of Otto's brain, his pencil, and his notebook. Although the qualification that Inga and Otto be cognitively the same is never made explicit, it is clearly necessary in order to challenge the orthodox understanding of the bounds of cognition. It would obviously be irrelevant to theories of the bounds of cognition to claim that Inga and Otto are physically and biologically the same. Almost as obviously, it is not enough merely that there be some loose sense in which Inga's normal internal memory and Otto's writings in his notebook are the same, or that they have the same function or same functional role. For example, one might think that a memory or a belief is simply any semantically evaluable trigger to action. But that is a weak, promiscuous theory of what constitutes a belief or a cognitive state. By such an account, a stop sign or a low fuel warning light in a car could be a belief. Stop signs and fuel warning lights are semantically evaluable and can trigger beliefs, such as that one should stop or purchase gasoline. Nor is it enough that Inga's normal memory and Otto's notes have the same semantic content and are both triggers to action. The challenge that the Inga–Otto thought experiment issues to those who believe that cognitive processes occur within the brain is to find some principled, non-question-begging reason for thinking that Inga and Otto differ in their *cognitive* processing. If this is the challenge, then we need some theory of what cognition is.

We have here given three reasons to think we need a theory of the mark of the cognitive, but we will consider more reasons later. Now, however, we to turn to a possible extended cognition defense of the import of the Inga–Otto example. In the preceding criticism of the Inga–Otto thought experiment, we assumed that human cognition was at issue.[10] Human cognition, however, may well be one species of a broader genus of cognition. Maybe Otto's use of his notebook does not constitute a normal human memory process or involve normal human cognitive processing, but it does not follow from this that Otto's use of his notebook does not constitute a memory process or cognitive processing at all. It does not follow that Otto does not have some more generic form of memory or cognitive processing. One might think that Inga and Otto are exactly alike in having a more generic kind of memory or more generic kind of cognitive processing.

The sense that the advocates of extended cognition are envisioning some broader notion of the cognitive is encouraged by the examples used in complementarity arguments.[11] One might readily admit that the use of pencil and paper to compute large products does not result in normal human cognition. Instead, these tools create a synergy in which the whole

---

[10]   Given the way in which the example is set up, we think this is a reasonable assumption. It is the one we made in Adams and Aizawa (2001). It is also one made in Rupert (2004).
[11]   Clark (forthcoming b, p. 20) apparently has this in mind.

is greater than the sum of its parts. A human with pencil and paper has greater reasoning abilities and greater mathematical abilities than a human left to her own brainy devices. Similarly, when Otto avails himself of a notebook to remember information that is valuable to him, he becomes cognitively more than the sum of his parts, paper, and pencil. Much of Clark (2003) can be viewed as an elaboration of the kinds of ways in which human cognition will be transformed into some alternative kind of cognition through increasing reliance on tools.

Advocates of extended cognition may, or may not, be interested in embracing the hypothesis that it is some broader notion of cognition than mere human cognition that is extended. On the one hand, this might seem to be a more plausible hypothesis, but on the other, this hypothesis might not be radical enough to suit the tastes of those who are attracted to extended cognition. In any event, in the chapters to come, we will consider the version of the hypothesis of extended cognition that is based on a broader conception of the cognitive. We shall argue that this does surprisingly little to advance the cause of extended cognition.

2.3 The Possibility of Extended Cognition

The preceding two sections have laid out something of the landscape of the issues regarding cognition and its boundaries. Here, we want to begin to evaluate the hypothesis that *it is possible* that cognition extends into the body and surrounding environment on this landscape. In Chapter 1, we noted the difference between the hypothesis that cognition extends into the body and surrounding environment and the hypothesis that *it is possible* that cognition extends into the body and surrounding environment. While the latter hypothesis, we argued, should not be accepted uncritically, it is a consequence of many functionalist views of cognition. It is, therefore, not beyond the pale of orthodoxy. By contrast, the former view is radical insofar as it asserts that extended cognition *actually occurs* in mundane human actions, rather than in exotic philosophical thought experiments. Crudely speaking, the non-modal hypothesis of extended cognition is more radical in proportion to the pervasiveness it attributes to extended cognition. Consider some of the discussions there have been of the possibility of extended cognition.

At one stage of his book, Noë maintains that it is possible for items in the extracorporeal environment to be part of the necessary physical substrate for perceptual experiences.[12] This sounds like the claim that it is possible for external objects to constitute perceptual experiences. For example, he proposes that it may well be that the only biologically possible way to produce a particular perceptual experience of the taste of a particular wine is by rolling the wine over the tongue. In such a case, one might say that the corporeal and extracorporeal items are part of the necessary physical substrate of the experience – that is, that the corporeal and extracorporeal items constitute the experience. Further, insofar as perceptual experiences involve cognitive processing, this suggests that, in such cases, we have extended cognitive processing. So, Noë is explicitly committed to the possibility of extended cognition, and apparently not more.

Most recently, there is the work of Clark. There are times when he appears to defend only the modal claim that it is possible for cognition to extend.[13] There are, however, other times when he seems to suggest that it is human biological nature to interact with external objects in such a way as to extend our cognitive processing from our brains into our tools.[14] This suggests that he believes extended cognition is a common or even pervasive feature of human life. It is what makes us "natural-born cyborgs." Then there are still other times when he claims that the kinds of conditions that would lead to extended cognition rarely obtain, so that it would be a mistake to think that extended cognition is rampant.[15]

One approach to modal versions of the extended cognition hypothesis is simply to ignore them as within the realm of orthodoxy, but to argue that, as a matter of contingent empirical fact, extended cognition is not a common or pervasive feature of our everyday world. Perhaps there are exotic conditions that philosophers entertain in thought experiments, but they are not part of normal human experience at the start of the twenty-first century. This is the line of response we adopted in earlier publications. Yet this line can be unsatisfying insofar as there is some vagueness about what it means to say that extended cognition is common or pervasive. Just how often must human cognition extend for it to be common or pervasive?

---

[12]   Cf., Noë (2004, ch. 7). In our Chapter 9, we shall explore another line of argumentation Noë gives that provides at least *prima facie* support for a special case of the hypothesis of extended cognition, a version of the hypothesis of extended perception.

[13]   Cf., e.g., Clark (2005, p. 1). Menary (2006, p. 329) cites this passage with approval as a statement of the extended mind (cognition?) hypothesis.

[14]   Cf., e.g., Clark (2003, p. 6; 2005, p. 9).

[15]   Cf., Wilson and Clark (forthcoming).

Just exactly how and how often must humans have used tools to modify their performance for natural selection to have lead to the fixation of tool use in the species? We have said that extended cognition is not as widespread as human tool use, but there are times when this does not enable us to engage the issue of extended cognition.[16] We still believe this view is correct, but there is perhaps a better way to meet the challenge of the possibility of extended cognition. This would be to address the different hypotheses about what makes extended cognition possible. This would be to challenge the theories of the conditions under which cognition would extend from the core of the brain into the body and environment. The advocates of extended cognition can share with orthodoxy the idea that it is possible for cognition to extend beyond the boundaries of the brain. Yet they can, and evidently do, differ about the sorts of conditions that would actualize that possibility. The new approach we will explore here, and later in the book, is to challenge those conditions.

Return to Noë's reasons for thinking that the perceptual experience of the taste of the wine extends into the mouth and tongue. Concede, merely for the sake of argument, that the only possible way to produce a given perception of the taste of a wine is by rolling it over the tongue in a particular way. Why does the uniqueness of the cause of the perception provide any reason to think that the cause – that is, the rolling – is part of the physical substrate of the perceptual experience? Why does the uniqueness of the cause provide any basis to think that the rolling process constitutes part of the process of experiencing? Suppose that the only physically possible way in which to initiate a nuclear fusion reaction involving hydrogen would be through an explosive nuclear fission reaction involving ^{238}U. Would that be any grounds for saying that the fission of ^{238}U is fusion of hydrogen? Noë appears to commit a version of the coupling-constitution fallacy in which Y's being the *unique* (kind of?) cause of a cognitive process makes Y a part of that (kind of?) cognitive process. But, in general, Y's being a unique (kind of?) cause of an X process does not make Y a part of the X process. These kinds of coupling-constitution arguments will come in for much greater attention in Chapters 6 and 7.

We think that a much more plausible basis upon which to say that extended cognition is possible is through reliance on (one reading of) Clark and Chalmers's *parity principle*. According to this principle, "If, as we confront some task, a part of the world functions as a process which, *were*

---

[16]   This issue emerges clearly in Clark (forthcoming b).

it done in the head, we would have no hesitation in recognizing as part of the cognitive process, then that part of the world *is* (so we claim) part of the cognitive process" (Clark and Chalmers, 1998, p. 8). One way to read this is as saying that if some transcorporeal process is cognitively just like an intracranial cognitive process, then that transcorporeal process is a cognitive process too. We think that the possibility of cognitive equivalence between the intracranial and transcranial processes allows for the possibility of extended cognition. But while we think that such cognitive equivalence is possible, we also think that this possibility is rarely, if ever, realized in these early years of the twenty-first century. Exactly why we think that there are cognitive differences between what typically goes on in the brain and the kinds of processes that typically span brain and body or brain, body, and environment will be the topic of Chapter 8.

As just mentioned, one way to read Clark and Chalmers's parity principle is as founding extended cognition on an equivalence or parity between the cognitive processes that go on inside the brain and what goes on in brain–body–world transactions. This seems to us the most natural reading of the principle and the one that is most commonly adopted. Wilson and Clark (forthcoming), however, have recently offered another reading, or a correction of this more common reading. According to Wilson and Clark, the parity principle points to certain sorts of conditions on the coupling that must obtain between a largely free-standing cognitive unit, such as a brain, and bodily and environmental objects and processes. Clark and Chalmers (1998) provide the following conditions, which they find intuitively plausible coupling criteria for a dispositional belief:

> First, the notebook is a constant in Otto's life – in cases where the information in the notebook is relevant, he will rarely take action without consulting it. Second, the information in the notebook is directly available without difficulty. Third, upon retrieving information from the notebook he automatically endorses it. Fourth, the information in the notebook has been consciously endorsed at some point in the past, and indeed is there as a consequence of this endorsement. The status of the fourth condition as a criterion for belief is arguable (perhaps one can acquire beliefs through subliminal perception, or through memory tampering?), but the first three features certainly play a role. (Clark and Chalmers, 1998, p. 17; cf., Clark, forthcoming a, for a slightly modified set of conditions)

We will argue (in Chapter 7) that these conditions are technically flawed, insofar as we think they yield counterintuitive results. We will also argue (in Chapters 6 and 7) that the entire "coupling" approach to extending cognition is wrongheaded. What makes a process or routine in some resource cognitive is not whether it is hooked up to a cognitive process or how intimately or intricately it is hooked up to a cognitive process. What matters is the nature of the process itself. The process or routine should bear the mark of the cognitive. As suggested above, we will time and again return to the issue of the mark of the cognition.

So, our plan for addressing the possibility of extended cognition in the foregoing kinds of cases will be to focus on the proffered conditions under which cognition is hypothesized to extend. We will argue that the conditions under which advocates suppose that it is possible for cognition to extend are not valid conditions. This should help integrate our discussion of the possibility of extended cognition with our discussion of the non-modal hypothesis of extended cognition.

2.4 Conclusion

In this chapter, we have refined the relevant landscape concerning the bounds of cognition. A theory of the bounds of cognition needs (a) at least the outlines of a theory of what cognition is and (b) a theory of where cognition is to be found. Without a theory of the mark of the cognitive, or at least a plausible approach to determining what cognition is, the claim that cognition extends into the body and the environment lacks substance. With a theory of cognition in place, it is much clearer how one might try to justify localizing cognition in some restricted regions of the brain, in the central nervous system, in the brain and body, or in the brain, body, and tools. We have also been at pains to emphasize the important interactions between these two theories. The principal interaction is that the more permissive one's theory of the mark of the cognitive, the more likely it is that one will be able to find cognition spanning the brain, body, and environment. We can make the point in another way. One way to defend the hypothesis of extended cognition is simply to invoke a lax theory of the cognitive – or better, perhaps, simply do not draw attention to any presuppositions as to the nature of cognition. We provided some simple illustrations of this idea, but we also considered a more subtle interaction between the hypothesis of extended cognition and the theory of the mark of the cognitive, namely, its role in formulating the challenge of the Inga–Otto thought experiment.

We also drew attention to an important distinction that may, or may not, be in the minds of those advocating extended cognition. This is the distinction between human cognition and some broader conception or theory of cognition. We believe that there is good reason to think that there are non-human forms of cognition. Nevertheless, we also will argue that having recourse to a theory of non-human cognition will do little to support the ultimate plausibility of the hypothesis of extended cognition.

Finally, we proposed a strategy for addressing the claim that it is possible for cognition to extend. We think that the possibility of extended cognition is not radical; that many functionalist conceptions of cognition will allow for it. The possibility will be realized any time the "right kind" of cognitive causal mechanisms are found in the processes spanning the brain and body, or brain, body, and environment. In earlier work, we set aside any concern for the mere possibility of extended cognition. Now, however, we will try to address this possibility by challenging the plausibility of the conditions under which advocates of extended cognition have thought that extended cognition is possible or actual.

Chapter 3

Original Content

There seem to us a number of good reasons to believe that the debate over extended cognition needs to pay greater attention to the matter of what distinguishes the cognitive from the non-cognitive. If we are trying to determine what portions of spacetime contain cognitive processes, we should have some idea what cognitive processes are. If we are trying to determine the links in the causal chains of world events that are cognitive links, rather than mere biological, chemical, or physical links, we need some plausible way to distinguish cognitive links from non-cognitive links. Although it is too much to say that we are actually able to offer a complete theory of what distinguishes cognitive processes from non-cognitive processes, we think we have two important clues. In the first place, cognition involves non-derived representations, representations that mean what they do independently of other representational or intentional capacities. This is an idea we borrow from the *naturalized semantics* literature, and the idea that we propose to develop and defend in this chapter. In the second place, we think that the cognitive is to be individuated by specific kinds of information processing mechanisms. We conjecture that human and many non-human brains contain forms of information processing that manipulate and transform information in ways unlike those found in processes spanning the brain, body, and environment. Although this falls short of a complete, detailed theory of what cognition is, we maintain that it is refined enough to establish the legitimacy of the current cognitive psychological presupposition that cognitive processes are to be found almost exclusively within the brain. We think that merely recognizing this approach will do a great deal to bolster the orthodox view of the bounds of cognition.

3.1   Part of the Mark of the Cognitive: Non-Derived Content

Part of what we think distinguishes genuine cognitive processes from non-cognitive processes is that cognitive processes involve representations. More specifically, cognitive processes involve non-derived, rather than derived, representations. Homely examples point to the distinction we have in mind. Traffic lights, gas gauges, and flags are paradigm cases of items bearing derived content. Thoughts, experiences, and perceptions are paradigm cases of items bearing non-derived content. Roughly speaking, the idea is that derived content arises from the way in which items are handled or treated by intentional agents. For the most part, things with derived content are assigned that content by intentional agents who already have thoughts with meaning. Underived content arises from conditions that do not require the independent or prior existence of other content, representations, or intentional agents.

Why hypothesize that cognitive processes involve representations? Within cognitive psychology, the principal reason has long been that representations are posits that help explain how it is that cognitive agents are not merely stimulus driven. Rodney Brooks's robot, Herbert, is a fine example of a stimulus driven device.[1] It can roam the halls of MIT searching for aluminum cans, resetting its internal states every three seconds. What it does at any moment is determined by its fixed internal structure and what its sensors currently tell it. By contrast, normal humans appear to be able to record information that informs future actions. Humans remember names, dates, and places that influence their future behavior. Many non-human animals remember such things as where they have stored food caches and what traps look like.[2] The foregoing explanatory motivation in cognitive psychology has been complemented by parallel developments in neuroscience. Beginning in the late 1950s, neuroscientists developed single-cell recording techniques that enabled them to measure the action potentials of individual neurons. Since then, single-cell recordings have suggested that there are neuronal representations of a vast array of environmental features. Seminal work by Jerome Lettvin and Humberto Maturana revealed cells in the frog retina that respond to moving black

---

[1]   Brooks (1999).
[2]   Emery and Clayton (2004) comment on the cache management abilities of corvids.

dots in regions of the frog's visual field.[3] Pioneering work by David Hubel and Torsten Wiesel revealed the response properties of cells in the lateral geniculate nucleus and area V1 as well.[4] This has culminated in an extensive theory of hypercolumns that appear to enable a more or less detailed combinatorial representation of an organism's visual field.[5] There are also motion-processing cells in primate V5,[6] shape-sensitive cells in the inferior temporal cortex in macaques,[7] and action/performance cells (mirror neurons) in the macaque area F5,[8] to name but a few. We would not want to claim that these neurons are representations simply in virtue of their causal connections to environmental stimuli, but we do think they are likely to turn out to be representations.[9] These considerations seem to us to provide defeasible reasons to accept what cognitive psychologists typically presuppose, namely that cognitive processes involve representations.

Part of what motivates the view that cognitive processes involve *underived* representations is that such content appears to be required to explain lone thinkers. Some hundreds of millions of years ago, the brain of some primitive fish evolved in such a way as to incorporate a fundamentally new type of state. That primitive fish's brain contained a thought or belief. That primitive fish may have thought it was about to be attacked, or that there was something to eat nearby. One can speculate about what that first primitive content was. Perhaps it was not "I am about to be attacked!" or "I am about to be eaten!" or "There is something to eat." Perhaps it was something simpler like "Ah, there!" Whatever that first content was, it must have appeared in some one organism, either as a passing thought or perhaps some guide to action. And, whatever that first content was, it could not have been had in virtue of the contentful states of another organism, since *ex hypothesi* there were no such states. Similar considerations apply in historic times. Consider a solitary orangutan in a rainforest in Borneo. She

---

[3]   Lettvin et al. (1959).

[4]   Many of the most important papers are collected in a beautiful volume, Hubel and Wiesel (2005).

[5]   For a textbook account, see Sekuler and Blake (2002, ch. 4).

[6]   Zeki (1974).

[7]   Cf., e.g., Gross et al. (1972).

[8]   Di Pellegrino et al. (1992). For a review, see Rizzolatti and Craighero (2004).

[9]   Specifying the difference between causal connection and meaning was the central theme of "informational" approaches to naturalizing semantic content. Many of the papers in Stich and Warfield (1994) bear this out.

might reach for a piece of fruit because she sees the fruit, is hungry, and wants to eat it. A natural explanation of the animal's behavior is that she has cognitive states that are about the fruit and the state of her dietary needs. Yet, alone in the forest, the current contents of her thoughts are not the product of any neighboring cognitive agents. And, in fact, what appears to go on in the lone thinker seems to be plausible for groups of thinkers. The average human being is capable of thinking about things all by him- or herself.

In what follows, we presuppose that thoughts have non-derived semantic content, but that natural language has merely derived content. This is, of course, not entirely unproblematic. There are philosophers who think that meaningful language comes first, and then thoughts derive their semantic content from language.[10] Perhaps vervet monkey calls have semantic meanings, such as that there is a predator above or a predator below, that do not derive their meaning from content-bearing mental states. Thereafter, vervet mental content derives from these calls. We resist this order of derivation, however, since the system of vervet monkey calls, like many systems of animal communication, does not appear to be sufficiently elaborate to do justice to the range and diversity of mental representations that vervet behavior suggests. There are few vervet calls, but many vervet thoughts. We also resist this order of derivation since we do not think it can do justice to evolutionary history. The vervet monkey kind of story might work for many social animals, such as some insects, birds, and primates, but it looks much less plausible as a theory of, say, reptilian cognition. There are many organisms that appear to think, but that have at best minimal systems of interorganismal communication. In any case, this issue alone does not challenge the existence of non-derived content.

For philosophers who propose to take these kinds of observations seriously, there are obvious questions. How exactly does non-derived content emerge and how is derived content actually derived? In what follows, we will review what we think are some familiar types of answers to these questions, and then address three critiques of the hypothesis that cognition involves non-derived content. The first predates much of the debate over extended cognition. It is Dennett's (1990) critique of Searle's position on non-derived content. The second is Clark's (2005) criticisms of our appeal to non-derived representations as part of the mark of the cognitive.

---

[10]   Cf., e.g., Speaks (2006).

The third is a brief exposition of the dynamical systems and mobile robotics challenges to representationalism. Our contention is that neither Dennett (1990) nor Clark (2005), nor the dynamical systems theorizing, nor the mobile robotics theorizing, provide any compelling reason to doubt the existence of non-derived content, the viability of the derived/non-derived distinction, or the hypothesis that non-derived content is distinctive of cognitive processing. In choosing to address just this limited set of criticisms of an appeal to non-derived representations, we do not assume that we have exhausted all the extant and possible future criticisms of the hypothesis of non-derived content and its possible role in cognition. Such an exercise would likely constitute a book in itself. Instead, we take up only the challenges that appear to us to be most intimately involved with the extended cognition hypothesis. We merely wish to show that this portion of the mark of the cognitive deserves more serious and detailed consideration than it has so far received in the extended cognition literature.

3.2 The Basics on Derived and Underived Content

The central challenge facing those who hypothesize underived content is specifying the conditions under which an object "X" bears some non-derived content X. There is, in fact, a cottage industry in the philosophy of mind dedicated to attempts to answer this question. This literature attempts to explain, not how non-derived content can emerge *ex nihilo*, but how non-derived content can come from the content-free. This body of work attempts to specify naturalistic conditions that might constitute a basis for non-derived content.[11]

Searle is one well-known defender of the derived/non-derived distinction, who has also offered a theory of the basis for non-derived content.[12] He has frequently argued that a computer cannot be intelligent simply in virtue of running a particular program, since running a particular program does not suffice to endow the computer with non-derived

[11] The collection by Stich and Warfield (1994) is an excellent introduction to the area.
[12] Searle uses the term "intrinsic" content. Although we used this term in Adams and Aizawa (2001), we have stopped using it here, since we have found Searle's term to cause confusion.

representations.[13] According to Searle, the basis of non-derived representation is fundamentally different and strikingly simple. It is the brain. Just as digestion is a biological process of the stomach, so representation is just a biological process of the brain. Digestion is a causal power that stomachs have; representation is a causal power that brains have.

We are inclined to agree with Searle that merely running a computer program is not sufficient for generating non-derived representations or non-derived intentionality. We are, however, dissatisfied with Searle's view that representation is merely a causal power of the brain. We think that as this stands it does not tell us much about how the brain actually gives rise to representation or intentionality. We can read biology textbooks that explain how acids and enzymes in the mouth, stomach, and intestines cause the breakdown of certain molecules in food, but we have yet to find a chapter in a neuroscience textbook that provides a comparable explanation of how brains generate non-derived representations. This last point, however, should not be taken to mean that neuroscience is not committed to representations. It is. What neuroscience does not (yet?) tell us are the conditions in virtue of which, say, a particular neuron or the firing of a particular neuron represents, say, an oriented line at a particular position in the visual field, a color, or an action. This is something that is very much needed in the philosophy of neuroscience and the philosophy of mind. Nevertheless, the correctness or completeness of Searle's theory of non-derived content is a separate matter from the tenability of the derived/non-derived distinction. The distinction can be viable, even if Searle's theory of the origin of non-derived representation is incorrect or incomplete. This point can be reinforced by noting that there are any number of more detailed alternatives to be found in the philosophical literature.

Dretske (1981, 1988) provides a theory of the semantic content of thoughts that does not derive from prior semantics. According to Dretske, thought content arises due to acquisition of an indicator function. "X" comes to mean X when "X"s come to have the natural function of indicating Xs. If "X" is a syntactic symbol in the brain, it acquires a non-derived content when it comes to mean X. It means X via a process of neural recruitment for its ability to indicate Xs. Indicating the presence of Xs (carrying/conveying information about Xs) is not the same as semantically meaning X. The natural recruitment process is not driven by a mind or intelligence, but by the same kinds of natural causes that drive natural

---

[13]   Cf., e.g., Searle (1980, 1984).

selection for the function of the heart or kidney. This is what makes "X"s coming to mean Xs a theory of non-derived content. That is, the content is not derived from other states, objects, or processes with semantic content.

Jerry Fodor, for his part, has also offered a related naturalistic theory of content. This is his asymmetric causal dependency theory.[14] On Fodor's proposal, an object "X" will non-derivedly come to mean X if:

(1) Xs cause "X"s is a law.
(2)   Some "X"s are actually caused by Xs.
(3)   For all Y other than X, if Ys *qua* Ys actually cause "X"s, then Ys causing "X"s is asymmetrically dependent on Xs causing "X"s.
(4)   There are some non-X caused "X"s.

One can worry about the completely proper interpretation of Fodor's theory and whether or not it is a viable theory of non-derived content, but the ambition to have content emerge from the previously non-contentful is clear.[15]

As another example, on the picture theory of representation, developed by Robert Cummins, "X" means X if:

(1)   "X" is part of a relational structure R.
(2) X is part of a relational structure C.
(3)   The relational structure R is isomorphic to the relational structure C.
(4)   "X" is mapped to X under this isomorphism. (Cummins, 1996)

As with the Fodorian example, one can worry about exactly how one is to interpret Cummins's theory and its viability as a theory of non-derived content, but the goal of having content emerge from the previously non-contentful is again obvious.[16]

The question about derived content – namely, how the process of content derivation works – has been less thoroughly explored by

---

[14]   Cf., Fodor (1987, 1990).
[15]   For a discussion of Fodorian semantics, see Adams and Aizawa (1994).
[16]   Cf., Aizawa (2003), for a critique of Cummins's picture theory of representation.

philosophers of mind.[17] Dennett suggests that mere willing can endow something with a derived content.[18] Perhaps "X" means X, if some normal human being wills that "X" means X. Perhaps a string tied around one's finger means to remember to bring home coffee, if some normal human being simply wills to have the string bear this meaning. Yet mere acts of will appear to be insufficient to make sense of all cases of derived content. Perhaps merely willing could work for a string tied around a finger, but it could not make a word meaningful to others. Nor is it clear that some sort of performative act, such as saying "By this flag I will mean peace and nothing else," is sufficient to establish a corresponding derived meaning. Witness how such performatives might fare in attempts to assign new meanings to the swastika, the Confederate battle flag, or a burning cross.

Suffice it to say that there is no consensus in the philosophical community on what conditions enable "X" to bear non-derived content X, or on what conditions enable "X" to bear derived content X. A fortiori, there is no consensus on a more subtle question that has figured into the plausibility of hypothesizing both derived and non-derived content. If "X" means X in virtue of satisfying the conditions of some true theory of derived content, does this preclude "X" from meaning Y (or X) in virtue of satisfying the conditions of some true theory of non-derived content? If we pitch the question quite abstractly, asking whether satisfaction of conditions on derived content precludes satisfaction of conditions on non-derived content, or vice versa, we can see that the answer is not obvious, barring a specification of these conditions. Surely it is not an obvious logical or conceptual truth that satisfaction of one set of conditions precludes satisfaction of the other. For all anyone knows, satisfaction of conditions on derived meaning does not preclude the satisfaction of conditions on non-derived meaning, and vice versa.

Indeed, it seems to us crucial to the project of developing genuinely intelligent, cognizing machines that an object's satisfying conditions on derived meanings does not thereby preclude the object's satisfying other conditions on non-derived meaning. Suppose one wanted to build a genuine thinking machine. To do this, one would have to design the machine in such a way that the machine's symbols meant something to the machine in virtue of satisfying some conditions for non-derived content,

---

[17]   But see Lewis (1969).
[18]   Dennett (1990, p. 54).

conditions such as those in Cummins's or Fodor's or Dretske's theory of meaning. But the symbols in the mind of this machine would likely have meanings to the designers and builders, insofar as they would have to understand the machine and its design to build it. Yet, because the machine would have to be designed so as to meet the conditions of a true theory of non-derived content, the symbols would also have meanings for the machine. Indeed, somewhat surprisingly perhaps, the symbols in the machine "X," "Y," and "Z" could mean X, Y, and Z in virtue of satisfying conditions for both derived and non-derived content. It is in virtue of satisfying the conditions of a theory of non-derived content that the meanings of the machine's symbols would not be semantically derived or dependent upon us. The syntactic items in the machine would be causally produced by us, but they would not have their contents derived exclusively from us.

In advancing the hypothesis that cognition involves non-derived representations, we do not presuppose that machines or other objects outside the head *cannot* bear non-derived content. Maybe an argument could be given for this view, but we do not have one. Instead, our conjecture is merely that as a matter of contingent empirical fact, they do not. Although there is room for dispute about just which objects in the world might be bearers of non-derived content, we think that for at least some of the cases that matter to the extended cognition debate, there will be some consensus about which objects do not.

3.3 Dennett's Critique of Original Content

In "The myth of original intentionality," Dennett appears to want to argue for four claims involving the distinction between original and derived intentionality:[19]

1 Humans lack original intentionality.[20]
2 Humans have derived intentionality only.[21]

---

[19] There is, of course, a distinction between representation and intentionality. For present purposes, however, will set aside these differences as tangential to our present concerns.
[20] Cf., Dennett (1990, p. 59).
[21] Cf., Dennett (1990, pp. 59 and 60).

3   There is no distinction between original and derived intentionality.[22]
4   There is no such thing as original intentionality.[23]

Dennett's case for these four claims has two principal components. The first is an argument concerning the relationship between derived and non-derived content and the other is a "survivorship" argument. We will review these in this order.

Dennett contends that "No artefact of ours, no product of AI, could ever have original intentionality simply in virtue of the way it conducted itself in the world or in virtue of its 'formal' design" (Dennett, 1990, p. 57). Here Dennett is echoing Searle's (1980, 1984) view of the matter. Dennett's case for this begins with a consideration of an encyclopedia with derived intentionality. Even if we were to make an electronic version of this encyclopedia with automated question-answering capacities, thereby giving the system additional "formal" design features and additional capacities for interacting with humans, it would still contain only derived content. Similarly, no matter how we program a chess-playing program, he supposes, it will have only derived intentionality with derived goals of defeating human opponents, concealing what it knows from its opponents, and tricking its opponents. Suppose, simply for the sake of argument, that Dennett's contentions are correct, that no artifact could have original intentionality merely in virtue of its programming or the way it interacts with other agents. One can concede this while still maintaining that there are conditions other than "formal" properties of machine design and conduct in the world that enable a machine to have original, underived content. Other conditions, such as those in Dretske's indicator function account, Fodor's asymmetric causal dependency theory, or Cummins's picture theory of representation might suffice. So, if we review Dennett's paper, we find that, technically, he does not really even attempt to establish a conclusion as strong as that artifacts cannot have original intentionality, or that an object's having derived content precludes its having non-derived content. Such a case does not appear to be on his philosophical radar. Instead, just as he implicitly promises, Dennett argues for the claim that no artifact could ever have original intentionality simply in virtue of the way it conducted itself in the world or in virtue of its "formal" design. So, as things stand, it appears that one cannot simply move from the observation that "X" is an artifact and has

[22]   Cf., Dennett (1990, pp. 56 and 62).
[23]   Cf., Dennett (1990, pp. 43, 54, and 62).

derived content to the conclusion that "X" lacks non-derived content. Such a move requires more argumentation than Dennett has provided.

So much for the relationship between derived and non-derived content. We are now ready for Dennett's "survivorship" argument, an argument that begins with an analogy. Dennett invites us to imagine someone who creates a robot to carry her in suspended animation for four centuries. To insure the passenger's survival, this robot is designed to navigate about the world, seeking energy sources and avoiding danger. It is further designed to interact with humans and perhaps other robots in order to further the survival of its passenger. Such a robot, Dennett supposes, has only derived intentionality or derived content, since it is a *mere artifact*. Exactly here we have the *non sequitur* we have explained above. The claim that the robot's content is merely derived does not follow as a logical or conceptual truth from the fact that the robot is an artifact. Still, it is Dennett's example, so we will simply add an additional assumption that the robot does not satisfy the conditions of any true theory of non-derived content. Once we concede that the robot has merely derived content, however, the game is supposed to be over. The derivation relation that obtains between the robot and the designer of the robot is supposed to be the same as the semantic derivation relation that obtains between a normal human being and her genes. From this, we are supposed to see that human cognitive content is derived and that humans don't have original – that is, underived – intentionality. In other words, Dennett evidently thinks that this argument establishes the first two conclusions we attributed to him at the start of this section.

As we see it, Dennett does not establish either of these two conclusions. Let us consider, first, the idea that all human cognitive content is derived. It turns out that Dennett is somewhat equivocal here. At times, he appears to think that human cognitive content derives from our genes in the sense of being a product of natural selection during our evolutionary history.[24] At other times, he appears to think that human cognitive content derives from our genes in the sense of being a causal product of the developmental process.[25] So, a thorough refutation of Dennett's argument will have to

---

[24]   Cf., "We may call our own intentionality real, but we must recognize that it is derived from the intentionality of natural selection" (Dennett, 1990, p. 62).

[25]   Cf., "But this vision of things, while it provides a satisfying answer to the question of whence came our own intentionality, does seem to leave us with an embarrassment, for it derives our own intentionality from entities – genes – whose intentionality is surely a paradigm case of mere *as if* intentionality!" (Dennett, 1990, p. 60).

address both the phylogenetic and the ontogenetic interpretation. We will try to be thorough.

For Dennett's argument to show that all of our cognitive content is phylogenetically or ontogenetically derived from our genes, the sense in which our cognitive content derives from our genes must be the same as the sense in which the contents of stop signs, flags, and words of English derive from human minds. Although a maximally compelling case for the difference between content derivation and these ontogenetic and phylogenetic derivations might involve having secured a true theory of content derivation, one can still draw attention to significant differences between these types of derivations. Dennett is simply wrong to maintain that "our intentionality is highly derived, and in just the same way that the intentionality of our robots (and even our books and maps) is derived" (Dennett, 1990, p. 62).

Consider the fact that organisms derive from their genes in a developmental sense. Content derivation is essentially a meaning-conferring process, where ontogenetic development is not essentially a meaning-conferring process. The product of content derivation must be a content bearer, but the product of ontogenetic development need not be a content bearer. Ontogenetic development does not necessarily make an organism, or any of its parts, a representation or a content bearer. Organisms do not represent anything to, or mean anything for, their genes. A penguin doesn't mean anything. It is not a representation. It is not a content bearer. A penguin does not stand for or mean anything to the DNA that causally contributed to its development. A stop sign means something, is a representation, and typically means something to many humans. If you don't like penguins or their ontogeny, take plants or fungi as your example.

Next, consider the idea that humans are derived to some degree by natural selection. Essentially the same observations hold again *mutatis mutandis*. Where content derivation is essentially a semantic process, evolution by natural selection is not. Humans and penguins are not representations. They do not mean anything. Nor do they mean anything to natural selection. Humans and penguins are not representations that natural selection uses. Mother Nature just doesn't use humans, penguins, plants, or fungi to represent anything. So there is nothing like the *assigned meaning* model of derived content going on in natural selection.

Still, Dennett is clearly suggesting that since natural selection is intentional, and our thought symbols may have derived from processes of natural selection, then our thoughts too have derived content. The idea is that our thoughts have derived content because they are derived from selectional processes that are intentional. The problem with this view is that the causal processes involved in natural selection do not have semantic meaning. For example, nothing in them can be falsely tokened. False tokening is necessary to move from the level of information or indication (smoke in the forest means fire, and there is no fire without smoke) to the level of semantic meaning ("fire" means fire). At the semantic level one can produce a symbol or set of symbols, "There is fire here now," that are false (there is no fire here now). Semantic meaning has this feature of being able to be detached from the immediate surroundings, and to be false.

It is true that there can be *selection for* a trait or characteristic. But this sense of *selection for* is not the same as reflective, purposive selection for, say, a new car. In the latter case, one has to have the idea of what a car is and a desire for one. In natural selection for, say, a heart, there is no *idea* of what a heart is, nor a *desire* that creatures have operational hearts. The foregoing considerations give us reason to think that the notion of derivation used with regard to derived content is not the same as the notion of derivation found in natural selection.[26]

Here is another difference between the kind of derivation found in derived content versus the kinds of derivation found in ontogeny and phylogeny. Where content derivation is essentially a process of conferring meaning, ontogenetic and phylogenetic derivations are not meaning conferring. They are, instead, a species of causal production. A bird is developmentally derived from its genes in the sense that the genes are causally relevant to its growth and existence. A bird is historically derived by natural selection in the sense that natural selection is causally relevant to its form and existence. Yet an item bearing derived content need not be causally produced by a cognitive agent for whom it is meaningful. It is not the blue-collar manufacturer of a stop light who makes the red light mean stop and the green light mean go. It is not the person who waves the white flag who makes it mean what it does. It is not the typist who makes the letters on the page mean what they do. Though there are cases in which making (causal production) and making meaningful (deriving content) coincide, the process of making an object is distinct from the process of making an

---

[26] Perhaps the human ontogenetic process gives rise to some innate representations and innate knowledge, but they are not representations for the genes. Such knowledge does not consist of representations that genes use.

object meaningful. The process of tokening a representation is distinct from the process of making that token meaningful.

Even if there is a sense in which DNA encodes instructions from which symbols in the brain are built, this does not mean that those symbols in the brain acquire their semantic content from the DNA. First, the structure in the brain formed during development, and which will become a symbol, may have to acquire its content by causal interaction with information from the world. The genes may endow us with "belief boxes," but DNA hardly fills those boxes with beliefs. Second, even if DNA represents, it cannot be falsely tokened (as can a thought, belief, or intention). So there is little in DNA or its causal activity during development that resembles the way in which meaning is assigned by a human mind to an artifact or symbol. So, there are good reasons to think that the derivation of the human mind from the human genome is unlike the derivation of derived content from prior content.

Suppose, however, that Dennett could solve all these problems, that he could secure the claim that there is human cognitive content that is either an ontogenetic or phylogenetic artifact of the human genome. That is, suppose that he could secure the claim that there are things in the human brain that have their derived content in virtue of satisfying some set of conditions on non-derived content (Dennett's second claim cited above). Still, from what we have said before, one cannot infer just from the fact that human brain states have some *derived* content in virtue of one set of conditions that human brain states lack *underived* content in virtue of another set. Additional argumentation must be given to support the idea that satisfying the conditions on derived content for some objects precludes the satisfaction of any set of conditions on underived content. Yet, as emphasized above, Dennett provides no such argumentation.

So far, we have rejected Dennett's argument for the view that human cognitive states lack original content and his view that human cognitive content is only derived. Suppose, however, that we concede to Dennett the two claims he defends. Even with these generous concessions, Dennett still has no arguments for his other claims about original and derived intentionality. Take the claim that there is no distinction between derived and non-derived intentionality. Even if Dennett were correct in his view that human cognitive content is derived from our DNA or from our evolutionary history and that we lack original intentionality, his robot thought experiment does nothing to show that the distinction is false or ill considered. Dennett seems simply to be mistaken about the consequences of his own thought experiment.[27]

Finally, there is Dennett's claim that there is no such thing as original intentionality and, in fact, that the notion of original intentionality is "incoherent."[28] Suppose that Dennett's robot thought experiment did secure the conclusion that humans have only derived intentionality. Still, that does not show that there is no original intentionality. Perhaps original intentionality could be found in either DNA or "Mother Nature." So, why would DNA or Mother Nature not have original intentionality? Dennett *claims* that they do not have original intentionality in the sense we have been considering; instead, they have their intentionality in virtue of the intentional stance.[29] But there is no argument for this, because Dennett does not explain this derivation.

This last point bears some further exposition regarding Dennett's views about *the intentional stance*. Dennett (1981) believes that when it comes to explaining the behavior of a system, one of three things happens: one adopts the *physical stance* (one explains behavior in terms of the system's physical properties), or one adopts the *design stance* (one explains behavior in terms of the structural and programmed properties that nature or the engineer put in place), or one adopts the *intentional stance* (one explains behavior in terms of the goals, beliefs, desires, and intentions of the system). For instance, only adopting the intentional stance seems to work in making arrangements to pick someone up at the airport. Knowing all the physical or biological properties of the person's body alone won't tell you where or when to meet the person, or why she will be there. But knowing she has agreed to come for a job interview, wants the job, and believes this is the best way to get it helps you predict and explain her behavior. In taking this stance, one asks only whether attributions of "beliefs," "desires," or "intentions" help predict and explain the behavior of the system. One need not find physical structures inside the system that correspond to these intentional states; nor need one know how a naturally existing system could develop internal structures with meaning or content on their own (independently of our taking this stance towards them). To return to the problem for Dennett's intentional stance, we have to ask how it gets started. How does the practice of taking the intentional stance get under way? If person

---

[27] Cf., Dennett (1990, p. 56).

[28] Dennett (1990, pp. 54 and 62).

[29] Dennett (1990, pp. 59–60).

A takes the stance with respect to system B, person A must have intentional mental states himself in order to be able to take the stance. But how it is that person A gets these mental states? Nowhere in Dennett's corpus does he come to grips with this question.[30] That is, Dennett is quite happy to make use of talk of "beliefs," "desires" and "intentions" while taking the intentional stance toward another system, but he does not ask how such stance taking is possible in the first place.

So, in "The myth of original intentionality," Dennett has given no good reason to think that humans have only derived content. Nor has he given any reason to think that humans lack original (non-derived) content. For that matter, he has not given any reason to think that non-derived content is a myth or to doubt the derived/non-derived distinction. Finally, we do not see that Dennett has provided a viable alternative to hypothesizing non-derived content in cognition.

3.4   Clark's Critique of Original Content

Clark (2005) offers, among other things, a challenge to our hypothesis that cognition involves non-derived representations. We find this reply surprising, since in earlier work Clark defended a view of the nature of cognition that accords strikingly well with our general approach. He and Rick Grush argued that cognition involves a particular type of non-derived representation and that this type of representation figures in certain kinds of functional economies:

> The problematic distinction (between systems that can be usefully understood, from the outside, in representational terms and those in which the representations are actually for the system) is thus revealed as genuine. (Clark and Grush, 1999, p. 9)

> Instead, we are suggesting that, as a matter of empirical fact, the capacities most strongly associated with the traditional notion of cognition will turn out to be supported (made possible) by the presence of robustly representational inner states or processes: inner states or processes that are a) scientifically (non-semantically) identifiable and b) serve as stand-ins for specific extra-neural states of affairs. (ibid., p. 10)

---

[30]   See Adams (1991).

What happens if humans turn out not to have intrinsic content? Would they not be cognitive agents? No. Then our theory will have turned out to be false. (ibid.)

Although we do not specifically endorse the theory of representationalism broached in Clark and Grush's paper, we nevertheless view them as working within a broadly "rules and representations" kind of approach to demarcating the cognitive from the non-cognitive. Clark and Grush's approach at least bears a family resemblance to the kind of approach we endorse. However Clark ultimately comes down on the role of representation in cognition, we think that his subsequent criticism of the original/derived content distinction and the hypothesis that cognition involves original content is not compelling.

Consider how Clark proposes to rebut our claim that cognition involves non-derived representations. His response has three components. First, he claims that, "it is unclear that there is any such thing as intrinsic content anyway" (Clark, 2005, p. 1). Why is this? Three pages later, Clark claims that the distinction between intrinsic and derived content is unclear (cf., Clark, 2005, p. 4). He does not, however, say why it is unclear. In fact, he gives a reasonably clear account of the distinction. More importantly, even if the distinction were not that clear, that would not suffice to show that there is no such thing as intrinsic content.[31] So, Clark gives no good reason to think that the original/derived content distinction is flawed or that there is no such thing as intrinsic content.

Clark's second claim is that, "in so far as the notion [of intrinsic content] is intelligible at all, there is no reason to believe that external, non-biological structures are incapable of supporting such content" (Clark, 2005, p. 1). Here, we are quite sympathetic with Clark. We do not propose that non-biological structures are incapable of supporting non-derived content. Our view is that, as a matter of contingent empirical fact, cognitive processing typically occurs within brains, even though it is possible for it to extend. To keep this view consistent with the hypothesis that cognition involves non-derived content, we have to maintain that it is possible for non-derived

---

[31]   At one point, Clark was apparently appealing to Dennett (1990) as having shown that there is no such thing as intrinsic content. Although Clark did not know this when writing his 2005 *Analysis* paper, we had a forthcoming critique of Dennett (1990). This paper has since appeared as Aizawa and Adams (2005).

content to occur outside the brain and body.[32] Clark's real challenge to our view begins with the observation that humans can have mental representations involving Venn diagrams, which are surely conventional. This suggests that thought might involve non-derived representations. As we see things, however, Clark's observation adds nothing more than a wrinkle to the basic story that cognition involves non-derived representations. Venn diagrams mean what they do in virtue of Venn's convention. This is common ground between us and Clark. When someone, say Gary, imagines Venn diagrams, however, we think that his mental representation of the Venn diagrams means what it does in virtue of satisfying some conditions on non-derived representations. It also doesn't follow from the fact that the content of Gary's thought is of an object with content derived by (social) convention that Gary's thought itself has the content it does in virtue of that social convention. Gary's mental image can, in principle, have both derived and non-derived content. This is a point that we made in connection with our discussion of Dennett's survivorship argument.[33]

Clark evidently anticipates our response here; hence in the next paragraph he invokes an example in which there are Martians whose biological memories store bit-mapped images of text. These images are supposed to be conventional, derived internal representations of conventional derived external representations. That is, texts are conventional representations of words and the Martian bit-mapped images of the texts are supposed to be a conventional way of representing the conventional representation. *Ex hypothesi*, these bit-mapped images of texts do not have non-derived content. Throw in additional assumptions about these Martians using these representations to engage in some apparently cognitively demanding task, such as flying a spaceship. Clark thinks it is simply obvious that we should say that the Martian brain states involving these representations are cognitive. The only resistance to this conclusion, he thinks, must be "skin-and-skull based prejudice." Thus, we should not expect that cognition requires non-derived representations.

[32]   Clark notes that this is, in fact, our view in the following: "But since Adams and Aizawa stress that they are defending only a contingent, humans-as-currently-constituted, form of cognitive intracranialism, I suspect that they will concede this general point without much argument" (Clark, 2005, p. 4).

[33]   We make this same point in another way in Aizawa and Adams (2005). We do not think Clark saw this paper prior to submitting Clark (2005). Further discussion of this point may be found in Adams and Aizawa (forthcoming a).

Here, we think it is perfectly reasonable for us to stand by the view that these Martian representational states are not cognitive states. We have a theory of what cognition involves. The Martians in Clark's thought experiment do not satisfy the conditions of that theory. So we must either reject the hypothesis that the Martians have cognitive processing or the hypothesis that cognition involves non-derived representations. Why can we not rationally choose to stand by our theory? Our theory is an empirical conjecture about the nature of cognition, not a definition of cognition. Thus, future scientific developments could undermine our theory and force revisions. Alternately, our theory could turn out to be so successful and well-confirmed that we determine that Martians are not cognizers. What their spaceship handling abilities, for example, might show is merely that they have managed some trick of flying without thinking. Exactly which course of action should prevail depends on exactly how the future develops on a number of fronts, not just one single case. This said, Clark has not shown how things have gone badly for our view.

Consider another example that we think might bear out the potentially difficult choice to be made between a bizarre discovery and a well-entrenched theory. Suppose that future science discovers things that look like ducks, walk like ducks, and quack like ducks. They are probably ducks, but not necessarily. Suppose these things lack DNA in their cell nuclei. Instead of DNA, these things have some other chain molecule that works in much the way that DNA works in previously studied ducks. The remaining meiotic and mitotic biochemical apparatus of the cells in these newly discovered things is the same as the biochemical apparatus of the cells in ducks. The chain molecules found in these new creatures fit into the other biochemical apparatus of the cells of these new creatures in just the way that duck DNA fits into the biochemical apparatus of old-fashioned duck cells. This would certainly be a surprising and baffling discovery, but it seems to us to be perfectly defensible to maintain that these new things aren't ducks. What we have in Clark's Martian case and our duck-like creature case are instances in which we are invited to entertain surprising and even bizarre possible findings that appear to conflict with our theories of what constitutes cognition and what constitutes a duck. It might be that, on balance, we should reject our current theories of cognition and of ducks, but, then again, perhaps we should stand by them. At this point, we don't see sufficient reason to abandon our theory of cognition.

Clark's third objection to our view about intrinsic content is that even if external, non-biological structures were incapable of supporting intrinsic content, "this would not actually compromise the case for the extended mind" (Clark, 2005, p. 1). It is not clear to us that Clark really tries to substantiate this particular charge. He does, however, have something more to say about our view of the role of intrinsic content in cognition. In our paper, we noted that

> Having argued that, in general there must be non-derived content in cognitive processes, it must be admitted that it is unclear to what extent every cognitive state of each cognitive process must involve non-derived content. (Adams and Aizawa, 2001, p. 50)

Having quoted us on this, Clark claims that, "this concession, I submit, removes the entire force of the appeal to intrinsic content as a reason for rejecting [extended mind]. For it was no part of [extended mind] to claim that one could build an entire cognizer out of Otto-style notebooks" (Clark, 2005, p. 6). Here, we think Clark misses the importance of the foregoing qualification. In the passage above, we were concerned about what to say about the possibility of there being things like punctuation marks and parentheses in our hypothetical language of thought. Perhaps the cognitive punctuation marks and parentheses aren't representational items at all, and hence bear no content at all, non-derived or otherwise. We don't think we have good reason to hypothesize that every component of every state of every cognitive process must bear non-derived content. That is a pretty strong empirical hypothesis, which, had we advocated it, would have been subject to challenge for being too strong or being undermotivated. Clearly, we need the view that our requirement of non-derived content, though not maximally demanding regarding the pervasiveness of non-derived content, is still demanding enough. We think it is. Our view is that at least some components of cognitive states require some non-derived content, where the states of a notepad for arithmetical computations, Otto's notebook, video games, and most mundane tools do not. We think this is an empirical hypothesis that may well need refinement in the light of further investigation, but it is not for that reason unprincipled.[34]

---

[34]   A subsequent paper, Clark (forthcoming b) appears to accept our clarified reading of the qualification broached in Adams and Aizawa (2001).

3.5   Anti-Representationalism in Dynamical Systems and Mobile Robotics

Some discussions of extended cognition refer to work in dynamical systems theory and mobile robotics that is supposed to provide reason to think that cognition does not involve representations. We do not think this is a consensus view of what these research programs show.[35] Nevertheless, the supposed implications merit some attention. We do not have sufficient space in this book to do complete justice to the complexity of current work on dynamical systems and mobile robotics. Instead, we will present the reasons we have to be skeptical about the supposed anti-representationalist implications of this work. In fact, we will narrow our focus to what seems to us to be the principal problem with the anti-representationalist inspiration coming out of both of these traditions.

In an early philosophy paper entertaining the hypothesis that cognitive processes might be the changes in the state-space of a dynamical system, van Gelder (1995) drew attention to two ways in which one might adjust a throttle valve from a steam engine to maintain a flywheel at constant speed. One might be through an algorithm that involves measuring the speed of the flywheel, comparing that speed to a target speed, and then making adjustments to the throttle valve, if necessary. Another way might be to link the flywheel to a vertical spindle. On this spindle, one might add rotating arms holding metal balls at their ends. The rotating mechanism of the arms might then be linked to the adjustable throttle. If the flywheel rotates too quickly, the centrifugal force on the rotating arms increases, extending the arms outward, thereby slowing the throttle. If the flywheel rotates too slowly, the centrifugal force on the rotating arms decreases, lowering the arms inward, thereby speeding up the throttle. This organization constitutes the Watt governor. Suppose, for the sake of van Gelder's argument, that the first method is a computational method involving

---

[35]   Giunti (1995), for example, proposes that dynamical systems theory is a sufficiently general theory of cognition that it might encompass traditional symbolic models. In the mobile robotics tradition, when Brooks reprinted his paper, "Intelligence without representation," he added a prefatory comment in which he says, "I must admit that the title is a little inflammatory – a careful reading shows that I mean intelligence without conventional representations, rather than without representation at all" (Brooks, 1999, p. 79).

representations and the second is a non-computational method in a dynamical system that does not involve representations, and that these are genuinely different methods.[36] The suggestion, then, is that if cognitive processing consists of changes in the state-space of a dynamical system that does not use representations, then cognitive processing does not require representations.

We think this argument has little force against our hypothesis that cognition involves representations, derived or underived. Van Gelder's argument observes that there are two ways of completing or performing a task – in this case, regulating the flow of steam from a steam engine. One way is by computer and the other by a dynamical system (that does not use representations). Suppose this is so. Now take a task such as obtaining food. One way to perform this task might be to deploy cognitive processing mechanisms, such as visual recognition, evaluating individual objects for edibility, planning a course through the environment, and so forth. Many animals apparently use one or another such cognitive strategy for obtaining food. But, another way to obtain food apparently involves no cognition at all. The Venus flytrap, like all insectivorous plants, evidently uses an entirely non-cognitive method. This plant secretes a sweet mucous that attracts insects. When an insect approaches the mucous and appropriately triggers one of the hair structures in the trap, the trap snaps shut. Over the course of the next several days, a trapped insect will be completely enveloped and digested by glands in the leaf. Does the way in which a Venus flytrap obtains food show that cognition does not require representation? No. A perfectly reasonable thing to say is that the task of obtaining food simply does not require cognition. The point, therefore, is that showing that some task is accomplished by some dynamical system that does not use representations does not show that cognition need not involve representations. Instead, it may show only that the task does not need to be performed using cognitive processing at all, and hence does not need to be performed using representations.

One might contend that obtaining food is not a cognitive task, so that the example is misleading. That's fine. Suppose, then, that the task is more complicated. Suppose that the task is to move about a building, looking for aluminum soda cans. Humans will do this one way, employing patently

---

[36] Chemero (2000) challenges van Gelder's anti-representational interpretation of the Watt governor.

cognitive mechanisms, perhaps mechanisms of visual search, object recognition, and planning. Exactly which cognitive mechanisms will be involved and exactly what they are like is certainly a topic for investigation, but beyond much scientific doubt humans will use at least some cognitive mechanisms. Now suppose that some scientist or engineer develops a dynamical system that completes this task without using any representations. One thing one might say is that this shows that cognition does not involve representations, but we think that that inference is too quick. All that this might show is that, prior expectations notwithstanding, the task does not really requires cognitive processing, and hence does not really require representations.

But one might persist. Perhaps one needs something more demanding than looking for aluminum soda cans in a building. Suppose, instead, one wants to build creatures that have the following capacities:

- A Creature must cope appropriately and in a timely fashion with changes in its dynamic environment.
- A Creature should be robust with respect to its environment. Minor changes in the properties of the world should not lead to total collapse of the Creature's behavior; rather one should expect only a gradual change in capabilities of the Creature as the environment changes more and more.
- A Creature should be able to maintain multiple goals and, depending on the circumstances it finds itself in, change which particular goals it is actively pursuing; thus it can both adapt to surroundings and capitalize on fortuitous circumstances.
- A Creature should do *something* in the world; it should have some purpose in being. (Brooks, 1999, p. 86)

At first glance, one might expect *these* conditions to be attainable only by agents who perform cognitive processing. But, unless one takes care to interpret the conditions with this aim in mind, one should be prepared to discover that some non-cognitive organisms meet these conditions. Some plants are likely to meet these conditions. Plants cope with their environments insofar as they can survive, reproduce, and even flourish. They often respond to their environments by sending out roots in appropriate directions and displaying phototaxis. Many can thrive in a wide range of climates or environments. They can have multiple goals, if one counts producing leaves, roots, stems, taking in carbon dioxide, collecting water, and so forth. Perhaps they also do something in the world and have some purpose in essentially the same sense in which cognitive animals do. So, possible initial expectations to the contrary, we should not assume that these conditions can only be satisfied by cognitive agents.

The application of the foregoing considerations to mobile robotics should be clear. Brooks (1999) describes a mobile robot, Herbert, which has the task of finding soda cans in offices at MIT, picking them up, and bringing them back to a start point. Just for the sake of argument, grant that Herbert lacks representations, derived or underived.[37] Further, suppose that Herbert meets the design criteria that Brooks describes above, those involving coping appropriately and in a timely fashion with changes in the environment, performing in a robust manner in the environment, and so forth. From this one might infer that Herbert has intelligence, or is a cognitive agent, even though Herbert lacks representations. Anyone running this argument, however, apparently presupposes that any mechanism for finding aluminum cans in the rooms at MIT requires cognitive processing or intelligence, that any device that can accomplish this task must use cognitive processing or be intelligent. Yet once we challenge this estimation of the task, a different analysis becomes available. That is, it could be that, while some tasks, such as the soda can collection task, can be accomplished in the way humans do it – namely, by deploying cognitive mechanisms – other devices or organisms can also accomplish the task through chains of simple non-cognitive mechanisms. Perhaps this shows that, rather than using cognitive mechanisms to accomplish the task, one can perform the task using purely stimulus-driven, non-cognitive mechanisms. Just as might in some sense be best for an organism to try to perform some task without representations, so it might in some sense be best for an organism to try to perform some task without thinking about it.

The present considerations reinforce one of the principal points of this book, namely that the advocates of extended cognition need to develop a plausible theory of cognition. In the absence of a plausible theory of cognition, one has little reason to say that Herbert, or some dynamical system lacking representations, is in fact a cognitive agent. It could be a merely non-cognitive machine. It could be more like a plant than an animal. We will return to this topic in Chapter 5, when we discuss some of the theories of the mark of the cognition that are found, implicitly or explicitly, in the extended cognition literature.

---

[37] Brooks (1999, p. 79) explicitly disavows this interpretation of his work.

3.6   Conclusion

In this chapter, we have offered an empirical hypothesis concerning what all cognitive processes have in common, namely, that they all involve non-derived representations. We do not take this to be part of a definition of the cognitive. Nor do we mean to stipulate what we shall mean by the word "cognitive." Nor do we mean to stipulate that non-derived representations are found only in the brain, core regions of the brain, the central nervous system, or anywhere else for that matter. We do not maintain that non-derived representations must be found in the head. That cognition involves non-derived representations is one empirical hypothesis; that non-derived representations are to be found in some particular regions of spacetime is another. In addition to our hypothesis that cognition involves non-derived representations, we want to advance the further empirical hypothesis that, as a matter of contingent empirical fact, non-derived representations happen to occur these days only in nervous systems. Insofar as this latter hypothesis is true, we have some non-question-begging, defeasible reason to think that, contrary to what the advocates of extended cognition propose, cognitive processing is by and large to be found within the brain.

There are some limitations in using this hypothesis to delimit the bounds of cognition. These are limitations that arise because of what (we think) is not currently known about cognition. In the first place, there is the fact that philosophers and psychologists have yet to develop a theory of naturalized semantics that enjoys much widespread acceptance. It remains unclear just exactly what naturalistic conditions give rise to non-derived content; hence it remains correspondingly unclear just exactly what objects bear non-derived content. There will be hard cases aplenty here. A second limitation is that it is unclear just how completely cognitive states must be representational. This is a point we noted earlier. Must every component of every cognitive state be a representation? This seems to be an overly strong empirical hypothesis not warranted by any data we know of. Take one epistemic possibility. As far as we know, cognitive processes might involve representations that include a small fixed set of non-representational functional elements, such as punctuation marks and parentheses. Such items might count as part of a language of thought based on the manner in which they interact with items having non-derived content. If this happens, then cognitive states will to some extent be less than maximally dependent on non-derived content. Not every part of every cognitive state will be content bearing.

Despite these limitations, we believe that there are instances in which an appeal to the hypothesis of non-derived representations will support the rejection of the analysis of some examples as instances of extended cognition. Support for this contention, however, will have to wait until we have developed our positive view in more detail and come to the actual application of our positive view to the case for extended cognition.

Chapter 4

Cognitive Processes

In Chapter 3, we defended the idea that one difference between cognitive processes and non-cognitive processes is that the former involve non-derived representations. In this chapter, we advance a second kind of difference. The cognitive differs from the non-cognitive in virtue of the kinds of mechanisms that are involved. For the purposes of locating cognition, this is perhaps a more practical guide than the hypothesis of non-derived representations, because cognitive psychologists have invested so much effort in developing experimental protocols that promise to reveal the nature of cognitive processes and the mechanisms underlying them. Moreover, we believe they have enjoyed some success in this. This is not, we believe, an idiosyncratic view. In a review of the embodied cognition literature, Wilson (2002) observed that the advocates of extended cognition frequently do not take account of the processing characteristics commonly supposed to be found in human cognition. Further, we view Rupert's (2004) discussion of the nature of memory processing to be quite sympathetic to the general kind of critique broached in our "Bounds of cognition" paper. What we propose to do in this chapter is simply clarify and emphasize the point we have already made by reviewing a number of concrete examples from theories of memory and vision. We do not claim that all cognition must contain exactly the mechanisms found in human cognition. There could be robot cognition that does not contain these specific human mechanisms, but we should not suppose that robot cognition could contain just any arbitrary mechanisms that might mimic cognition. Theorizing about cognition and its location must be sensitive to the kinds of mechanisms that implement cognitive processes. To date, insufficient attention has been paid to mechanisms that implement cognitive processes.

4.1   Individuating Process Types in Science

To begin, note that our contention that the difference between the cognitive and the non-cognitive ought to be made out by reference to the nature of the underlying processes is not a mere assertion or assumption on our part. It is a common, although not universal, practice in more developed sciences, such as physics, chemistry, and biology.[1] Let us consider some examples of taxonomy-by-mechanism in action.

In the *Novum Organum*, Francis Bacon proposed a set of methods for determining the causes of things. According to one of these methods, to find the cause of X, one should list all the positive instances of things that are X, then find what is common to them all. As an example, Bacon applies this method to the "form of heat." On his list of hot things, Bacon includes the rays of the Sun, fiery meteors, burning thunderbolts, eruptions of flame from the cavities of mountains, all bodies rubbed violently, piles of damp hay, quicklime sprinkled with water, horse-dung, the internal portions of animals, strong vinegar which when placed on the skin produces sensation of burning, and keen and intense cold that produces a sensation of burning. Bacon conjectured that what was common to these was a high degree of molecular vibration and that the intensity of heat of a thing is the intensity of molecular vibration. Bacon clearly intended to carve nature at its joints, but it simply turns out that, as a matter of contingent empirical fact, the things that appear hot, or produce the sensation of being hot, do not constitute a natural kind. The rays of the Sun, meteors, friction due to heat, body heat, and so forth simply do not have a common cause or underlying mechanism. There is no single scientific theory that encompasses them all; the phenomena are explained by distinct theories. Heat due to friction is described by physics. Heat from decomposition falls to biology. Exothermic reactions are described by chemistry.

As a second example, there are the late nineteenth century developments in the theory of evolution. By this time, Darwin's biogeographical, morphological, taxonomic, and embryological arguments had persuaded many biologists of the theory of evolution by common descent. Despite this, the majority of biologists were reluctant to accept Darwin's hypothesis that evolution is caused primarily by natural selection. In this intellectual

---

[1]   We made a case for this in Adams and Aizawa (2001, pp. 51–2), by providing illustrations of the principle in action in other sciences.

environment, biologists returned for a second look at Lamarckian theories of the inheritance of acquired characteristics. In support of their theory, neo-Lamarckians pointed to cases that, in retrospect, proved to be instances in which a mother would contract some disease, then pass this disease on to her offspring *in utero*. Phenomenologically, this looks like the inheritance of acquired characteristics, but, in truth, inheritance and infection involve distinct causal processes. Inheritance involves genetic material in the sex cells of a parent being passed on to offspring; infection is the transmission of an alien organism, perhaps via the circulatory system, in isolation from the sex cells. To a first approximation, inheritance is a process in the germ line of an organism, where infection is a process in the soma line of an organism. It is only after the true causal differences between inheritance and infection are made clear that one can conclude that we have one less instance of the inheritance of acquired characteristics than we might at one time have thought. Throughout the episode, Lamarckians were aiming to carve nature at its joints, but in the absence of a true understanding of the nature of the processes underlying inheritance and infection, these distinct kinds of processes had to appear to be the same, both as instances of the inheritance of acquired characteristics.

Evolutionary biologists draw a contrast between homologous and analogous structures. Homologous structures in distinct species of organisms are those that are similar in virtue of the distinct species sharing a common ancestor. The most famous cases of homology, of course, are the forelimbs of vertebrates. Bats, moles, dogs, and humans share the same number and relative placement of bones in their forelimbs, even though each combination of bones is modified to meet distinct specific needs. Homologous structures are the product of divergent evolutionary pathways. Analogous structures in distinct species, by contrast, are those that are similar in virtue of adaptation to common environmental demands. Analogous structures are the product of convergent evolutionary pathways. The tail fins of sharks and cetaceans are analogous structures, as are the overall streamlined shapes they share. Sharks are cartilaginous fish of relatively great age. Cetaceans are mammals of relatively recent appearance that migrated back into the ocean after their ancestors had adapted to terrestrial life. Here, superficial similarities of form are categorized in terms of the underlying mechanisms that brought them into existence.

Notice that through these examples we take ourselves to be describing a common, but not universal, feature of science. There are exceptions. In physics, there is the concept of an oscillator. The pendulum in a grandfather clock is an oscillator. A hydrogen molecule composed of two covalently bonded hydrogen atoms is an oscillator. This does not look to be a case of individuation by underlying mechanism. Nevertheless, we maintain that there is some principled basis for cognitive scientists to assert that the processes that occur within a neuronal core of the brain are distinctly cognitive in a sense in which transcranial and extracranial processes are not. For this purpose, all that is needed is the mere existence of *some* scientifically valid, non-question-begging basis upon which to distinguish the intracranial cognitive from the putative transcranial and extracranial. We do not need the much stronger assumption that taxonomy by underlying process is the only scientifically legitimate taxonomy. We do not need to deny the scientific legitimacy of other kinds of scientific taxonomy. In our appeal to the nature of processing, we think we have a principled basis for delimiting the bounds of cognition in this familiar manner.

4.2   Individuating Processes in Cognitive Psychology

We think that developed sciences regularly categorize processes by reference to their underlying laws or mechanisms. Further, we think that cognitive psychologists aspire to do this as well and that they have discovered experimental methods that aid them in their work. What, for example, are the differences between attentional, linguistic, memory, and visual processing? There are certainly differences in the kinds of information processed, but there are also likely to be differences in the way information is processed. Part of the difference is in the nature of the processes.

Before we get to examples that illustrate this, we will qualify what we need and do not need in order to apply a taxonomy-by-mechanism to cognitive psychology. These qualifications have the same theoretical role as the qualifications we introduced in the last chapter regarding theories of non-derived content. That is, although we have more refined views within the space of hypotheses defined here, we do not wish to appeal to these more restrictive views in making our case for orthodoxy. We do not wish to appeal to stronger premises to run our arguments than are necessary.

As mentioned in Chapter 3, there is an affinity between our view that cognition is a matter of cognitive principles governing non-derived representations and the so-called "rules and representations" view of cognition.

Our appeal to representations and cognitive processing principles, however, is less restrictive than is commonly presupposed in the rules and representation framework. For example, in the rules and representations framework, it is commonly assumed that the representations are digital. We do not assume this. In addition, in the rules and representations framework, it is commonly assumed that the set of processes operating on representations form a set of Turing-equivalent computational processes. We do not make that assumption here. It might be, for example, that there are psychological processes that relate real-valued mental representations to other real-valued quantities. Some psychophysical laws relating the perceived intensity of a stimulus to the physical intensity of a stimulus might be of this character. Insofar as real-valued quantities are not part of a Turing-equivalent computational formalism, the existence of such processes would fall outside the scope of the standard rules and representations conception.[2] Our view of the individuation of the cognitive by reference to the nature of underlying processes, however, allows for real-valued mental representations and processes that operate over them. So, the view we are appealing to here does not discriminate between analogue and digital processes. For present purposes, we note only that our theory of the mark of cognitive does not presuppose that cognitive processes are Turing-equivalent computational processes.

Psychologists sometimes postulate laws. There is, for example, Thorndike's (1911) *law of effect* which, at least in some formulations, claims that reinforcers strengthen stimulus–response connections, where punishers weaken them. There is a power law of learning, which asserts that the amount of time a memory is retained is proportional to the amount of practice raised to some power (Newell and Rosenbloom, 1981). There is the Yerkes–Dodson law, which claims that there is an optimal level of arousal for the performance of any task. There is Weber's law, which asserts that the ratio of the size of just noticeable differences in stimuli is proportional to the intensity of the stimulus. Insofar as such laws govern processes in the core of the brain, but not combinations of brains, bodies, and environment, there are principled differences between intracranial brain processes and processes that span brains, bodies, and environments.

---

[2] Perhaps there could be digital Turing-equivalent computations that approximate the real-valued processes, but such approximations would not constitute a digital, Turing-equivalent realization of those real-valued processes. The approximations would not be those cognitive processes.

Not every feature of cognitive psychology, however, is readily couched in terms of such putative laws. For example, the hypothesis that there is a distinction between long-term and short-term memory is not typically conceived in terms of laws. Theories of attentional mechanisms provide further plausible illustrations. The hypothesis that attention is a kind "spotlight" that agents can project here or there in the visual field is not easily conceived in terms of psychological laws. Biedermann's (1987) hypothesis that, in the perception of objects, one constructs a representation of an object using a set of primitive geometrical representations, such as "geons," also strains any attempt to articulate a set of laws. What this indicates is that, while an appeal to psychological laws provides one means of trying to provide a principled cognitive distinction between the cognitive and the non-cognitive, it is not the only way. Our view is that there is some more generic, but nonetheless principled, notion of types of cognitive processes and mechanisms that distinguishes the intracranial and the transcranial. This notion allows, but does not require, an appeal to laws of cognition.

Providing an apt description of what is discussed in cognitive psychology provides one reason not to appeal exclusively to cognitive laws in demarcating cognitive processes from non-cognitive processes. Another reason stems from worries about psychological laws coming from philosophers of science.[3] In psychology, such regularities as one finds are not physically necessary and they are, at best, probabilistic. What one finds in psychology are not natural kinds with covering laws over their properties, but entities that engage in particular kinds of activities. So, in neuroscience, one should not think of voltage-gated ion channels as natural kinds; one should think of them as entities. One should not think of voltage-gated ion channels as covered by natural laws; one should think of them as engaged in activities, such as receptor binding and ion transport. In psychology, one might think that a short-term memory store is not a natural kind, but merely an entity, and that Miller's (1956) "magic number seven" does not indicate any natural law of memory, but reflects an activity of short-term memory, such as that it removes or loses any more than about seven items that might be stored there. Talk of mechanisms and activities at times provides a natural description of things that cognitive psychologists care about. So, we mean our appeal to cognitive processes to be neutral on this dimension of the ontology of the cognitive. For our purposes, we are indifferent between describing cognitive processes in terms of laws and natural

---

[3]   Machamer et al. (2000).

kinds versus activities and entities. We will shift between the two as seems natural.

4.2.1   Memory

Qualifications on the table, we are now in a position to review some examples where cognitive psychologists strive to individuate cognitive processes by reference to underlying laws or mechanisms. We begin with a part of cognition commonly discussed in the extended cognition literature, namely, memory. In Chapter 1, we mentioned Miller's (1956) theory of a short-term memory capacity – experimental work revealing something about the processes underlying short-term memory. This, however, is just the smallest tip of the memory research iceberg. Here, we review some familiar sorts of results to be found in one textbook on learning and memory.[4]

Consider a free recall task in which subjects hear a list of 20 words at a fixed rate of one word every two seconds and in which they are asked to recall those words in any order. If one plots the probability of recall of any word, averaged across lists and subjects, one finds that the words at the beginning and at the end of the list have the highest probability of being correctly recalled (see Figure 4.1). Further, the words near the end of the list are even more likely to be recalled than the words at the beginning of the list. The benefit of early occurrence in the list is the primacy effect; the benefit of late occurrence in the list is the recency effect.

In one study of the effect of practice on memory formation, Anderson (1981) presented subjects with 20 paired associates, such as *dog-3*. They were asked to respond with the second member of the pair when presented with the first. After one practice pass through the list, subjects had an error rate of almost 50 percent. With successive passes through the list – that is, more practice – their error rates declined. In addition, with more practice, the time to recall also declined. These results are illustrated in Figure 4.2. They suggest to some cognitive psychologists that practice affects the "strength" of a memory trace. Many studies of the relationship between the amount of practice, P, and retention of memories over time, T, can be described by an equation of the form of $T = cP^{-d}$, where c and d are constants.

---

[4]   Each of these is discussed in Anderson (1995).

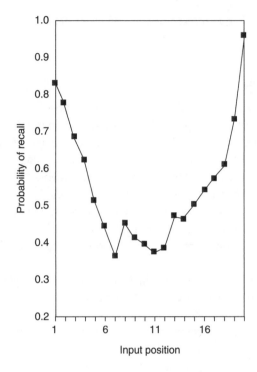

Figure 4.1

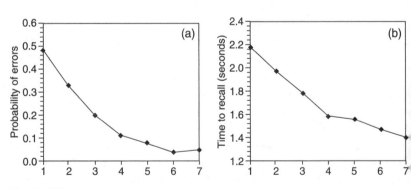

Figure 4.2

Other results indicate factors, in addition to the amount of practice, that influence the ability to recall. For example, Craik and Tulving (1975) hypothesized that "depth of processing" influences memory. In this study, the investigators showed subjects a word, such as "table," and then asked them one of three questions. The first was the case of the letters in the word, either upper or lower case. The second was whether the word rhymed with another word, such as "label." The third was whether the word could be used to complete a sentence, such as "He put the plate on the _____." Subjects were later asked if they recognized words on a test list. What the investigators found was that the second question improved recall over the first and the third improved recall even more (see Figure 4.3). Anderson (1974) reports a related finding. Subjects were asked to remember a target sentence, such as "The missionary shot the painter." They were later asked to identify which of four related sentences they had heard:

1   The missionary shot the painter.
2   The painter was shot by the missionary.
3   The painter shot the missionary.
4   The missionary was shot by the painter.

Subjects typically could reject sentences 3 and 4, since they differed in the relatively "deep" property of the meaning of the sentence, where they could not recall whether they had heard 1 or 2, since these differed in the relatively "superficial" property of active versus passive voice.

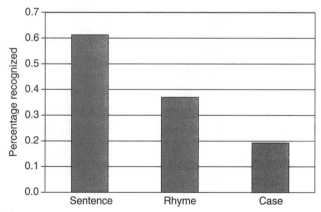

Figure 4.3

Another factor influencing memory is described as the "generation effect." In a "read" condition, Slamecka and Graf (1978) asked subjects to memorize word pairs, such as *sea–ocean* and *save–cave*, that they read off a list. In a "generate" condition, subjects were given a word and asked to come up with a new word that meets a rule and fits a constraint. So, given the word *sea*, the rule that the generated word must be synonymous with *sea*, and the constraint that the generated word begin with "o," the subject must come up with *ocean*. Given the word *save*, the rule that the generated word must rhyme with *save*, and the constraint that the generated word must begin with "c," the subject must come up with *cave*. In this experiment, Slamecka and Graf found a depth of processing effect in which recall of synonyms was superior to recall of rhymes. But they also found superior recall of generated synonyms to read synonyms and superior recall of generated rhymes to read rhymes (see Figure 4.4). These latter results are taken to be the product of having generated the items; they constitute the generation effect.

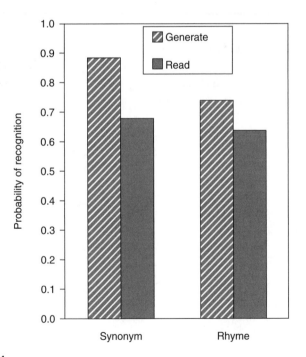

Figure 4.4

Glenberg and Adams (1978) found that even if subjects did not increase the depth of processing, the mere verbal articulation of items could enhance the memory trace for rehearsed items. Subjects were asked to try to remember sets of digits flashed on a screen. After the digits disappeared, subjects were asked to rehearse unrelated word pairs such as "green–walk" while they were to hold the digits in memory. Since the subjects believed they were being tested on the digits, they were giving minimal processing to the distractors. Yet Glenberg and Adams found recognition memory on the distractor word pairs to be significantly above chance. The cognitive mechanism for articulating the word-pairs seems to have enhanced the memory trace for the words even though there is good reason to believe that the distractor paradigm prevented the subjects from trying to enhance the memory trace or increase the depth of processing.

Yet another apparent factor influencing memory is the spacing of practice. In one study of the spacing effect, subjects were asked to learn 50 Spanish–English vocabulary items (Bahrick, 1984). Subjects studied these items before going through five test-study cycles in which they were tested on the vocabulary list, and then given the opportunity for further study. The test-study cycles, however, were separated over greater or lesser temporal intervals. In the first version of these cycles, subjects underwent all five test-study cycles in one day, and then took a final test 30 days later. In the second version of the cycles, subjects took one of the five cycles per day for five days, followed by a final test 30 days later. In the third, and final, version of the cycles, subjects took one of the five cycles every 30 days, then the final test 30 days after this (see Table 4.1). Among the things this study revealed was that in preparing for a test 30 days hence, it is better to space one's study cycles over 120 days (five test-study cycles separated by 30 days), rather than over five days or a single day.

Table 4.1 The percentage of recall of Spanish vocabulary items for various delays between test-study cycles

Intersession interval	Test					Final 30-day test
	1	2	3	4	5	
0	82	92	96	96	96	68
1	53	86	94	96	98	86
30	21	51	72	79	82	95

In these experiments, cognitive psychologists take themselves to be finding out facts about memory that are, at least potentially, helpful in determining the nature of the underlying memory processes or mechanisms. These data are the observable phenomena that cognitive psychologists use to inform their theories of memory. They are the data that are meant to illuminate the nature of memory and memory processing. So, for example, Miller's magic number seven is thought to reveal the existence of a short-term memory buffer and give us some insight into its storage capacity. Atkinson and Shiffrin (1968) used the existence of the primacy and recency effects to support a theory of short- and long-term memory. They contend that subjects fill a short-term memory buffer with words as they read them. When more words are encountered and the buffer is full, a new word replaces an old word. Recency effects are explained by the fact that they were most likely not to have been replaced. Primacy effects are explained by the fact that the longest-standing words are more likely to have been encoded in a more durable form in long-term memory. Our point, of course, is not to champion the merits of individual psychological hypotheses. Instead, it is to illustrate our claim that cognitive psychologists are, at least at times, engaged in research that attempts to discern the mechanisms or processes underlying behavior.

4.2.2   Vision

One reason we have for thinking that cognitive processes are, in all known cases, neuronally bound is the vast differences in the kinds of processes and principles that take place in nerves versus those found elsewhere. We are materialists, so we believe that all cognitive processes are in some sense determined by lower-level biological, chemical, or physical processes. Given, however, that cognitive processes are not spread throughout the whole of spacetime, one would expect that processes as distinctive as cognitive processes would supervene on correspondingly distinctive lower-level processes. Roughly speaking, lower-level processes should be as distinctive as the higher-level processes they realize. One might ask, then, what sorts of things have a sufficiently unusual structure and organization to give rise to cognition. We think it is eminently plausible to conjecture that neurons have sufficiently distinctive forms of information processing that they are plausibly construed as realizing, or serving as a supervenience base, for cognitive processes. The idea is really scientifically pedestrian. One reason to think that the liver, muscles, and brain do different things is the fact that these tissues have radically different cellular structures. Cells of the liver help regulate synthesize, store, and break down many different substances in the body. Muscle cells contain fibers that enable them to shorten, thereby effecting muscular contractions and bodily movement. Neurons, we suppose, process information in ways that enable cognition. Functionalists about cognition might, at this point, observe that, in principle, anything could be organized in such a way as to give rise to cognitive processing. But our point is that, even though many things *could*, in principle, be organized to form a cognitive processor, it is reasonable to conjecture that only neuronal processes are in fact so organized. A fine way to make out this point is to draw attention to the differences between the processes inside the first neurons dedicated to sensation and perception and the processes that transpire prior to sensory transduction. For this, any sense modality would do, but vision might work best because of its familiarity.

The propagation of light is, of course, governed by laws of reflection, refraction, and so forth. Many of the very same laws apply to light as it propagates through the cornea, the lens, the aqueous humor, and the vitreous humor. The refractive indices of these structures as well as the radii of curvature of the surfaces of these elements have an important role to play in focusing the light entering the eye more or less sharply on the retina. Like essentially any other optical system, the eye produces various distortions. There are spherical and chromatic aberration and oblique astigmatism. Again, the optical properties governing the propagation of light within the eye are very generally the same as those in the extracorporeal world.

When light enters the retina, however, fundamentally different kinds of processes begin. Photons entering the photoreceptors can be absorbed by molecules of rhodopsin, initiating a biochemical cascade leading to the release of neurotransmitters. The photoreceptors in the human retina are arranged into a cone system that enables high-resolution processing of color in bright light and a rod system that enables low-resolution visual processing under low light. The photoreceptors interact with other cells in the retina via processes such as lateral inhibition to give rise to distinctive response properties in the retinal ganglion cells (RGCs). Some RGCs leaving the eye typically fire more frequently in response to spots of light in a given circular region, but less frequently in response to spots of light in a surrounding annulus. These so-called "on-center, off-surround" RGCs are complemented by so-called "off-center, on-surround" cells. RGCs also disproportionately represent the activity of color-sensitive, high-resolution cones found in the fovea of the retina. RGCs in humans converge on the lateral geniculate nucleus (LGN) in what is called a retinotopic map, so that adjacent regions of the left and right retinas are represented by adjacent regions of the LGN. In humans, the majority of cells from the LGN project to the striate cortex, area V1. Here again, we find such features as disproportionate representation of the activity of the cones of the fovea. We also find cells that are responsive to activity in both retinas, rather than just one. We also find cells that are sensitive to oriented lines and edges. We find cells that are motion sensitive and, indeed, sensitive to the direction of motion. And, of course, this is just the beginning.

The aim here is not to provide an introduction to optics or to the neuroscience of sensation and perception. It is merely to draw attention to the physical and biological differences between the kinds of processes that occur in neuronal networks and the kind that occur in the extraneuronal world. On the hypothesis that differences in realizer properties and processes produce differences in realized properties and processes, we have some non-question-begging, defeasible reason to suppose that cognitive processes are typically brain bound and do not extend from the nervous system into the body and environment.

4.3   A Broader Category of Cognition

One way to think about our strategy for demarcating cognitive from non-cognitive processes is to begin with paradigms of cognitive processing, those involving normal humans. We have been drawing on features of human cognition as a first step toward demarcating the cognitive from the non-cognitive. But surely the category of the cognitive encompasses more than this. Surely a definition of the cognitive exclusively in terms of normal human cognition is too parochial. For one thing, there are cases of abnormal human cognition. This is, in fact, a branch of psychology unto itself. Surely, an otherwise normal human being who consistently has a memory capacity of five items, plus or minus two, on Miller's experimental protocols would not, thereby, become a non-cognitive agent. Nor would such a person be said not to possess memory. Such a person would surely be said to have a rare or unusual or abnormal form of short-term memory.[5]

---

[5]   This kind of argument is advanced by Clark (forthcoming b) and, perhaps, Sutton (2004).

The idea that there are non-human forms of cognition gains considerable independent support by reflection on animal cognition. Many non-human animals are plausibly construed as being both cognitive agents and as having cognitive processes unlike those found in humans. Most obviously, to all appearances humans have a capacity for linguistic processing that outstrips any such capacity found in any other known organisms. Surely we want to maintain that human cognition differs from animal cognition in this regard. But, even within what is commonly treated as a single cognitive domain, such as visual perception, we should expect cognitive differences among the distinct species of the animal kingdom. Among the things the frog's eye tells the frog's brain are facts about the movement of little black dots in the environment. In human and primate vision, however, motion processing does not begin in the retina. Another difference among species is that humans and other primates have color vision, where other mammals, such as seals and raccoons, do not. Still another difference is that humans and other primates have one component of their visual system, the cone system, dedicated to vision in bright light and another, the rod system, dedicated to vision in low light. By contrast, some organisms have only a rod system. Certain fish that are adapted to the dimly lit environment of the ocean depths only have rod systems. Some owls that hunt in nocturnal environments only have rod systems. Other organisms, such as birds of prey, have only a cone system for high-acuity, bright light visual perception. The list of differences in the visual capacities of distinct species could obviously go on. In addition, similar stories might be told for the other sense modalities of taste, audition, olfaction, touch, pain, and proprioception. Then there is that loose conglomeration of skills that one might group under the heading of reason. Humans have the capacity to do logic and mathematics, solve cryparithmetic problems, play chess, checkers, and poker, design computer programs, develop systems of government, and think philosophically. However these skills might be analyzed, however reasoning figures into them, and whatever mechanisms might underlie them, there is good reason to believe that these skills involve cognitive abilities that are not found in any significant degree among many non-human animals.

Animal cognition, however, is a springboard to further possible kinds of cognition and cognitive processing. It seems to us reasonable to speculate that evolution has yet to exhaust the possible ways in which to process information in a way that can plausibly be construed as cognitive. Perhaps it is eminently practical for organisms to become perceptually sensitive to light. Electromagnetic radiation of wavelengths in the neighborhood of 400–700 nanometers has a number of properties that make it a useful tool for gaining information about the environment. It is produced by stars, is absorbed and re-emitted by the surfaces of many objects, and propagates rectilinearly at a high velocity. The fact that the Sun produces light means that this form of radiation is abundant on Earth. The fact that the surfaces of terrestrial objects absorb and re-emit light that propagates rectilinearly enables light to impart information about the form of those objects. These properties might explain why so many distinct animal forms have developed mechanisms for detecting light. This also probably explains why so many plant forms have used it to their own ends, as in the development of colored fruit. Colored fruit attracts the attention of frugivorous animals when the plant seeds are ready to be dispersed by animal intervention. And the kinds of things that have been said for light might also be said for airborne and waterborne molecules, and vibratory disturbances in air and water. These media make olfactory and auditory sensory mechanisms useful tools for determining features of an organism's environment. So, to reiterate, we think there are grounds for a more general conception of cognition than just human cognition.

These observations suggest a complication in the evaluation of the hypothesis of extended cognition. They suggest that we cannot refute the hypothesis of extended cognition simply on the grounds that the combination of brain, body, and environment does not form a conglomerate that is like a normal human cognitive processor. The combination could have some more general, non-human kind of cognition. Perhaps the combination realizes a kind of cognitive processing that is related to human cognition in only a "family resemblance" kind of way.

Here, we wish to make a few replies, some of which will be fleshed out in greater detail in later chapters. To begin with, as we shall see in Chapter 5, the advocates of extended cognition simply do not have a plausible theory of cognitive processing. They are, therefore, that much farther from having a plausible theory of what these more general cognitive processes are. They do not have a theory of the family resemblances between human cognition and some other kinds of cognition. The lack of a plausible theory of human cognition compounds the problem of finding a plausible theory of this more general kind of cognition. Human cognition is the subject of great scientific scrutiny, but if we cannot develop a sound theory of this, then an even more general theory will be all that much harder to find. If we do not know what human cognitive processes are, then how can we know what all animal cognitive processes are? But the matter is even more difficult than this. The advocates of extended cognition apparently want a theory of cognition that covers an apparently open-ended set of combinations of brains, bodies, and tools. They apparently want a theory of cognition that applies to humans and computers, humans and Rolodexes, humans and notebooks, humans and cell phones, humans and personal digital assistants. What could the processes found in all of these combinations have in common that would warrant their being called "cognitive processes"? Or, if there is nothing that they all have in common that makes them cognitive processes, what are the family resemblances that could carry the weight of these differences? And, if there is nothing that they all have in common, what is the scientific payoff for grouping them together under the rubric of "cognitive processes"?

The foregoing points are challenges of articulation; they are questions about what this more general theory of cognition is supposed to be. There are, however, other problems to be faced by the idea of a more general theory of cognition. Even if we were to formulate the hypothesis of extended cognition in terms of a broader notion of cognition, this does not as dramatically alter the argumentative landscape as one might at first suspect. For one thing, there still remains the possibility that these hypothetical general categories of cognition could well break down. Science no longer accepts Bacon's general theory of heat, but instead recognizes disparate sciences that relate to heat. Bacon's theory of heat gave way to more refined sciences that partitioned phenomena into distinct kinds according to the underlying mechanisms. Similarly, a more general theory of cognition, were we to have one, might well give way to more specific theories based upon distinct mechanisms. We can see this kind of scientific development in the making insofar as we recognize a distinction between short-term memory and long-term memory, or between episodic memory and procedural memory. We also see this possibility in the emergence of the sundry "two visual systems" hypotheses.[6] Insofar as there is something like a "what" and a "where" pathway in vision, the general theory of "visual processing" threatens to break down.

There are also still other challenges to be faced by the advocate of extended "general" cognition. Even if we were to develop a theory of extended "general" cognition, most of the kinds of arguments that have been given in the extended cognition literature would still be fallacious.

[6]   Cf., e.g., Ungerleider and Mishkin (1982) and Milner and Goodale (1995).

As we shall see in Chapters 6 and 7, observations about the many complex causal relations between intracranial cognitive processes, on the one hand, and bodily and environmental processes, on the other, simply do not warrant the inference that cognitive processes, no matter how generally or loosely conceived, span brain, body, and environment. The coupling-constitution reasoning is fallacious even within a broader understanding of what is cognitive. Nor are evolutionary arguments going to help with "general cognition." Why would anyone think that evolutionary theory would provide any way to classify the causal processes that span brains, bodies, and environments into some that are cognitive and some that are not? And what of the "complementarity arguments"? Is the hypothesis of extended cognition really committed to saying something to the effect that the combination of Otto and his notebook is just like what goes on in, say, bonobo cognition or alligator cognition, or some other such form of animal cognition? There is clearly a pathological human condition encountered with Otto in isolation – namely, Alzheimer's disease – but is there supposed to be another (pathological human) condition that is mirrored by Otto and his notebook? The principal challenge raised by "general cognition" comes when one examines cognitive equivalence arguments. The advocate of extended cognition might observe that, insofar as one is unsure of what cognitive equivalence really amounts to, one cannot be so sure that the differences between Inga and Otto show that they are not cognitively equivalent. But this observation cuts both ways. If we cannot be sure that Inga and Otto are not cognitively equivalent, then, Clark and Chalmers's contentions notwithstanding, we also cannot be sure that they are. Put more generally, insofar as a theory of cognition avoids refutation simply by being insufficiently articulated, we have so much the more reason to take it less seriously as a scientific hypothesis. These are points to which we shall return in later chapters.

4.4   Conclusion

In all of the foregoing discussion, we have written of a need for the mark of the cognitive. Yet, having considered the different types of processes and mechanisms that seem to be involved in memory, attention, and vision, one might worry that there will be nothing in common to these different types of processes and mechanisms, save perhaps that they all operate upon non-derived representations. In such a case, it might turn out that there is no such thing as cognitive processing *per se*, but only memory processing, attentional processing, visual processing, linguistic processing, and so forth. It could turn out that cognitive processes are a kind of grab bag of processes.

Were cognitive psychologists to find that there is nothing common to all forms of cognitive processing, save perhaps the use of non-derived representations, it seems to us that a natural conclusion to draw is that there would be no extended cognition. If there is no cognition, then there is no extended cognition. This point aside, discovering that there are only specialized forms of cognition processing, such as attention processing, linguistic processing, visual processing, and so forth, would not change much of the argumentative structure surrounding the issues. The coupling-constitution fallacy would be just as fallacious for, say, visual processing as it is for cognitive processing. The "visual equivalence" arguments would be just as problematic as are the cognitive equivalence argument. The complementarity arguments and the evolutionary argument would be just as problematic. Given these considerations, just for the sake of simplicity of exposition, we will continue to write of a mark of the cognitive and treat all of cognitive processing as of a single kind. We do not want to have to re-introduce all the plausible types of cognitive processing at every key point in our discussion. This said, we will now turn to an examination of such extended cognition theories of the cognitive as we have found, with the aim of showing how our theory supports the view that the most familiar arguments for the hypothesis of extended cognition are not compelling.

Chapter 5

The Mark of the Cognitive, Extended Cognition Style

A theory that claims that cognitive processing extends into the body and the extracorporeal environment requires, at a minimum, an account of what cognitive processing is and how far beyond the boundaries of the brain it extends. Thus, we need some kind of specification of what cognitive processing is in order to assess the claim that cognition extends. After all, if one maintained the empirical hypothesis that, say, chaotic dynamical systems extend from the brain into the body and the extracorporeal environment, one would be obliged to provide some theoretical account or explication of what a chaotic dynamical system is. Advocates of the extended cognition hypothesis have not been entirely silent on what cognition might be, but the proposals they have offered up to now are clearly inadequate. What they tend to have in common are low standards for what counts as a cognitive process. Of course, the more promiscuous the standards for what constitutes cognition, the less surprising it should be to find that cognition extends into the body and environment. In earlier chapters, we have charged the advocates of extended cognition with this kind of promiscuity. In this chapter, we shall try to make good on that charge.

5.1 Cognition as Information Processing, as Computation, and as Abiding in the Meaningful

We begin our review of theories of the cognitive with a relatively simple example. Clark (forthcoming a) and Rowlands (1999) suggest that cognition is information processing.[1] We have considerable sympathy for something like this as a part of a theory of the cognitive, but we think that cognitive processing is only a narrow subspecies of information processing. Not all information processing is cognitive processing. CD players, DVD players, FM radios, digital computers, cell phones, and so forth are all information processors, but none of them are cognitive processors. Any theory of the cognitive that does not explain the difference is clearly missing something relevant to cognitive psychology. This difference is presumably part of the difference between a scientifically interesting cognitive psychology and a scientifically uninteresting take on consumer electronics.

Just as one might think that cognition is information processing *simpliciter*, one might hypothesize that cognition is computation *simpliciter*. This appears to be how Edwin Hutchins motivates the view that in many group interactions cognition is extended throughout the group in a kind of "supermind," over and above the minds of the individuals. In describing navigation of a navy destroyer, he writes,

> Having taken ship navigation as it is performed by a team on the bridge of a ship as the unit of cognitive analysis, I will attempt to apply the principal metaphor of cognitive science–cognition as computation – to the operation of this system. In so doing I do not make any special commitments to the nature of the computations that are going on inside individuals except to say that whatever happens there is part of a larger computational system. But I do believe that the computation observed in the activity of the larger system can be described in the way cognition has traditionally been described – that is, as computation realized through the creation, transformation, and propagation of representational states. (Hutchins, 1995a, p. 49)

In the same vein, this is how Hutchins (1995b) motivates a cognitive analysis of the process of landing a commercial airliner. He proposes that this can be understood in terms of the representations that two pilots use and the manipulations and transformations they perform on these representations. Now, if cognition is supposed to be just any sort of computation,

---

[1]   In both cases, there should be emphasis on the word "suggest." See Clark (forthcoming a,b). For his part, Rowlands has a complicated view of what constitutes cognitive processing, which we will examine below. At times, however, he also writes things that sound as though they support a simple information processing view of the nature of cognition. Cf., Rowlands (1999, pp. 26, 115, 119, and 122).

any sort of transformation of representations, then it should be no surprise that such cognitive processing spans brains, bodies, and environments. By this standard, using an abacus or pencil and paper to work an addition problem will right away be a cognitive process. Either involves the manipulation of representations – in this case, the representation of numbers. By this standard, ordinary digital computers and CD players would be cognitive processors. By this standard, we do not need arguments based on complex interactions between brains, bodies, and environmental structures to argue for the existence of extended cognition. We do not need to appeal to the complementary properties of brains and tools. We do not need to appeal to significant cognitive equivalences between intracranial brains processes and transcranial brain–body–environmental processes; that is, we do not need to appeal to equivalences over and above the involvement of representations and transformations of them.[2] Here is a theory of the cognitive that even advocates of extended cognition may not have fully embraced. If they had, they may well have simply set aside these other (fallacious) arguments. Moreover, this theory of cognition, like the theory of cognition as information processing, is too simple to capture what is of interest to cognitive psychologists.

Haugeland (1998) urges another theory of the cognitive, what he describes as a theory of human intelligence. His approach is based on a contrast between representations and things that are meaningful. Representations are symbolic markers that denote or refer to or mean things; they are the data structures of computational theories of mind. The meaningful, however, is a broader kind. Representations have one kind of meaning or significance, but there are others. Cognition, Haugeland proposes, involves this broader kind of non-representational meaning. Cognition abides in the meaningful. As with the other thin theories of the cognitive, we might note that, even if there were a science of the meaningful in Haugeland's sense, this would not necessarily constitute a cognitive psychology. Surely, the vast differences between hammers and saws, on the one hand, and what appears to take place within human brains, on the other, are part of what interests cognitive psychologists. Surely a cognitive psychology that ignores such differences is ignoring something important.

---

[2] As an aside, this theory of cognition would not underwrite putative cases of extended cognition that do not involve representations in the body or environment.

5.2 Operationalism

We think that few advocates of extended cognition explicitly wish to endorse the idea of operationalizing cognition. Still, we can see intimations of operationalism in some of what they write and their sources of inspiration. Whether or not the advocates of extended cognition really want to endorse operationalism, we want to be sure to make a case against it.

In Chapter 3, we saw how one might wish to draw anti-representationalist conclusions from Rodney Brooks's work on mobile robotics. One might also think that Brooks's conditions on Creatures provide for an operational definition of a cognitive agent. Recall that Brooks's goal was to develop Creatures that meet the following specifications:

- A Creature must cope appropriately and in a timely fashion with changes in its dynamic environment.
- A Creature should be robust with respect to its environment. Minor changes in the properties of the world should not lead to total collapse of the Creature's behavior; rather one should expect only a gradual change in capabilities of the Creature as the environment changes more and more.
- A Creature should be able to maintain multiple goals and, depending on the circumstances it finds itself in, change which particular goals it is actively pursuing; thus it can both adapt to surroundings and capitalize on fortuitous circumstances.
- A Creature should do *something* in the world; it should have some purpose in being. (Brooks, 1999, p. 86)

One might suppose that the foregoing conditions provide an operational definition of "cognitive agent." Creatures, anything that meets the foregoing conditions, are cognitive agents, so whatever mechanisms they use to meet these conditions are cognitive mechanisms that engage cognitive processes. On this kind of operational definition of cognitive processes, it would not be a surprise to find that Otto and his notebook constitute a cognitive agent, with the processes of writing and flipping through the notebook counting as cognitive processes. In Chapter 3, however, we observed that, on the face of it, non-cognitive organisms meet these specifications. On a natural reading of these conditions, many plants meet them. The point here is not to challenge either the scientific interest or legitimacy of Brooks's research or research in mobile robotics more generally. There are indeed difficult technical and scientific problems associated with the design and construction of robots that can function autonomously. Our point is to draw attention to what appear to be some mistaken morals or methodological proposals one might draw from this research.

There are other intimations of operationalism elsewhere. Haugeland (1998) invites us to consider the ability to go to San Jose. Going to San Jose is a task that requires coping with something that is out of view, a feature he suggests is indicative of cognition. He then observes that there are many ways one might accomplish this task, such as retaining a horse that is trained to go to San Jose or picking a road that leads to San Jose. And, of course, he is right. Further, he is right that many of these ways need not involve the data structures that are postulated in computational theories of cognition. Having conceded this, it is also the case that not all of the ways to get to San Jose involve cognitive processing. A train on rails has the ability to go to San Jose from a point out of sight. An ICBM has the ability to go to San Jose from a point out of sight. These abilities require no intelligence, no cognition. There are lots of combinations of cognitive abilities that one might deploy to get to San Jose, but not every way of getting to San Jose involves cognition. Once one asks whether the ability to move to a point out of sight is a proper (operational?) definition of a cognitive task, one can immediately see its inadequacies.

Clark also makes comments suggestive of operationalism: "What makes a process cognitive, it seems to me, is that it supports genuinely intelligent behavior. . . . To identify cognitive processes as those processes, however many and varied, that support intelligent behavior may be the best we can do" (Clark, forthcoming b). In offering this proposal, Clark wishes to explicate the notion of a cognitive process by appeal to cognitive tasks, just the opposite order of our approach. We think that cognitive tasks are those that engage cognitive processes, where cognitive processes in turn are understood as specific kinds of operations on non-derived representations. One problem with Clark's account, as he hints, is that it is not very illuminating to be told that what makes a process cognitive is that it supports cognitive behavior and only slightly better to say, as does Clark, that what makes a process cognitive is that it supports genuinely intelligent behavior. In both cases, one immediately wants to know what cognitive behavior or genuinely intelligent behavior is. Clark's claim that cognitive processes are those used to support genuinely intelligent behavior only pushes the question about the nature of cognitive processes back one step.

And even a solution to that problem leaves another. Respiration, glucose metabolism, and blood circulation are all processes that support intelligent behavior, but surely these are not cognitive processes. Clark needs to provide a theory of the "right kind" of support. This is where we would suggest that he needs to say something to the effect that they are processes that support cognitive behavior through certain kinds of information processing involving non-derived representations. Perhaps there is room for him to offer a different theory of the nature of cognition, but we do think Clark needs to adopt our order of theoretical dependence. Do not try to explain cognitive processes in terms of cognitive behavior. Cognitive processes come first; cognitive or intelligent behavior is the product, in part, of cognitive processes.

Rowlands, at one point, offers a proposal strikingly similar to Clark's: "I propose to take the notion of a cognitive task as basic, and as defined by ostension – by pointing. That is, cognitive tasks are those tasks we say are cognitive. Cognitive processes, then, consist in those information-processing operations that are essential to the solution of cognitive tasks" (Rowlands, 2003, p. 158). Rowland's appeal to ostension is no more illuminating than Clark's appeal to genuinely intelligent behavior. Surely it would be a mistake to point to some plant and claim that it is remembering where the sun is, or is learning algebra or performing any other kind of cognitive activity. This problem aside, Rowlands's analysis of cognitive processes seems to us more plausible than Clark's, since it is information-processing operations, rather than any old type of operations or processes, that are supposed to support the solution of cognitive tasks. Rowlands's, thus, has a *prima facie* way of rejecting respiration, glucose metabolism, and blood circulation as cognitive processes. They are, in some sense, not dependent on information-processing operations. This, however, is flirting with the approach that we take.

In an earlier work, Rowlands advances a still more complex theory of what distinguishes cognitive processes from non-cognitive processes. This is found in Rowlands's (1999) discussion of perception, where he proposes that cognitive tasks involve the acquisition and employment of information, information in the sense of a nomological dependence between event types. On this theory, cognitive tasks are not specified by ostension. Next, Rowlands suggests that a cognitive process is one that is essential to the accomplishment of some cognitive task and that involves operations on information-bearing structures.[3] This appears to be exactly the idea from Rowlands (2003).

Consider, first, a task that Rowlands would call cognitive, then an information transforming process that nonetheless fails to be a cognitive process. Here is the task: make sure that when the electric garage door opener lowers the door, the door does not close on anyone. This task evidently requires the employment of information in the sense of a nomological dependence between event types. More specifically, it requires information about the presence of a person beneath the door. So, by Rowlands's account, this task is a cognitive task. Now consider an electric garage door opener that passes a light beam from a source on one side of the entrance of the garage door to a detector on the other side. If some object, such as a person, breaks the beam, the door opener will raise the door. Presumably, the light source, detector, and accompanying wiring are essential to the accomplishment of the task, and they use information about the presence of objects in the light's path. Thus, by Rowlands's account, the operation of the light source, the detector, and its accompanying wiring constitutes a cognitive process. Yet, *prima facie*, a Sears garage door opener is not a cognitive agent.

Suppose, however, that Rowlands were to insist that the garage door opener is in fact a cognitive agent. As far as we can tell, this really does not matter. Consider the electric garage door openers that were more common 20 years ago. With the older door openers, whenever the garage door was to be closed, a person would position herself so as to have a clear view of the space where the door would close, then start the garage door opener when she could see that the path was clear. Clearly there is some difference between the new way and the old way of operating an electric garage door opener. A very reasonable empirical hypothesis is that the process by which the electric eye works to detect objects beneath the door is different from the process by which the human eye and visual system detects objects beneath the door. It also seems very reasonable to us to suppose that figuring out what is going on in the human eye and visual system is part of what has interested cognitive psychologists who have studied vision in recent years. It is this difference that makes the study of the human eye and visual system intellectually challenging, where the electric eye is a boring piece of

[3]   This seems to be Rowlands's "official" theory of the mark of the cognitive, where the idea that cognition is simply information processing is merely a view suggested by stylistic variations in Rowlands's writing. Cf., e.g., Rowlands (1999, pp. 102–3, 116, and 137).

hardware anyone can buy at Sears. So, even if we give Rowlands the term "cognitive" to use as he pleases, there still appears to be a natural kind of process, at least reasonably construed as cognitive, that is worthy of scientific investigation. Further, this kind of process appears to take place only within the brain.

5.3   Is This Merely a Terminological Issue?

When we argue that, as a matter of contingent empirical fact, cognitive processes take place only in core neurons of the brain, we are not merely trying to enforce linguistic purity in the use of the word "cognitive." We are not trying to appoint ourselves language police. There already exists informal talk of cars not "wanting to start," of computers "outthinking" humans in a game of chess, and the weather being "temperamental." And, of course, there is the fact that we routinely speak of computer "memory" and miraculous "memory foam" mattresses. Those linguistic ships have already sailed. And even if they had not, we do not think that our arguments would counterbalance the forces that drive common linguistic usage. Philosophical arguments rarely, if ever, stop the emergence of new ways of talking. As best we can tell, no party to the debate over extended cognition wants the matter to degenerate into a mere terminological dispute. We will now evaluate at least some evidence that the other parties to the dispute wish to avoid a mere battle over linguistic usage.[4]

Clark and Chalmers (1998), for their part, are clearly concerned that the debate be construed as substantive. They write, "in seeing cognition as extended one is not merely making a terminological decision; it makes a significant difference to the methodology of scientific investigation" (p. 10). Unfortunately, this observation does not provide good grounds for our common position. Make up some terminological shift. Consider using "cognitive" to mean avian. Surely such a terminological shift will have dramatic methodological implications for the new "cognitive science." This looks like a pretty clear change of topic, but there will also be important methodological implications. Obviously, the use of birds will have to become much more common in this new cognitive psychological research. So, as we said, there is reason to be dissatisfied with the solution Clark and Chalmers propose.

---

[4]   Susi et al. (2003), for example, charge that the dispute is terminological.

Another way to try to avoid the present extended cognition debate degenerating into a mere terminological dispute would be to propose that on the old-fashioned view there are processes that take place within the brain that do not take place outside of the brain. This would eliminate the use of the problematic term "cognitive." By parity of reasoning, one might think that the advocate of extended cognition could settle for the claim that there are processes that take place within the brain that are identical to processes that cross from the brain into the body and the environment. This, too, would avoid the problematic term "cognitive." These proposals certainly have the virtue of avoiding disagreement over use of the word "cognitive," but do so at the cost of avoiding any substantive disagreement as well. The advocate of extended cognition might well concede that there are processes that take place within the brain that do not take place outside of the brain.[5] Those processes might well be specifically neuronal processes, such as the firing of action potentials or the actions of ATP-driven sodium ion pumps. Such a concession, however, would not be tantamount to the concession that cognitive processes are entirely intracranial. Moreover, the advocate of intracranialist cognition could readily concede that there are some processes that are common to brain and body. These might be biological, chemical, or physical processes. The advocate of intracranialist cognition could readily concede that there are physical and chemical processes that pass between brain, body, and environment, without thereby acquiescing to the hypothesis of extended cognition.

Evidently, the dispute must be joined by a substantive theory of the cognitive. This is why we offer the conjecture that cognitive processes involve non-derived representations that are embedded within (largely unknown) cognitive mechanisms. This is not a definition of the cognitive, let alone a stipulative definition of the cognitive. It is a theory that we think is implicitly at work in a lot of cognitive psychological research. Cognitive psychologists have not, in general, definitively established what mechanisms are at work in cognitive processing, but they generally assume that cognitive mechanisms exist and that they are discoverable through clever experimental techniques. We very briefly described just the tip of the iceberg of research there is on memory, leaving aside the vast literature on such topics as linguistic processing, attentional processing, and reasoning. We think these examples lend considerable plausibility to the claim that there are processes that are plausibly construed as answering to our

---

[5]   Clark (forthcoming a) apparently overlooks the need for this qualification.

common-sense and orthodox conception of the cognitive that occur only within core neurons of the brain.

5.4   Conclusion

In this chapter, we have reviewed the diversity of ways in which advocates of extended cognition have abetted the plausibility of their hypothesis by advancing generous theories of what counts as cognitive processing. If one has a lower standard for the mark of the cognitive, then one greatly increases the chances of finding cognition extending. Advancing a generous theory of the cognitive is a plausible first move in developing the view that cognitive processes cross the boundaries of the brain. It does not, however, do much to bolster the idea that locating cognitive processes within the brain is merely a matter of prejudice. There still could be principled reasons for thinking that cognitive processes as we have hypothesized them to be are found almost exclusively within brains. Moreover, it is only a first move, for in addition to having a generous theory of the cognitive, one needs to have this theory turn out to be scientifically explanatory. A lax theory of the cognitive that merely allows one to re-describe phenomena using cognitive vocabulary, for example, is of little scientific value.

In Chapter 2, we offered a number of reasons for thinking that we need a theory of cognition and promised to return to the issue at a later point. So, consider now an argument given by van Gelder against worrying too much about what separates cognitive from non-cognitive processing. Van Gelder claims that "Knowledge is now only one indicator of cognitive status; others include intelligence, adaptability, and coordination with respect to remote states of affairs. The concept now resists capture in terms of any concise set of strict conditions" (van Gelder, 1998, p. 619). In this chapter, we have indicated some of the shortcomings of van Gelder's last two indicators of cognition. In discussing Brooks's Creatures, we noted that many plants are adaptable, but are still non-cognitive. In considering Haugeland's example of going to San Jose, we observed that all sorts of non-cognitive mechanical devices can be coordinated with respect to remote states of affairs. Of course, it seems that having knowledge and intelligence are hardly separable from cognitive processing. More to our present concern is van Gelder's claim that, "This paper simply takes an intuitive grasp of the issue for granted. Crudely put, the question here is not what makes something cognitive, but how cognitive agents *work*" (ibid.). Our charge has been that the advocates of extended cognition have *not* taken an intuitive grasp of the issue. They have, instead, opted for promiscuous theories of the cognitive that include things other than those that cognitive psychologists have traditionally concerned themselves with. The theories allow such things as consumer electronics devices and grandfather clocks to count as cognitive agents. Turning specifically to van Gelder's point, we note that it will not help to change the question. Suppose we let the question be how cognitive agents *work*; one then has to know what a cognitive agent is. Suppose we know how Brooks's robot Herbert works. Is this knowing how a cognitive agent works? Maybe; maybe not. It depends on whether Herbert is a cognitive agent. How would we know that without a theory of what a cognitive agent is, and hence what cognition is? Van Gelder's apparent dismissal of the question about what cognition is evidently only pushes it back one step.

Here is another way one might challenge the need for a mark of the cognitive. Maybe trying to develop a theory of the difference between cognitive processing and non-cognitive processing is misguided. To try to define cognition or articulate a theory of cognition in advance of research is to put the cart before the horse. Perhaps we should, instead, simply develop theories of what takes place prior to and during the movements of certain animals, and then see how things turn out. Cognitive psychological research should not be put on hold until one comes up with a plausible theory of what cognition is. Just the opposite! Cognitive psychological research should be conducted with the long-term aim of developing a plausible theory of the cognitive. After all, the vast majority of cognitive psychological research does in fact proceed without great worries about the nature of cognition.

We think it is completely correct to observe that vast areas of cognitive psychological research can proceed without a definition or theory of *cognition*, and we don't propose to change that. This is just like the observation that many research projects in biology can proceed without a definition or theory of what life is. One can surely explore the mechanisms of mitosis and meiosis, for example, without a theory or definition of life. One can surely even attempt to reconstruct much of the evolutionary "tree of life" with a definition or theory of what life is. The point to observe, however, is that even though *many* projects in psychology can proceed without a theory of the cognitive, just as *many* projects in biology can proceed without a theory of life, not all projects are like this. In particular, the hypothesis of extended cognition would seem not to be such a project. If one maintains that, say, the brain, body, and environment sometimes form a chaotic dynamical system, one would naturally expect an explanation of what a chaotic dynamical system is. Similarly, if one maintains that the brain, body, and environment sometimes give rise to an extended cognitive process, one expects a theory of what cognition is. Indeed, the more radical the proposal about the bounds of cognition, the greater the need there is for such a theory. Consider how things might go in biology. It is not so surprising to be told that single-cell organisms are alive. It is somewhat more surprising to be told that viruses are alive. One might, at that point, wonder what is meant by being alive. But, faced with the assertion that crystals are alive, one surely wants to hear some account of what is meant by saying that crystals are alive. So it is with cognition. For most purposes, cognitive psychologists can get by without much in the way of a theory of what cognition is. But, faced with the assertion that cognitive processes extend into pencils and paper, one should want to know what conception of cognitive processes is in play.

Chapter 6

The Coupling-Constitution Fallacy

One of the most common themes in the extended cognition literature is the observation of the numerous ways in which cognitive processes involve and depend upon the body and environment. Solving a large addition problem with pencil and paper may involve computing simple sums in one's head, making marks on the paper, and then computing another simple sum and making further marks on the paper. Writing a philosophy paper may involve thinking, consulting some notes, and reading a book. The localization of the source of a sound sometimes involves turning the head left to right and right to left in ways that influence some of the cues humans use to localize sounds. These motions change differentials in the times at which the sound waves reach the two ears and the differentials in intensity with which they arrive at the two ears. In other words, rotation of the head influences interaural time differences and interaural intensity differences.

Sometimes these kinds of observations are taken to be interesting in their own right – as, for example, showing how the body shapes or influences what we think and what we think about. They show a kind of dependency of the mind on the body or environment. Lakoff and Johnson (1999) explain how the mind depends on the body by offering a theory of ways in which much of our conceptual apparatus is derived by metaphorical extension from our concepts of our bodies. Gallagher (2005) does this by elaborating a theory of body image and body schema.[1] Sometimes, however, there is a more or less subtle move from the observations about the causal

---

[1] Gibbs (2006) touches on both of these topics in his review of the topics to be found under the heading of "embodiment and cognitive science."

dependencies between cognitive processes, on the one hand, and the body and environment, on the other, to a conclusion that there is some constitutive dependency between the cognitive processes and the brain–body–environmental processes. There is a kind of inattention to the difference between causal dependencies and constitutive dependencies. The basic move is articulated in different ways by different individuals. Sometimes the move is describing in terms of "causation" and "constitution," as in Noë (2004). Van Gelder (1995), Haugeland (1998), and Clark and Chalmers (1998), however, use the term "coupling" (each in their own proprietary sense) as the term to denote the relevant causal dependencies. Rowlands (1999) uses the term "manipulation"; Menary (2006) the term "integration." Sometimes the constitutional basis for the cognitive is described as the physical substrate of cognition (Noë, 2004, p. 220), the embodiment of cognition (Rockwell, 2005, pp. 72), the realizers of cognition (Wilson, 2004), or the supervenience base for cognition (Rockwell, 2005, p. 71; Clark, forthcoming b). For reasons that will become apparent below, we think it is worthwhile drawing attention to the prevalence of this kind of argumentation.[2] Here are some of the passages that strike us as presenting the shortest, clearest articulations of the move from a causal or coupling kind of dependency to a constitution or supervenience kind of dependency:

> In this vision, the cognitive system is not just the encapsulated brain; rather, since the nervous system, body, and environment are all constantly changing and simultaneously influencing each other, the true cognitive system is a single unified system embracing all three. The cognitive system does not interact with the body and the external world by means of the occasional static symbolic inputs and outputs; rather, interaction between the inner and the outer is best thought of as a matter of coupling, such that both sets of processes continually influencing [*sic*] each other's direction of change. (van Gelder, 1995, p. 373)

> In these cases, the human organism is linked with an external entity in a two-way interaction, creating a *coupled system* that can be seen as a cognitive system in its own right. All the components in the system play an active

---

[2]   One immediate reason to provide all these quotations is that when Rob Wilson read our account of the coupling-constitution fallacy in personal communication, he denied that he or anyone else he knew reasoned this way. Maybe this is right, but at the very least there is a lot of text here that we think could have been clearer. After all, Block (2005), Prinz (2006), and Rupert (forthcoming a,b), have also "misread" the literature on this point.

causal role, and they jointly govern behavior in the same sort of way that cognition usually does. If we remove the external component the system's behavioral competence will drop, just as it would if we removed part of its brain. Our thesis is that this sort of coupled process counts equally well as a cognitive process, whether or not it is wholly in the head. (Clark and Chalmers, 1998, p. 2)

If . . . there is a constant close coupling between the ant and the details of the beach surface, and if this coupling is crucial in determining the actual path, then, for purposes of understanding the path, the ant and beach must be regarded more as an integrated unit than as a pair of distinct components. This is the simplest archetype of what I mean by *intimacy*. (Haugeland, 1998, p. 217)

. . . cognitive processes are not located exclusively inside the skin of cognizing organisms because such processes are, in part, made up of physical or bodily *manipulation* of structures in the environments of such organisms. (Rowlands, 1999, p. 23)

We solve the problem by continually looking back to the board and trying to figure out sequences of moves that will get us closer to our goal, all the time exploiting the structure of the environment through continual interaction with it. We look, we think, we move. But the thinking, the cognitive part of solving the problem, is not squirreled away inside us, wedged between the looking and the moving, but developed and made possible through these interactions with the board. (Wilson, 2004, p. 194)

. . . perhaps the only way – or the only biological way – to produce just the flavor sensations one enjoys when one sips wine is by rolling a liquid across one's tongue. In that case, the liquid, the tongue, and the rolling action would be part of the physical substrate for the experience's occurrence. (Noë, 2004, p. 220)

According to active externalism, the environment can drive and so partially constitute cognitive processes. Where does the mind stop and the rest of the world begin? If active externalism is right, then the boundary cannot be drawn at the skull. The mind reaches – or at least *can* reach, *sometimes* – beyond the limits of the body out into the world. (Noë, 2004, p. 221)

If we abandon the mind–brain identity theory, what would stop us from saying such counterintuitive things as "Because the tree I am observing outside my window is causally connected to my psychological state, my mind is partially instantiated by that tree?" But there are far more arguments for biting such a bullet than one might first suppose. (Rockwell, 2005, p. 46)

The real disagreement between internalists [like Adams and Aizawa] and integrationists [like Menary] is whether the manipulation of external vehicles *constitutes* a cognitive process. Integrationists think that they do, typically for reasons to do with the close coordination and causal interplay between internal and external processes. (Menary, 2006, p. 331)

There are other passages where this kind of argument is presented, but they are less quotable primarily because they involve greater amounts of text.

The basic problem with all of these moves is that none of them provides a plausible argument for going from the causation claim to the extended cognition claim. The point applies whether cognition is understood as human cognition or as some more general kind of cognition. It applies even to cognition conceived as a set of family resemblances. It simply does not follow from the fact that process X is in some way causally connected to a cognitive process that X is thereby part of that cognitive process. Consider the expansion of a bimetallic strip in a thermostat. This process is causally linked to the motion of atoms of the air in the room the thermostat is in. The expansion of the strip does not, thereby, become a process that extends into the atoms of the air in the room. It is still restricted to the bimetallic strip in the thermostat. The liquid Freon™ in an older model air conditioning system evaporates in the system's evaporator coil. The evaporator coil, however, is causally linked to such things as a compressor, expansion valve, and air conditioning ductwork. Yet, the evaporation does not extend beyond the bounds of the Freon™. So, a process may actively interact with its environment, but this does not mean that it extends into its environment.

Each of the individuals cited above commits, in one way or another, some version of what we have called the "coupling-constitution fallacy" (Adams and Aizawa, forthcoming b). The name is meant to capture what is going on in several of the arguments with a name that is moderately descriptive. Still, it may not be the perfect name, since it suggests that the fallacy arises because of an invocation of a causation-constitution distinction. In truth, one can point out the fallacy without relying on the distinction. We originally ran the argument without this distinction in Adams and Aizawa (2001). There, the argument pointed out that one cannot simply move from an observation of a causal dependency between cognition and the body and the environment to the conclusion that cognition extends into the body and environment. Perhaps a better name would have been the "coupling-extension fallacy" or maybe the "causation-extension fallacy." But, who knows, there could be some other problem with these names that we do not currently foresee. For the present, we will stick by our original title, warts and all, in hopes that the principal idea still comes through. Perhaps one can see the basic form of the problem, then adapt it *mutatis mutandis* to the sundry formulations found in the literature.

Although we first articulated the core idea of the coupling-constitution fallacy in Adams and Aizawa (2001), we thought it was just a quirky little argument given by Clark and Chalmers (1998). Since then, we have recognized its pervasiveness and commented on some of its numerous variants in Adams and Aizawa (forthcoming b). Still, we do not think we have yet done complete justice to the problem. For one thing, we have not managed to articulate the problem in a way that is acceptable to those who propose the coupling-constitution kinds of arguments.[3] Clark objects that our talk of "cognitive objects" is unintelligible, that our notion of parts of cognitive processes is implausible, and that we have not fully addressed the details of his theory of the coupling between brains, bodies, and environments. Hurley (forthcoming) and Rockwell (2005) challenge the reliance on a coupling-causation distinction. We think all of these issues can be addressed rather easily.

To organize our discussion into smaller chapters, we shall divide it. This chapter will concern the simpler versions of the coupling-constitution fallacy, paying some attention to disentangling the argument for extended cognition from other related observations and issues. What will be common to all these versions is the move directly from some causal dependency claim to a constitution/supervenience/embodiment claim. We will also address some of the concerns expressed by advocates of extended cognition. These concerns appear in Rockwell (2005), Menary (2006), and Hurley (forthcoming). In the next chapter, we shall turn to "systems" versions of the fallacy. These versions of the argument have two steps. The first is a move from the observation of some sort of causal connection to the claim that the brain, body, and relevant parts of the world form a cognitive system. The second step is a tacit shift from the hypothesis that something constitutes a cognitive system to the hypothesis that it is an instance of extended cognition. This is the kind of coupling-constitution argument found in van Gelder (1995), Haugeland (1998), Clark and Chalmers (1998), and Clark (forthcoming b). Each of these system versions

---

[3]   Cf., e.g., Menary (2006), Clark (forthcoming a), and Hurley (forthcoming).

of the coupling-constitution fallacy involves a theory of what it means to be a cognitive system; hence each will need some attention to its specifics.

As a final preliminary, we should note that the nature of the fallacy in no way depends on whether we assume that the kind of cognition under consideration is human cognition or some more generic kind of cognition. The basic problem is that, in general, one cannot assume that a causal coupling with a process of type Y is sufficient to render the process coupling to Y itself a Y process. More specifically, we cannot assume that casually coupling a process X to a cognitive process Y is sufficient to make X a cognitive process. This point does not depend on the details of the theory of cognition.

6.1   Some Examples of the Coupling-Constitution Fallacy

In what we call the simple coupling argument, all that is invoked in arguing for an extended cognitive process is a causal connection between the cognizing organism and its environment. The inference is most commonly made in the suggestion that in the use of pencil and paper to compute large sums, one's cognitive processes include processes in the pencil and paper. But other examples are invoked as well. Robert Wilson, for example, describes a children's puzzle game, Rush Hour, wherein one moves wooden rectangles around in a wooden frame. The inference from coupling to constitution is made quite succinctly in the following passage:

> We solve the problem by continually looking back to the board and trying to figure out sequences of moves that will get us closer to our goal, all the time exploiting the structure of the environment through continual interaction with it. We look, we think, we move. But the thinking, the cognitive part of solving the problem, is not squirreled away inside us, wedged between the looking and the moving, but developed and made possible through these interactions with the board. (Wilson, 2004, p. 194)

One might think that these examples are not meant to support extended cognition over intracranial cognition; rather, they are meant only to illustrate how the two views are applied to specific cases. Yet Wilson says nothing of this sort. Instead, in the text leading up to the example, he suggests that he plans to make a case for transcranialism (cf., Wilson, 2004, pp. 188–93).[4]

Alva Noë (2004), in his chapter 7, provides a nice illustration of the casual shift between causation and constitution. He begins by describing perceptual experiences as being external in the sense that they depend on causal interactions between the animal and the environment. He then frames a slightly different question that has more the nature of a constitution issue, namely, "What is the causal substrate of an experience?" As an answer, he writes, "perhaps the only way – or the only biological way – to produce just the flavor sensations one enjoys when one sips wine is by rolling a liquid across one's tongue. In that case, the liquid, the tongue, and the rolling action would be part of the physical substrate for the experience's occurrence" (Noë, 2004, p. 220). This last sentence appears to be a claim about constitution, one with a minor twist on the coupling condition, roughly, that there be some unique nomologically possible way of achieving something. But why should the uniqueness matter at all? Suppose, for example, that the only physically possible way to produce a nuclear fusion reaction would be by an appropriately placed nuclear fission reaction. Would that be any reason to suppose that the nuclear fission was part of the physical substrate for the fusion reaction? Not likely. The physical substrate for the fusion reaction would be the combining of atomic nuclei.

However, maybe the uniqueness of cause is not even that important for Noë. Discussing the use of pencil and paper in complex calculations, Noë makes a coupling-constitution move without any conditions regarding the nomological uniqueness of the cause. He writes, "Indeed, for a great many calculations that we can perform, the pencil and paper are necessary. If the pencil and paper are necessary for the calculation, why not view them as part of the necessary substrate for the calculating activity?" (Noë, 2004, p. 220). Noë is even more explicit in his commitment to the causation-constitution claim when he cites, with apparent approval, an idea he

---

[4]   In defense of Wilson, one might note that, while Wilson does deny that the cognitive part of the processing is intracranial, he does not go so far as to assert that cognitive processing extends transcranially. Rather, cognition is only developed and made possible through interactions with the environment. Thus, he is not really committing the coupling-constitution fallacy. Perhaps one can read Wilson in a way that does not have him committing the fallacy, but this defense does not have him providing an argument for transcranialism either. *Prima facie* the intracranialist can maintain that internal cognitive processes are developed and made possible through interactions with the environment.

attributes to Clark and Chalmers (1998), namely that, "According to active externalism, the environment can drive and so partially constitute cognitive processes? Where does the mind stop and the rest of the world begin? If active externalism is right, then the boundary cannot be drawn at the skull. The mind reaches – or at least *can* reach, *sometimes* – beyond the limits of the body out into the world" (Noë, 2004, p. 221). We think Noë's discussion here nicely illustrates our view that advocates of extended cognition are largely insensitive to the distinction between coupling and constitution and just casually slip between one and the other.[5]

Clark (2001) gives us another example that is strikingly similar to the ones we have just seen, a case of writing an academic paper:[6]

Confronted, at last, with the shiny finished product the good materialist may find herself congratulating her brain on its good work. . . . But if we look a little more closely what we may find often is that the biological brain participated in some potent and iterated loops through the cognitive technological environment. We began, perhaps, by looking over some old notes, then turned to some original sources. As we read, our brain generated a few fragmentary, on-the-spot responses which were duly stored as marks on the page, or in the margins. This cycle repeats, pausing to loop back to the original plans and sketches, amending them in the same fragmentary, on-the-spot fashion. This whole process of critiquing, rearranging, streamlining and linking is deeply informed by quite specific properties of the external media, which allow the sequence of simple reactions to become organized and grow (hopefully) into something like an argument. The brain's role is crucial and special. But it is not the whole story. In fact, the true (fast and frugal!) power and beauty of the brain's role is that it acts as a mediating factor in a variety of complex and iterated processes which continually loop between brain, body and technological environment. And it is this larger system which solves the problem. . . . The intelligent process just *is* the

---

[5]   Chapter 1 of Noë (2004) can also be viewed as a defense of the view that cognition extends into one's body. In that chapter, Noë defends the view that perceptual experiences are constituted, in part, by the exercise of sensorimotor skills. Given the assumption that the production of perceptual experiences is a cognitive process and that the exercise of sensorimotor skills is constituted in part by processes within muscles and peripheral nerves, one has the view that cognitive processing is constituted, in part, by bodily processes. In that chapter, Noë is pretty explicit in favoring the constitutive claim over the causal claim. We will return to critique this theory in Chapter 9.

[6]   Actually, the example first appears in Clark (1997), but its use to support extended cognition is less marked there.

> spatially and temporally extended one which zig-zags between brain, body, and world. (Clark, 2001, p. 132; cf., Clark, 2002, pp. 23–4)

The intracranialist can agree with everything up until that last sentence. Here we find a familiar pattern, a long description of the causal connections between the brain and environment followed by the move to the view that these causal loops constitute part of the cognitive process. This is the simple coupling-constitution fallacy. We can note as well that it is common ground that the brain and the tools are jointly responsible for the product, the journal article.[7] This, however, does not require that both the brain and the tools constitute components in a single *cognitive* process. It is the interaction between the spinning bowling ball and the surface of the alley that between them leads to all the pins falling. Still, there is no "extended bowling ball" meshing with the alley, nor do we see any particular *intimacy* between a bowling ball and the alley.[8] Moreover, the contingent intracranialist has no objection to saying that operation of the tools and the brain provides the basis for hypothesizing a single causal process. The problem is that this provides no reason to think that the tools and the brain constitute parts of a single *cognitive* process.[9]

Gibbs (2001) claims that "intentions are, in many cases, emergent products of interactions between individuals, and between individuals and the environment, and that therefore they exist in a distributed manner across individuals" (Gibbs, 2001, p. 106). Clearly, Gibbs is a transcranialist about at least some intentions and, as we saw above, is prone to committing the simple coupling-constitution fallacy. In addition, however, he

---

[7]   This jointly responsible idea figures more prominently in the version presented in Clark (1997). Haugeland (1998) runs the same "jointly responsible" line about navigating to San Jose. By driving the interstate, one relies on the structure of the interstate and on one's cognitive abilities in dealing with roads. Thus, the road and the brain are between them responsible for successfully navigating to San Jose and they constitute a single causal process. Still, that does not weave the road and brain into a single *cognitive* process. Establishing the latter stronger claim is what the extracranialist needs.

[8]   Cf., Haugeland: "If . . . there is a constant close coupling between the ant and the details of the beach surface, and if this coupling is crucial in determining the actual path, then, for purposes of understanding the path, the ant and beach must be regarded more as an integrated unit than as a pair of distinct components. This is the simplest archetype of what I mean by *intimacy*" (Haugeland, 1998, p. 217). Substitute "bowling ball" for "ant" and "alley" for "beach" and you are well on your way to committing Haugeland to something rather wild.

[9]   Haugeland (1998, p. 217) provides one more example.

advances some more complicated versions of the fallacy. We will consider just one.

One of Gibbs's arguments is based on a dialogue he observed in a bar. The dialogue begins after John spills a beer:

JOHN: I wonder if there is a towel behind the bar.
NICOLE (goes over to the bar and grabs a towel): Here you go.
JOHN: Oh thanks! I wasn't actually asking you to get a towel for me. I just was thinking aloud about whether there might be a towel that I could get from the bartender. But thanks. (Gibbs, 2001, p. 109)

Gibbs begins his analysis of this dialogue by saying that, "John intends his utterance with a particular meaning, but changes his mind and accepts Nicole's interpretation of what he said" (ibid.). We think that Gibbs's treatment of this case is flawed in many ways, so it will take a while to work through these problems before we can ultimately relate it to the other coupling arguments. So, first off, we think that Gibbs simply misunderstands John's comment. John is not changing his mind about anything. He is not adopting Nicole's interpretation of what he said; in fact, he is explicitly rejecting it. John says, "I wasn't actually asking you to get a towel for me," which is an explicit rejection of what he thinks Nicole thinks (or might think) he intends. When he says, "But thanks," he means that, even though he didn't intend for Nicole to get him a towel, he is thankful that she did it anyway. It looks as though John's initial intention and his interpretation of it remain constant throughout the whole episode.

Not to rest our argument too much on what Gibbs might take to be our idiosyncratic understanding of the foregoing dialogue, we might try to develop an imaginary scenario in which John does change his initial intention. How would the scenario have to be different in order for John to have really changed his original intention? Let's say that at t_0 he has the intention merely to wonder out loud and so he proceeds to utter, "I wonder if there is a towel behind the bar." Nicole then goes and gets the towel and says, "Here you go." Now at t_1 let John say, "Thanks. I'm glad you discerned what I intended." Now at least Nicole's actions have provoked a kind of conflict between the intention John had at t_0 and the intention he implies (at t_1) that he had at t_0. This, however, is still not an instance of actions at t_1 changing John's intentions at t_0. Indeed, the mechanics of this exchange are those of Inspector Clouseau in a comic film scene. Clouseau clearly intends one thing, has something unexpected arise, but then tries to play off the surprise as what he intended all along. What reason is there to think that John changed the intention he had at t_0, rather than that he changed *his interpretation of* the intention he had at t_0? It could be that John suffers from a failure of memory or self-deception. Gibbs provides no reason to prefer the view that John changed his intentions at t_0 to the view that John merely changed his assessment of his intentions at t_0.

However, suppose we set aside the infelicity of Gibbs's original example wherein John says, "I wasn't actually asking you to get a towel for me." Further suppose that at t_1 John really is able to do something to alter the intention he had at t_0. In particular, let us suppose that there are no problems with backwards causation, that there is nothing wrong with events at t_1 causally influencing temporally prior events at t_0. (We think we're being especially generous here.) Still, Gibbs must come to grips with the fundamental flaw in coupling arguments, namely, the fact that events at one time causally influence cognitive events at another time does not make it the case that those first events constitute part of a single cognitive process that includes the events causing the cognitive events. More concretely, the fact that Nicole's actions or John's actions made some cognitive difference to John's intention at t_0 is not enough to establish that Nicole's and John's actions are part of the same cognitive process or state as John's intention at t_0.

Further evidence that Gibbs is guilty of confusing constitution relations and causal relations in the analysis of this case is supported by his claims following another sample dialogue. He notes that, "speakers' intentions also clearly shift as a result of conversation and may at times not be viewed as solely a product of an individual speaker's mind" (Gibbs, 2001, p. 111). It is surely common ground that intentions change over the course of a conversation. I ask you to pass the salt. That, against a backdrop of other factors, might cause you to form the intention to pass the salt. And, of course, in such a case, there is a perfectly good sense in which your intention is not solely a product of your mind, namely, your intention is not caused exclusively by events within your own mind. Yet such an admission does nothing to challenge the intracranialist position. For all that has been conceded, the intracranialist can still maintain that your intention to pass the salt is entirely *constituted* by events and processes within your cranium. So, even under quite generous concessions, Gibbs has not produced a persuasive argument for transcranialism. He has only found so many ways of committing the coupling-constitution fallacy.

In all these cases, what we find is that the advocates of extended cognition do not take into consideration the possibility that what makes a process cognitive is something internal to the process, something to do with how it works, rather than what it is connected to. They do not consider the possibility that to be cognitive a process must meet internal conditions for being cognitive. What makes a process a cognitive process? – Perhaps something about the nature of the process. After all, what makes a process a process of nuclear fission? – Something about the nature of the process, namely, the division of an atomic nucleus. This is the kind of approach we tried to spell out in Chapters 3 and 4.

6.2   Replies to the Coupling-Constitution Fallacy

The core issue in the coupling-constitution fallacy is so simple that many critics seem to have come to it independently. Adams and Aizawa (2001) put it forth. Block (2005) and Prinz (2006) probably came to it independently of Adams and Aizawa (2001), and perhaps of each other. James Garson raised the issue in correspondence with Teed Rockwell, prior to Rockwell (2005). Rupert (forthcoming a,b) appears to have formulated the problem independently as well. In reply to the problem that the coupling-constitution distinction makes for the hypothesis of extended cognition, some advocates of extended cognition have begun to rethink the distinction. Hurley (forthcoming) asks why the distinction is necessary. Noë is reported to reject the distinction, even though he appears to be committed to it in print.[10] Rockwell (2005) argues that the distinction should be viewed with suspicion, although he also maintains that one can develop a principled version of distinction.[11] These issues merit attention.

6.2.1   Why is the coupling-constitution distinction necessary?

In a forthcoming paper, Hurley appears to demand that the *critic* of extended cognition explain what is meant by causation or coupling, on the one hand, versus constitution, supervenience, physical substrate, or embodiment, on the other. Yet it is the advocates of extended cognition who have put the distinction on the table. As seen from the numerous quotations provided at the start of the chapter, there is good reason to think it is one of the defining features of the hypothesis of extended

[10]   Block (2005, p. 266, fn. 12).
[11]   Cf., Rockwell (2005, pp. 44–5 and 48).

cognition. If the advocates of extended cognition want to rely on some distinction to present their view, surely they bear the burden of explicating their own view. Moreover, it is awkward to be a critic of extended cognition and have to explicate and defend a central distinction of extended cognition. Nevertheless, we will offer a conjecture about why so many advocates of extended cognition appeal to a causation/constitution distinction.

Given the consensus in cognitive psychology that cognitive processes are causally related to bodily and environmental events, how might one advance a radical new theory along the lines of extended cognition? One way is to claim that it is not merely that cognitive processes are causally dependent on bodily and/or environmental processes; it is that cognitive processes are constituted, in part, by bodily and/or environmental processes. As a clear case, Noë (2004) pushes for perceptual experiences being constituted, rather than merely caused, by the deployment of sensorimotor skills found, in part, in the body. The causation-constitution distinction, thus, does some theoretical work for extended cognition. It provides some basis for it to distinguish itself from orthodoxy and do this in a radical way. These seem to be what the fans of extended cognition want out of the distinction. So, *prima facie*, the advocates of extended cognition need to have the distinction to articulate their break from the orthodox and they need to avoid it because, in the guise of the coupling-constitution fallacy, it gives them a higher argumentative burden to establish.

Of course, the foregoing rationale for the advocates adopting the causation-constitution distinction does not show that it is an indispensable part of their theory. As far as anything we have said goes, it is logically possible that there exists an alternative. Maybe they could go for a theory of extended cognition that differs from orthodoxy, but not so dramatically as to claim that bodily and environmental processes constitute, in part, cognitive processes.[12] Fans of extended cognition are free to try their hands at this.

---

[12]   Hurley (forthcoming) suggests abandoning the causation-constitution distinction and relying on "how"-explanations without worrying about whether they invoke causal or constitutive factors. In explication of "how"-explanations, she writes, " 'How'-explanations explain the processes or mechanisms that enable mental states of a given content or quality type" (Hurley, forthcoming, p. 1). It is hard to discuss this proposal very seriously, since there is no exposition of what is meant by enabling mental states. The enabling relation is the bottom of the expository heap. Further, since she has no theory of what the causation-constitution distinction is for, either our theory or any other, it is unclear how, or whether, the search for "how"-explanations might serve to help the fans of extended cognition state their view.

Both Rockwell (2005) and Hurley (forthcoming) express skepticism about the coupling-constitution distinction, although neither expresses serious reasons for doubting the distinction. There is, it seems to us, some reason for their suspicion, namely, that it is hard to make out this distinction for the case of cognition. What is the difference between things that merely cause cognitive processes and things that constitute cognitive processes? If we restate the question slightly, the source of the difficulty should be clear. What, we should ask, is the difference between things that merely cause cognitive processes and things are cognitive processes? The problem lies in the uncertainty about what exactly cognitive processes are. In support of this diagnosis, consider a case in which we do have a well-established theory of what a given type of process is. Consider again the process of nuclear fission. The process of nuclear fission is constituted by the process of a large atomic nucleus being broken into smaller atomic nuclei. Nuclear fission can be caused by bombardment of the nucleus with neutrons. The process of neutron bombardment causes nuclear fission, but does not constitute nuclear fission. Consider the isomerization of the retinal component of rhodopsin in the human eye. This process is constituted by a change in the molecular structure of the retinal component from 11-*cis* retinal to all-*trans* retinal. It is typically caused by absorption of a photon. Now the distinction is intuitively clear, although possibly difficult to explicate philosophically. Where we have a clear theory of the nature of a process, we have a very fair idea of the difference between what might cause it and what might constitute it.

6.2.2   Have we gotten confused about causation and constitution?

In a recent reply to Adams and Aizawa (2001), Menary (2006) includes what appears to be two distinct replies to our charge that there is a coupling-constitution fallacy in the extended cognition literature. The first reply is that we are begging the question against the hypothesis of extended cognition; the second is that we misunderstand how the argument is supposed to work. To meet Menary's first challenge, we need only tweak the details of the way in which we state the coupling-constitution fallacy. To meet the second, we think he either undermines the force of the coupling arguments or he begs the question against the advocate of intracranial cognition. (There is a nice bit of irony in this last case.)

Because Menary's comments are short and to the point, we would like to quote them at length:

> [Adams and Aizawa] (2001) claim that the causal coupling of X to Y does not make X a part of Y. The alleged fallacy assumes something like the following picture: an external object/process X is causally coupled to a cognitive agent Y. The Otto example fits this picture: a notebook coupled to a discrete cognitive agent, whereby the notebook becomes part of the memory system of that agent because it is coupled to that agent. Cognitive integrationists [those who support Menary's version of the extended cognition] should resist this picture. It is a residual form of internalism, because it assumes a discrete, already formed cognitive agent. And this is precisely the picture we are arguing against. If we accept the picture of a cognitive agent as implementing a discrete cognitive system, before they ever encounter an external vehicle, then we will have accepted the very picture of cognition we set out to reject. This does not fit with the aim of cognitive integration, which is to show how internal and external vehicles and processes are integrated in the completion of cognitive tasks (such as remembering the location of MOMA). (Menary, 2006, p. 333)

The suggestion appears to be that we should never think of a lone human being as a discrete cognitive system. Humans are, so this line goes, always cognitive systems integrated into a network of interacting components. Humans in their mere biological being are never cognitive systems. Put more boldly, perhaps, insofar as humans are cognitive beings, they are essentially users of external vehicles.

Suppose, just for the sake of argument, that it is true that, insofar as humans are cognitive agents, they are never entirely bereft of external vehicles that they manipulate. That is, suppose that every human cognitive agent always engages some external vehicle or another in her cognitive processing. Even this concession is not adequate to circumvent the coupling-constitution fallacy. We can simply reformulate the problem to incorporate Menary's idea. So, suppose, simply for the sake of argument, that Otto's biological mass never in itself suffices to form a cognitive system. Otto's cognitive being is always enmeshed in a network of tools. Still, think of "young Otto" before the onset of Alzheimer's disease. Young Otto was embedded in one network of tools. Presumably this network of tools will *not* include the notebook that will one day, say, 30 years later, be manufactured in some factory and subsequently purchased by "Old Otto," who has come to suffer from Alzheimer's disease. That is, assume that one's cognition does not extend into currently non-existent tools that one will use in the future. Now consider "Old Otto" following the onset of Alzheimer's, but prior to the purchase of the notebook. Still, the notebook lying on a store shelf never seen by Old Otto is not part of Old Otto's cognitive apparatus. How, then, does the notebook become part of Old Otto's cognitive apparatus on a coupling argument? One might suspect that it begins with Otto's coming to regularly use the apparatus. It begins when Old Otto begins to manipulate his notebook. But, it is right here that the coupling-constitution fallacy is committed. It is committed when one makes the move to include new cognitive processing mechanisms, such as the notebook. So, even Menary's strong hypothesis that cognitive agents are never without their cognitive processes extending into tools is not enough to avoid the coupling-constitution fallacy.

We should emphasize the importance of the foregoing reply to Menary. The reply lets the advocate of extended cognition dictate a case in which she can assume that a cognitive process extends from an individual's brain into that individual's body and a set of environmental tools at time t_0. Now suppose that the individual acquires a new tool at t_1, a tool that the individual uses a lot, one that the individual causally interacts with in some very intense way. The point of the coupling-constitution fallacy is that coupling is not sufficient for constitution, regardless of one's theory of the bounds of cognition. We are not begging the question against the hypothesis of extended cognition in drawing attention to the coupling-constitution fallacy. We are not presupposing our preferred way of localizing cognitive processes. We can concede a method of localizing cognitive processes to the advocate of extended cognition and the problem still remains.

Consider now Menary's second defense of coupling arguments:

For the cognitive integrationist the picture is like this: my *manipulation* of the notebook and my brain together constitute a process of remembering. In cases like these, the process of remembering cannot be described exclusively in terms of biological memory or solely in terms of the manipulation of external representations, because it is a hybrid process.

Schematically: X is the manipulation of the notebook *reciprocally* coupled to Y – the brain processes – which together constitute Z, the process of remembering. Once we have this picture, it is easy to see that [Adams and Aizawa] have distorted the aim of cognitive integration. The aim is not to show that artifacts get to be part of cognition just because they are causally coupled to a pre-existing agent, but to explain why X and Y are so coordinated that they together function as Z, which causes further behavior. (Menary, 2006, pp. 333–4)

One thing Menary may be saying is that he does not want to make an inference from coupling to constitution. He does not want to use the fact that Otto manipulates his notebook in certain ways as evidence for the hypothesis that Otto's use of his notebook constitutes an extension of cognitive processing. He simply wants to stipulate, or define, or hypothesize that Otto's manipulation of his notebook constitutes an extension of cognitive processing. This reading seems to be the import of the part about "The aim is not to show that artifacts get to be part of cognition just because they are causally coupled to a pre-existing agent." If that, however, is what Menary is about, then *that* is not a defense of what other extended cognition theorists have said. It seems to be an abandonment of coupling to constitution arguments, such as Noë's that, "According to active externalism, the environment can drive and so partially constitute cognitive processes" (Noë, 2004, p. 221). Indeed, it seems to be an abandonment of his own claim earlier in his paper that "The real disagreement between internalists [like Adams and Aizawa] and integrationists [like Menary] is whether the manipulation of external vehicles *constitutes* a cognitive process. Integrationists think that they do, typically for reasons to do with the close coordination and causal interplay between internal and external processes" (Menary, 2006, p. 331). Menary cannot defend a move from coupling (manipulation) to constitution simply by abandoning it.

Still, even setting aside the question of abandonment, this is not the only problem with Menary's reply. Menary claims that what we are supposed to do is explain why X and Y are so coordinated that they together function as Z, which causes further behavior. Here, there is an ambiguity about "functions as." Sometimes we say that a screwdriver functions as a hammer, as when we use the handle of the screwdriver to tap in a nail. Sometimes we say that a fork functions as a knife, as when one cuts pizza with a fork. In these cases, something functions as Z, even though it is not Z. A screwdriver functions as a hammer, even though it is not a hammer. A fork functions as a knife, even though it is not a knife. So, if Menary's idea is that we have to explain why the combination of Otto and his notebook function as the process of remembering, even though it is not remembering, then that's no problem for the internalist. After all, the internalist view is that when Otto manipulates his notebook, he is not remembering where the MOMA is. The notebook enables Otto, with his remaining cognitive faculties, to compensate for the fact that he does not remember.

But, maybe this "functions as" is not meant in this way. Perhaps that is simply an uncharitable reading. Suppose, instead, that what Menary has in mind is that what we are supposed to do is explain why the manipulation of the notebook (X) and the brain processes (Y) are so coordinated that they together constitute the process of remembering (Z), which causes further behavior. But wait! The internalist is not going to accept the obligation to explain this, because the internalist rejects the idea that the manipulation of the notebook and the processes are so coordinated as to constitute the process of remembering. According to the internalist, the only remembering that is going on is whatever happens to be in Otto's head. Demanding that the internalist explain why Otto's use of his notebook constitutes remembering is a question-begging demand.

6.3 Conclusion

The foregoing examples seem to us to show the pervasiveness of the fallacious move from the observation of ways in which cognitive processes causally depend on the environment, and body, to the conclusion that cognitive process constitutively depend on the environment, and body. These examples, however, are the simpler ones. In Chapter 7, we will move to the more complicated "system" versions.

Chapter 7

Extended Cognitive Systems and Extended Cognitive Processes

Our interest in extended cognition has centered on the hypothesis that cognitive processing extends beyond the boundaries of core regions of the brain into processes in bodily and environmental structures. This is a hypothesis about the bounds of cognition, about the regions of space-time in which one will find cognitive processes, but does not necessarily involve criteria for the identification of cognitive systems. The literature on extended cognition also contains, however, a range of hypotheses asserting that an animal's brain, body, and environment constitute an extended *cognitive system*. These latter hypotheses differ among themselves in their understanding of what is meant by a system. On one version of the extended cognitive system hypothesis, the claim is that the brain, body, and environment form a system in a sense implicit in the field of dynamical systems theory. Van Gelder (1995), for example, supports this form of the extended cognitive system hypothesis. Haugeland (1998), Clark and Chalmers (1998), and Clark (forthcoming a) offer their own versions of the hypothesis of extended cognitive systems based on their own of distinct theories of systems. While the notion of *system* implicit in dynamical systems theory is a more technical, mathematical notion, the ones found in Haugeland (1998), Clark and Chalmers (1998), and Clark (forthcoming a) are apparently supposed to be more pedestrian notions, such as might be involved in the idea of an air conditioning system or a sound system.

The reason the distinction matters is that, short of some stipulation to the contrary, the hypothesis that cognitive systems extend appears to be much less problematic than is the hypothesis that cognition itself extends. It seems pretty plausible to claim that a human being is a cognitive system in an ordinary pedestrian kind of way. Add to this the observation that a human's toe is a part of that human, hence part of that cognitive system, and right away one has the hypothesis of extended, or at least embodied, cognitive systems. Clearly, there is an informal sense in which the human cognitive system extends beyond the boundary of the brain and central nervous system into the body. By contrast, it is pretty bold to claim that cognitive processing extends into the human toe. What makes this so bold, by our lights, is that to all appearances the toes do not contain the kind of information processing that one finds in the normal human brain. Schematically, what makes the extended cognition hypothesis so much more problematic than the extended cognitive system hypothesis is that one cannot assume that an X process pervades every part of an X system, so that, in particular, one cannot assume that a cognitive process pervades every part of a cognitive system. (We will elaborate on this idea later in the chapter.) Applying the point to the case of extended cognitive systems and extended cognitive processes, it seems not wildly implausible to claim that Otto and his notebook form a cognitive system. This is little, if any, stretch of the ordinary view of what a system is. By contrast, this is a far cry from the claim that Otto's cognitive processing extends into his notebook. Claims by Clark and Chalmers notwithstanding, there are important cognitive-level information processing differences between what goes on in a normal human being's head and what transpires between brain, hand, and notebook. These differences warrant cognitive psychologists thinking that cognitive processes occur within the brain, even though there are numerous non-cognitive causal processes passing through the brain and interacting with the intracranial cognitive processes. This conflation between the extended cognitive system hypotheses and the extended cognitive processing hypothesis appears to be among the enabling conditions for confidence in the extended cognition hypothesis.

7.1 Dynamical Systems Theory and Coupling

Like many other advocates of extended cognition, van Gelder apparently conflates the extended cognition hypothesis and the extended cognitive system hypothesis. Van Gelder and Port claim that "Cognitive processes span the brain, the body, and the environment" (van Gelder and Port, 1995b, p. ix). In van Gelder (1995), we do not find the assertion that cognitive processing or cognition extends beyond the brain, only that the cognitive system does. Here is the first step in van Gelder's system version of the coupling-constitution fallacy:

> In this vision, the cognitive system is not just the encapsulated brain; rather, since the nervous system, body, and environment are all constantly changing and simultaneously influencing each other, the true cognitive system is a single unified system embracing all three. The cognitive system does not interact with the body and the external world by means of the occasional static symbolic inputs and outputs; rather, interaction between the inner and the outer is best thought of as a matter of coupling, such that both sets of processes continually influencing [*sic*] each other's direction of change. (van Gelder, 1995, p. 373)

In van Gelder's argument, the relevant notion of coupling is apparently the one from dynamical systems theory. According to this conception, two (or more) variables in a set of differential equations are coupled if their values are defined in terms of each other. So, suppose that the rates of change of variables x and y with respect to time are given by $dx/dt = x$ and $dy/dt = y$. In this case, the variables are not coupled. By contrast, if the rates of change of variables x and y with respect to time are given by $dx/dt = x + y$ and $dy/dt = y + 2x$, then the variables are coupled.

Does such a coupling claim justify an extension claim? We think not. Consider the swinging motion of a single pendulum in a vacuum. This is a process internal to the pendulum, constituted by the bob and its supporting line. Now suppose that this first pendulum is connected to a second pendulum via a spring, as illustrated in Figure 7.1.[1] This configuration of objects is a non-linear dynamical system in which the two pendulums are coupled in the sense of coupling used in dynamical systems theory. The equations of motion for this system are as follows:

$$d^2\theta_1/dt^2 = [\sin(\theta_1)\ \{m_1[l_1(d\theta_1/dt)^2 - g] - kl_1\} + kl_2 \sin(\theta_2)]/m_1l_1 \cos(\theta_1),$$
$$d^2\theta_2/dt^2 = [\sin(\theta_2)\ \{m_2[l_2(d\theta_2/dt)^2 - g] - kl_2\} + kl_1 \sin(\theta_1)]/m_2l_2 \cos(\theta_2),$$

where m_1 and m_2 are the masses of the bobs, l_1 and l_2 are the lengths of the pendulums, θ_1 and θ_2 are the angles of deviation from the vertical, g is the force of gravity at the surface of the Earth, and k is the spring constant.

---

[1]   Another example that works perfectly well for the following points is the double pendulum, in which a second pendulum is suspended from the center of mass of the first.

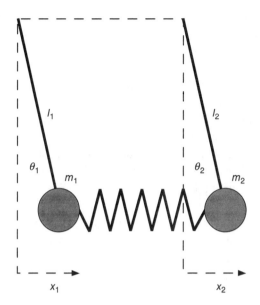

Figure 7.1

Here, we have a straightforward example of a system. In this second configuration, as part of a coupled non-linear dynamical system, the motions
of the first pendulum are still motions of the first pendulum. The motions
do not extend from the first pendulum into either the spring or the second
pendulum. Nor do we have any reason to think that there is no such thing
as the motions of the first pendulum.

There is another way to think about the difference between the first
pendulum prior to coupling and the coupling of the two pendulums via a
spring. Suppose that, once coupled, the masses of the bobs and the lengths
of the pendulums are such as to give rise to some new system-level feature
or process not had by the individual pendulums. Suppose, for example,
that the coupled dynamical system with the two pendulums and spring
gives rise to a chaotic process wherein the temporal evolution of the system
is sensitive to slight changes in the values of the masses and the lengths of
the pendulums. Perhaps this new process is more interesting than is the
process of a single uncoupled pendulum. This is not at all implausible,
since the single pendulum is relatively simple and well studied, where the
spring-coupled pendulums are relatively more complicated and less well

studied. Still, the existence of these higher-order system-level processes and complexity does not in any way provide evidence against the existence of the motions of the first pendulum.

The relevance to cognitive processing should be clear. Suppose that one has a cognitive process, either purely intracranial or not. (Recall the "young Otto – old Otto" example from our discussion of Menary in Chapter 6.) Now couple some further process to it to form a coupled non-linear dynamical system. Suppose, further, that this system is a cognitive system. If such a modification of the first pendulum does not show that the motion of that pendulum extends into the spring and the second pendulum, then why should a comparable modification of a cognitive process show that the first cognitive process extends into components of a newly coupled item? What is more, if such a modification of the first pendulum does not show that there is no motion in the first pendulum *alone*, then why should a comparable modification of a cognitive process show that there is no cognitive processing in the brain, or antecedently existing cognitive system, *alone*? Even if the dynamical system coupling of cognition with some other apparatus leads to some interesting new processes or types of processes, why does this support the view that there is no cognitive processing in the brain alone? Or, maybe more to the point, why suppose that it is this new kind of process that emerges with the recently implemented coupling that is *the real cognitive processing*, where what used to take place in the brain, or former cognitive system, alone was not cognitive processing? Van Gelder does not address these questions at all.

Having set up the coupled pendulum example to address the dynamical systems conception of coupling, we want to use it to make another important point. Tweak the example ever so slightly. Focus for a moment on just one of the pendulums, say, the one on the left, ignoring the spring and its connection to the other pendulum. Suppose we are totally oblivious to, or unaware of, the spring and the other pendulum. To aid in our imagination, we might suppose that the first pendulum bob and its supported cable are colored with a fluorescent pigment that is actively fluorescing, that no other part of the dynamical system is so pigmented, and that the entire system is illuminated only by a fluorescent light. Were we to observe the motions of the fluorescent pendulum under fluorescent light, it would be evident that it is not governed by the differential equation for the motions of a simple pendulum. That is, its motions would not be described by $d^2\theta/dt^2 + g/l \sin \theta = 0$, where θ is the angle of deviation of the pendulum from vertical, g is the gravitational constant at the surface of the Earth, and *l* is the length of the pendulum. It looks as though there is a perfectly good sense in which we could not understand the motions of this pendulum in isolation. To understand these motions, we need to consider the spring and the other pendulum. Nevertheless, it still does not follow that the motions of the first pendulum extend into the second. Obviously, the correct understanding of this case is that, while the motions of the first pendulum are causally influenced by the second pendulum and the spring, the motions are not constituted by the second pendulum and the spring. The need or desire to understand the motions of the first pendulum does not motivate the conclusion that those motions extend into the spring and the second pendulum. Nor does the need or desire to understand the motions of the entire system motivate the conclusion that the motions of the first pendulum are unimportant.

Again, the relevance of the foregoing observations to the case of cognitive processing should be clear. Suppose that it is true that a behavior cannot be understood in isolation from the environment, that one cannot possibly understand why a given cognitive process is taking its course without attention to the external environment.[2] We think this is often exactly the way things work with cognition. How could one understand why a person's eyes dilate at a given time, if one does not know that she is playing Texas Hold 'em and has just drawn the top full house? How could one understand why a person is thinking about a bandage without knowing that the person cut her finger with a knife? How could ethologists know about fixed action patterns, fixed behavioral sequences that run to a standard completion in response to a sign stimulus, without attending to an organism's stimuli? We think that cognitive psychologists typically do relate behavior and cognitive processing to environmental and bodily processes in order to understand them. Conceding all of this, as we did

---

[2]   Advocates of extended cognition often observe this sort of thing. Hutchins (1995b), in describing how pilots land a commercial jet, reports that, "The cockpit system remembers its speeds, and the memory process emerges from the activity of the pilots. The memory of the cockpit, however, is not made primarily of pilot memory. A complete theory of individual human memory would not be sufficient to understand that which we wish to understand because so much of the memory function takes place outside the individual" (Hutchins, 1995b, p. 286). Haugeland claims that, "We can only understand animals *as perceivers* if we consider them as inseparably related to an environment, which is itself understood in terms appropriate to that animal" (Haugeland, 1998, p. 221). Rowlands, for example, writes, "It is not possible to understand the nature of cognitive processes by focusing exclusively on what is occurring inside the skin of cognizing organisms" (Rowlands, 1999, p. 22).

for the case of the motions of a pendulum, does not provide any good reason to suppose that cognitive processing extends from the brain into the environment. It does not provide any grounds for thinking that the supervenience base of cognitive processes extends into the body or environment.

In the foregoing discussion, we have supposed that van Gelder intends to provide an argument for the hypothesis of an extended cognitive system. More specifically, we have supposed that he intends to give a form of coupling-constitution argument for this hypothesis. We think this is a natural reading of his claim that "since the nervous system, body, and environment are all constantly changing and simultaneously influencing each other, the true cognitive system is a single unified system embracing all three" (van Gelder, 1995, 373). Perhaps, however, all that van Gelder intends to do is to set up two competing hypotheses regarding the bounds of typical cognitive systems. The common hypothesis is that cognitive systems are found only in brains, where the new hypothesis is that cognitive systems are found in brains, bodies, and environments. As long as we can agree that the coupling-constitution argument is fallacious, or at least in need of further refinement, we can surely abide by the mere articulation and juxtaposition of the two hypotheses. We can leave it to further investigation to reveal the extent to which further scientific evidence supports one hypothesis over the other. Our present point can then be read as indicating the need for this further scientific evidence.

7.2   Haugeland's Theory of Systems and the Coupling of Components

In contrast to the technical, mathematical approach to dynamical systems and its notion of coupling, Haugeland wishes to explicate a more pedestrian conception of systems and the coupling of their components. This conception is supposed to show us how we can understand relatively complicated things (systems) by decomposing them into their simpler components. Thus, we can understand human cognition, or intelligence, by applying this strategy. In setting up his theory of systems and how they aid our understanding, Haugeland finds that there is no isolating a human cognitive processor as a separate component in the brain. Human cognitive processing is, thus, essentially embodied in the human body and embedded in the larger causal nexus of the environment.

To evaluate Haugeland's case for extended cognition, we need further details of his theory. Using televisions and stereo pre-amps as his models, Haugeland defines systems, interfaces, and components. He writes,

> A *component* is a relatively independent and self-contained portion of a system in the sense that it relevantly interacts with other components only through interfaces between them (and contains no internal interfaces at the same level). An *interface* is a point of interactive "contact" between components such that the relevant interactions are well-defined, reliable, and relatively simple. A *system* is a relatively independent and self-contained composite of components interacting at interfaces. (Haugeland, 1998, p. 213)

One attractive feature of this complex of definitions is that it captures much of our ordinary conception of a system as it might be defined in a dictionary. It also aptly describes televisions and stereo amplifiers as systems with components such as resistors and capacitors that interact via simple interfaces. By this analysis, it also turns out that blocks of marble and compost heaps are not systems. They are not systems because blocks of marble and compost heaps have no interfacing components.

Two features of Haugeland's theory bear on the hypothesis of extended cognition. First, one of the defining features of Haugeland's systems is they must have well-defined, relatively simple interfaces.[3] By a relatively simple interface, Haugeland means one with a narrow bandwidth of information passing through it, such as what occurs when current passes through a wire into a resistor, or when a teletype prints a message, or when one pushes a key on a computer keyboard. Relatively complex interfaces – that is, high-bandwidth interfaces – are a contradiction in terms. In the second place, he presupposes that genuine components of a system must be replaceable by functional equivalents. As an example, he claims that a resistor in a television set is a genuine component in virtue of the fact that it can be replaced by any other resistor with the same resistance value.[4]

To see how Haugeland uses his theory to support the hypothesis of extended cognition, we can review his case for saying that the human

---

[3]   Haugeland's theory of interfaces also, of course, requires that they be "reliable," but he does not invoke this in his argument against the hypothesis that there is an interface between the nervous system and the body.

[4]   He notes parenthetically that certain additional specifications might be in order as well. We conjecture that these might include something like size.

nervous system is not a component of the human cognitive system. In the first place, he claims that the human nervous system has a high-bandwidth interface with the world, so that there cannot in reality be an interface between the nervous system and the world. As we noted a moment ago, on Haugeland's view, a high-bandwidth interface is an oxymoron. Elaborating on what Haugeland appears to have in mind, we might note that each human retina contains on the order of 100 million photoreceptors, each human ear contains on the order of 20,000 hair cells, and the smooth hairless portion of each human hand contains on the order of 17,000 mechanoreceptors. This certainly makes the sensory input to the human cognitive system look to have a high bandwidth. In the second place, Haugeland claims that the human nervous system fails the replaceability test for genuine components. According to Haugeland, the particular patterns of action potentials in motor neurons that would be needed to perform some task, such as typing the letter "A" or tying one's shoes, would have to be attuned to the idiosyncrasies of an individual's body at a given time, to such things as the lengths of her fingers, the strengths of her muscles, the shapes of her joints, fatigue, what tasks she is doing before and after the principal task, feedback from the task, and so forth. In a word, nervous systems are individualized; they are tailored to individuals.

There are many details of Haugeland's theory of systems and its application that one might resist.[5] Here, we wish to focus on just one principal critical problem. Where Haugeland's theory might work well for some

---

[5]   For example, one might wish to know why we should not understand the inputs to the human cognitive system as a set of low-bandwidth channels. After all, textbooks on sensation and perception often include analyses of input systems in terms of systems and components where the components include rod and cones, rod systems, cone systems, inner hair cells, outer hair cells, and so on. As to the replaceability condition, it is also unclear why one could not replace the individual nerve cells of a human one by one. One would, of course, have to fit the new nerve cells in terms of size, but that was just the kind of additional specification that applies when one wants to replace a damaged resistor with a new one.

A second way in which Haugeland identifies components is in terms of intensity of interaction (Haugeland, 1998, p. 215). Thus, there are supposed to be relatively more "intense" interactions within components and relatively less "intense" interactions between components. Haugeland thinks that the intensity of interactions among the molecules of a connecting rod makes the molecules into one component and the intensity of the interactions among the faculty members of a single academic department makes them into one component. Fine, but doesn't this same intensity of interaction approach support the view that the brain is a component of the cognitive system? Don't the neurons of the brain interact more intensely with each other than they do with, say, muscle cells or bones?

electronic systems, it fares much less well for biological systems. In many biological systems, systems and their components are individuated, in part, by their structure and the kinds of processes they carry out, rather than exclusively by their interfaces or the simplicity of their interfaces. We will present two examples of this.

1   *The human muscular system.* The set of muscles in the human body constitutes the muscular system. In general, the muscles in the muscular system do not interface with each other; hence they do not constitute a system in Haugeland's sense. Even antagonistic muscles, such as the lateral and medial rectus muscles of the eye, which move the eye left and right, do not connect to each other. But, even if one were to say that antagonistic muscles have a kind of indirect interface, there are other combinations of muscles that do not stand in such antagonistic relations. The lateral and medial rectus muscles of the eye do not, for example, interface in any natural way with the gastrocnemius muscles of the calves. What appears to unify the muscles of the body into a system appears to be a commonality of function and a commonality of underlying mechanism.

2   *The endocrine system.* The endocrine system provides an even better illustration of the idea of a system and its components defined in terms of their function, rather than by their interfaces. The various glands of this system, its components, are located in anatomically distant portions of the body. They function by secreting hormones that influence particular target organs. In some cases, the organs in the endocrine system mutually influence each other, or interface with each other, by their secretion of hormones. As a case of this, the hypothalamus secretes hormones that stimulate the anterior pituitary gland, which in turn secretes hormones that stimulate the thyroid, the adrenal cortex, and the gonads to release still other hormones. There is, however, a component of the endocrine system that does not interface with other components of the system. The parathyroid glands tightly regulate calcium levels in the blood. In response to low calcium levels in the blood, the glands release more parathyroid hormone (PTH); in response to high calcium levels in the blood, the glands release less PTH. To increase calcium in the blood, PTH releases calcium from the matrix of bones, increases the resorption of calcium by the kidneys, and increases the absorption of calcium by the intestines. The parathyroid glands have well-defined, relatively simple, reliable interfaces with the

bones, kidneys, and intestines, mediated by PTH, but not with the other organs of the endocrine system. They nonetheless remain components in the endocrine system in virtue of the kinds of processes they perform. In this case, it is bodily regulation via the production of a class of chemical, a protein hormone. So, there are cases in which not all components of a system interface with each other, even in an indirect manner. In these cases, what makes a particular organ part of the system is the nature of the processes it carries out, such as the secretion of hormones.

In the foregoing examples, we have tried to point out an inadequacy in Haugeland's theory of systems by drawing attention to the fact that some biological systems are individuated by reference to the nature of the processing that goes on within those components, rather than exclusively by what interfaces with what. We can reinforce this point by reflecting on the adequacy of Haugeland's theory as a theory of the comprehensibility of systems. On Haugeland's theory of systems, the intelligibility of a system is supposed to follow from the decomposition of the system into components. In his section, "Intelligibility as the principle of decomposition," Haugeland paraphrases an idea of Herbert Simon's, saying that "So the point about comprehensibility can be paraphrased as follows: *finding*, in something complicated and hard to understand, a set of simple reliable interfaces, dividing it into relatively independent components, is a way of rendering it *intelligible*" (Haugeland, 1998, p. 216). Perhaps there are cases of the sort Haugeland envisions in which one understands a system simply in virtue of knowing how the components interface with each other. Nevertheless, there are surely plenty of cases where this is not the case. To understand the role of blood cells in the circulatory system, it is not enough to know that they interface via the plasma. One has to know something about what processes they carry out, processes such as the binding of oxygen and carbon dioxide to hemoglobin. Take a personal computer. To understand how a personal computer works, one surely needs to know more than how the parts are connected together. One needs to know what the components do. One needs to know what kinds of processes take place in each of the components. One needs to know that resistors are resistors, rather than, say, capacitors. One needs to know that RAM memory chips are RAM memory chips, rather than, say, a CPU. Maybe there are instances in which one can figure out these sorts of things from connectivity alone, but where one cannot it becomes apparent that one needs to know what kinds of processes take place within the component. At the very least, Haugeland's theory of the intelligibility of systems greatly understates the need to understand what the components do as part of what is needed to understand a system.

Haugeland's interest in what is causally connected to what, rather than the nature of the causal processes, seems to us not entirely idiosyncratic. We think this is another manifestation of an endemic feature of the extended cognition approach. There is in the extended cognition literature, we think, a relatively great interest in what is causally related to what, but a relative indifference, or inattention, to the kinds of causal processes there are in the world. To make the case that *cognitive* processes, and not merely *causal* systems, extend from the brain into the body and environment, one needs to attend to the kinds of processes that are the subject of investigation. As we have repeatedly claimed and argued, one needs some plausible way to distinguish cognitive processes from non-cognitive processes. In Chapter 5, we argued that Haugeland did not have one.

This point about the need to discriminate cognitive from non-cognitive processes, of course, leads us to the fundamental problem with the system versions of the coupling-constitution fallacy. It simply does not follow on Haugeland's account of a system that an X process must pervade all of an X system. Haugeland's version of an extended cognitive system hypothesis does not support the extended cognition hypothesis, the hypothesis that cognitive processes extend into the body and environment. Take an air conditioning system. Such a system typically includes a thermostat with electrical connections to the house's breaker box, a refrigerant, an expansion valve, an evaporator coil, a compressor, a condenser, a fan, and insulated pipes for carrying the refrigerant in a closed loop between the evaporator and the compressor. The system also has ductwork for distributing the cooled air through the house, duct tape covering the connections between the pieces of ductwork, outlet vents in the ceiling, walls, or floor, and a return vent. All of these components are linked by well-defined, relatively simple, reliable interfaces. Nevertheless, in an air conditioning system, not every component of the system "conditions" the air. Not every component cools the air. The evaporation coil cools the air, but the thermostat, the ductwork, the fans, and the compressor do not. Perhaps one can say that air is conditioned throughout the house, that the process of air conditioning takes place in all the rooms of the house.[6] After all, it is the

---

[6]   Shaun Gallagher made this point in conversation.

entirety of the air in the house that is cooled. Nevertheless, even on this understanding of what constitutes the relevant process of conditioning the air, the condenser and fan in the back yard do not condition the air. This example suggests an important feature of the claim that something is an *X* system: the fact that something is an *X* system does not entail that every component of the system does *X*. A number of further examples will bear this out.

A personal computer is a computing system in Haugeland's sense. Suppose, for the sake of argument, that we do not limit the notion of computing to what the CPU does. Suppose that we understand computing broadly so as to cover many sorts of information processing. Thus, we might count the process of reading a floppy disk, reading a compact disk, and turning the computer on as kinds of information processing, and hence as kinds of computing. Even on this very broad understanding of computing, it is still not the case that every process in a computing system is a computing process. There is the production of heat by the CPU, the circulation of air caused by the fan, the transmission of electrons in the computer's cathode ray tube, and the discharge of the computer's internal battery. Think of a sound system. Not every component in a sound system produces sounds (music). The speakers do, but the receiver, amplifiers, volume controls, tone controls, resistors, capacitors, and wires do not. Again, not every component of an *X* system can be presumed to do *X*. Even though we often identify systems in terms of processes that take place within them, we do not always identify systems in terms of processes that take place within all their components.

The drift of this line of reasoning is more than obvious. Grant that Otto, his body, and his pencil and notebook constitute a cognitive system. This does not suffice to establish that cognitive processing extends throughout Otto, his body, and his pencil and notebook. What the hypothesis of extended cognition claims about the case, over and above what the hypothesis of extended cognitive systems claims, is that cognition pervades the whole of the putative system. Clearly, the extended cognition hypothesis is the stronger claim. So, the truth of the cognitive system hypothesis does not suffice to establish the hypothesis of extended cognition. At the very least, some further argumentation will be needed in order to establish that Otto, his body, and pencil and notebook are the kind of system in which the system's identifying process pervades the whole of the system. Haugeland might simply stipulate that when one has a cognitive system in the sense that concerns him, then one has a cognitive system in which cognitive processing extends throughout the entire system. Of course, in that case, Haugeland will be guilty of committing an instance of a simpler version of the coupling-constitution fallacy of the sort described in Chapter 6. There is simply no easy road from coupling to constitution.

7.3   Clark's Theories of Systems and Coupling

As we saw in Chapter 5, there are times when Clark commits a straightforward version of the coupling-constitution fallacy. This is what we saw in his example of writing a philosophy paper.[7] At other times, however, he appears to commit a somewhat different version of the fallacy. Clark and Chalmers (1998), for example, appear to move from an observation about causal connections to a claim about cognitive systems, then slide from there to the hypothesis of extended cognition. They do this in their discussion of ways of playing the computer video game Tetris. In this game, a computer screen displays various irregularly shaped blocks, which fall down toward an array of blocks that is itself rising. The falling blocks can be rotated clockwise or counterclockwise so as to enable them to fit into gaps in the rising array of blocks. If a falling block forms a complete horizontal row of blocks in the array of rising blocks, the completed row disappears and the rising array of blocks is lowered just a bit. In the first way to play Tetris, a subject sits in front of the computer screen and uses mental rotation to determine how the current falling block might best fit into the rising array of blocks. In the second way to play, the subject can press a button on the game console that rotates the falling block. The actual rotation of the block on the screen obviates the need to perform mental rotation, thereby reducing the cognitive effort involved in determining where the falling block might best fit. The third way involves a bit of science fiction. In this version, there is a neural implant that is somehow supposed to carry out the equivalent of the actual rotation of the block on the screen, thereby eliminating the need to rely upon mental rotation to determine the best fit for a falling block. Not long after this example, Clark and Chalmers write,

> In these cases, the human organism is linked with an external entity in a two-way interaction, creating a *coupled system* that can be seen as a cognitive

---

[7]   Clark (2001, p. 132); cf., Clark (2002, pp. 23–4).

system in its own right. All the components in the system play an active causal role, and they jointly govern behavior in the same sort of way that cognition usually does. If we remove the external component the system's behavioral competence will drop, just as it would if we removed part of its brain. Our thesis is that this sort of coupled process counts equally well as a cognitive process, whether or not it is wholly in the head. (Clark and Chalmers, 1998, p. 2)

Although this passage is not as clear as it might be, there does appear to be the move from an interactive or coupling relation to the notion of a cognitive system and from there to something like the view that cognitive processes extend beyond the boundary of the head.[8] In what follows, we wish to address both of these moves. First, we will indicate why we should reject the coupling conditions that Clark proposes for understanding a cognitive system. The idea is that, even though it makes sense to say such things as that Otto and his notebook form a cognitive system, this is not a sense properly analyzed by Clark's theory of coupling and systems.[9] Second, we will review the basic problem with the move from the extended cognitive system hypothesis to the extended cognitive process hypothesis. We will also note how some of Clark's attempts to avoid committing the coupling-constitution fallacy do not help him.

7.3.1   Clark's trust condition(s) create a dilemma

Clark and Chalmers (1998) and Clark (forthcoming a) suggest that use of an external physical object, such as a notebook, constitutes part of an individual's cognitive processing if it meets three conditions:

1. The resource must be reliably available and typically invoked.
2. Any information retrieved from the resource must be more-or-less automatically endorsed. It should not usually be subject to critical scrutiny (unlike the opinions of other people, for example).

---

[8]   Part of what makes this passage less than perfectly clear is an apparent allusion to something like cognitive equivalence. This is the idea that "All the components in the system ... jointly govern behavior in the same sort of way that cognition usually does." We will return to this claim about cognitive equivalence in Chapter 8.

[9]   This section will meet, in some measure, the charge that we do not adequately address the specific kind of coupling relation that Clark and Chalmers (1998) had in mind. Cf., Clark (forthcoming b).

3.   Information provided by the resource should be easily accessible as and when required. (Cf., Clark, forthcoming a)

In support of these conditions, Clark claims that they yield what he takes to be intuitively correct results in a number of cases, in addition to Otto's case. A book in one's home library will not count, since (presumably) it fails the reliably available clause in the first condition. Mobile access to the Google search engine would not count, since it fails the second condition (Clark claims). By contrast, a brain implant that facilitates mental rotation would meet the conditions. Thus, Clark apparently applies his conditions as a set of necessary and sufficient conditions under which a resource is part of an agent's cognitive system. Clark can, of course, decide that he wishes his conditions only to count as sufficiency conditions, but in that event he will need some other basis upon which to say that a book in one's home library or the Google search engine are not part of one's cognitive system.

At one point, Clark describes his conditions as "conditions of trust and glue." This is a convenient name for Clark's general approach. It also provides us with a convenient description of the problem with Clark's approach, namely, that the trust condition is too strong. As a first set of examples, consider cases in which one might be "alienated" from one's own cognitive resources. By this, we have in mind the idea that one can have cognitive resources that one does not typically invoke, that one does not more or less automatically endorse, and that one does subject to critical scrutiny. Clark's conditions make such a situation an impossibility. One can evidently flesh out the form of this objection in any number of ways, but in an effort to make the problem more compelling we will offer some examples:[10]

1   *Dotto and the cabinet.* Let Dotto be a professor at a small liberal arts college. Let him be a normal human being with normal memory function. Dotto has taught at the college for a long time and can recall most

---

[10]   In reply to these kinds of examples, Clark suggests that his conditions are meant to apply only to cases of dispositional beliefs. So, it is not that something gets to be a cognitive resource if, and only if, it meets Clark's three conditions; it is that something gets to be a dispositional belief if, and only if, it meets those conditions. While narrowing the scope of the conditions may avoid the problem with blindsight, it does not fundamentally alter the nature of the problem. One can apparently be alienated from one's dispositional beliefs.

every faculty member's office phone number. Since the college is small and intimate, Dotto's ability requires no exceptional memory capabilities. One weekend, Dotto hits his head on a kitchen cabinet. Other than a bruise on the head, Dotto is not seriously injured. In particular, he suffers no cognitive impairment. Still, he has a strong reaction to his incident. He fears that his memory is, or might be, impaired, so he decides that he will try to reduce his dependence on it where he can. As part of this broader plan, he decides to reduce his reliance on his memory for phone numbers. Instead of calling people on the phone, he decides that he will communicate with his colleagues either face to face or via e-mail. He knows he can find their e-mail addresses on the college web page. He says to himself, "Given my accident, I think my memory for phone numbers may not be reliable. Rather than contacting my colleagues by phone, I will either meet them face to face or contact them via e-mail." He forms this resolution and sticks to it. *Ex hypothesi* the psychological processes in the recall apparatus of Dotto's brain are unchanged; Dotto has simply decided that he would rather not rely on their output. Were you to ask Dotto, "Do you know Professor Blotto's office phone number?," the correct number would occur to him. It would flash before his mind, so to speak. But, given his resolution, he would respond by saying, "I don't know." Dotto's memory, his dispositional belief regarding Dr. Blotto's office number, is evidently still reliably available, only he no longer typically invokes it. Indeed, he never invokes it. Further, he no longer endorses the phone numbers that flash before his mind when queried. By Clark's conditions, we would be forced to say that the processes that formerly constituted part of Dotto's memory no longer constitute a part of Dotto's memory. Dotto has lost part of his mind.

2   *Dotto and the scientific study of memory.* Perhaps one will not like the idea of a bump on the head initiating Dotto's change of heart regarding his memory. Suppose, then, that everything in the above example is the same, save for the fact that what provokes Dotto to change his attitude is reading about a scientific study of memory. In this version, Dotto reads about a study in which, in the days following the acquittal of O. J. Simpson, investigators asked undergraduates how they learned of Simpson's acquittal. Fifteen months later, the same undergraduates were questioned again and only half provided the same answers. Having read this, Dotto resolves to reduce his reliance on his memory, including his reliance on his ability to recall his colleagues' phone numbers.

It again looks as though we should say that Dotto has a cognitive resource that he simply does not invoke, he does not automatically endorse, and which he subjects to critical scrutiny. Clark, however, makes such a situation impossible.

3   *Dotto and his unreliable memory.* Of course, the foregoing scenarios are somewhat contrived. Nevertheless, once the idea is put forth one can see how mundane examples suffice. Suppose that Dotto is bad with names. Although he will realize that he has met someone before and should know her name, he does not trust his memory. Even if the person's name correctly comes to his mind – even if he has reliable dispositional beliefs about a person's name – he will still try to avoid relying on his memory. He will typically ask someone nearby that he knows to confirm his recollection. Dotto has a normal memory, but by Clark's condition of trust, Dotto would have to be missing some cognitive apparatus.

4   *Dotto and color illusions.* Memory is not the only cognitive resource susceptible to this sort of problem. Suppose that Dotto has completely normal human vision. One day, surfing the web, Dotto finds a gallery of visual illusions that includes some demonstrations of the ways in which a given color looks different on different backgrounds.[11] Given these illusions, Dotto decides that color perception is unreliable, and hence that he will not invoke color perceptions, that he will not endorse them, and that they should always be subject to critical scrutiny. While Dotto's color processing might be modified to some degree by viewing the color illusions, Clark must maintain that it has been so altered that Dotto no longer has a color-processing resource. The natural analysis, however, is that Dotto is simply alienated from his color processing.

5   *CLT and blindsight.* Those who accept or tolerate informal observations or thought experiments can clearly see how to generate further examples of this sort, but what about those who are skeptical of thought experiments as intuition mongering or bad armchair philosophizing? For them, there is a familiar scientific phenomenon that makes much the same point about trust, namely, some of the instances of blindsight. One cause of blindsight is a lesion to the primary visual cortex (a.k.a. the striate cortex, a.k.a. area V1). One example involves CLT, a 54-year-old male who had a right posterior cerebral artery stroke in 1987 (Fendrich et al., 1992). Magnetic resonance imaging confirmed a

---

[11]   Or think about the example of Jones, in Sellars (1956).

brain lesion to area V1 that deprived CLT of visual perception in most, but not all, of his left visual field. In the experiment run by Fendrich et al., CLT was asked to listen to two 0.6 second tones. During one of these tones, a one degree black circle was flashed three times for 96 milliseconds on a white background. Eye tracking equipment enabled the investigators to control the position of the display in the visual field. CLT's task was to make a forced choice regarding which tone co-occurred with the black circle. When the black circle was flashed in his right visual field, he was correct more than 95 percent of the time. When the black circle was flashed in his left visual field, CLT "insisted he 'never saw anything'" (Fendrich et al., 1992, p. 1490), but there remained a small island of preserved function in this left visual field, where CLT's detection was significantly above chance. What looks to be going on here is that CLT is doing some form of visual processing in detecting the flashing black circles, but he does not satisfy all of Clark's necessary and sufficient conditions. CLT's spared visual processing apparatus is reliably present in the sense that he always carries it with him. But it hardly appears that he typically invokes the information from it. He is not even aware that he has this apparatus or that it is doing anything for him. So, whatever apparatus CLT is using to detect the flashing circles appears to fail Clark's first condition for being a part of CLT's cognitive apparatus. Second, CLT does not at all automatically endorse the information from his spared neural apparatus, since he is entirely oblivious to its existence. Of course, CLT does not subject this apparatus or its information to critical scrutiny, since he is entirely oblivious to its existence. So, whatever apparatus CLT is using to detect the flashing circles appears to fail Clark's second condition for being a part of CLT's cognitive apparatus.

To recount, the problem Clark faces here is a dilemma. On the one hand, Clark needs his trust condition(s) to be necessary, so that such things as library books and Internet search engines will not count as part of one's cognitive apparatus. On the other hand, Clark needs his trust condition(s) *not* to be necessary, so that such things as the memory and visual processes one does not trust will count as part of one's cognitive apparatus. It is, of course, logically possible that Clark could amend his conditions in such a way as to steer clear of these objections. We do not deny that. Nevertheless, we conjecture that what enables these problems is that, ultimately, what makes something a cognitive process or resource is not whether a cognitive agent trusts it, but something about how it works. Perhaps part of what makes a process a cognitive process is that it involves non-derived representations. Recall that what makes a process nuclear fission is not what it is connected to, but whether or not it is the splitting of atomic nuclei. What makes the parathyroid glands part of the endocrine system is not what they are connected to, but their secretion of a protein hormone in the service of homeostasis. We think orthodox cognitive psychology places its bets on the individuation of cognitive processes in terms of mechanisms. We think Clark should as well.

7.3.2   Clark on cognitive systems and the coupling-constitution fallacy

Suppose, however, that we now simply set aside what might be taken to be mere infelicities in the details of Clark's theory of systems. Suppose that we concede the claim that, say, Otto, his pencil, and his notebook form a cognitive system in virtue of Otto's coupling with his tools. Does it follow from this that cognitive processing extends from Otto's brain into his arms, hands, pencil and notebook? Does it follow that cognitive processing pervades this entire region of spacetime? Not if the considerations brought forth in discussing Haugeland's view on systems are correct. It simply does not follow from the fact that one has identified an X system in terms of a causal process of type X that that X process pervades every component of the system. But suppose we take Clark to be treating the extended cognitive system hypothesis and the extended cognitive processing hypothesis as merely two ways of expressing the same idea. After all, Wilson and Clark appear to treat claims about systems and processes as interchangeable in the following passage:

> More radical forms of externalism about the mind abound, and go by a variety of labels. These include *locational externalism* (Wilson 2000, 2004a [2004]), *environmentalism* (Rowlands 1999), *vehicle externalism* (Hurley 1998) [1998a] and *the extended mind* (Clark and Chalmers 1998). One way or another, all these locutions aim to suggest that the mind and the cognitive processes that constitute it extend beyond the boundary of the skin of the individual agent. The extended mind thesis very explicitly identifies cognitive systems themselves as reaching beyond individuals into their physical and social environments. Such theses challenge individualism directly by implying that an individualistic psychology could only, at best, tell part of the story about cognitive processing: the inside story. (Wilson and Clark, forthcoming)

If, however, we are to read Wilson and Clark as simply stipulating the equivalence of the system claim and the processing claim, then we merely have to realize that Wilson and Clark are committing a simple version of the coupling-constitution argument of the sort discussed in the last chapter, rather than a more complex two-step system version of the sort that we are exploring in this chapter. It simply does not follow from the fact that Otto has intense causal interactions with his pencil and notebook – from the fact that he is coupled to his pencil and notebook – that the whole of this causal economy involves cognitive processing.[12] So, the situation seems to be this. Clark can equate the system hypothesis and the processing hypothesis by stipulation, in which case he commits the simple coupling-constitution fallacy, or he can let the system hypothesis and the processing hypothesis come apart, in which case he commits a system version of the fallacy. Either way, he does not yet have a way to move from a coupling claim to the hypothesis that cognitive processing extends beyond the boundaries of skin and skull.

Let us consider now two kinds of replies to the coupling-constitution fallacy that Clark seems to have in mind. The first appears to be intended to cast doubt on the propriety of asking whether a subprocess of cognitive process is itself a cognitive process.[13] The hypothesis of extended cognition claims that the processing that occurs in Otto's brain, arms, hands, pencil and notebook constitutes a cognitive process. In drawing attention to the

---

[12]   Notice that in putting the point in this way, we need not state the coupling-constitution fallacy in such a way as to suppose that Otto's pencil and notebook are cognitive objects. Rather, we rely only on cognitive processes in the pencil and notebook. This way of formulating the objection, found originally in Adams and Aizawa (2001), avoids Clark's (forthcoming b) concern that talk of "cognitive objects" is unintelligible. Whether or not this is so, it is beside the point of the objection underlying the coupling-constitution fallacy.

[13]   Clark (forthcoming b, pp. 3–4) runs the problem in terms of cognitive objects, which he finds unintelligible, so we restate what we take to be his point using cognitive processes. Cf. Clark (forthcoming b): "But this talk, of an objects [sic] being or failing to be 'cognitive' seems almost unintelligible when applied to some putative *part* of a cognitive agent or of a cognitive system. What would it mean for the neuron *or* the pencil to be, as it were, brute factively 'cognitive'?" This seems intelligible to us. What does it mean to say that the left hemisphere of the brain is cognitive? Cognitive processes take place there. What would it mean for the neuron or the pencil to be cognitive? Cognitive processes take place there. The question is intelligible, although we might well say that neither the neuron nor the pencil are cognitive, on the grounds that they do not bear the mark of cognitive processes. We should not think the question is unintelligible when all that is going on is that the answer to the question under investigation in negative. Cf., Wilson and Clark (forthcoming).

coupling-constitution fallacy, the critic of extended cognition asks whether or not the coupling suffices to extend a cognitive process into some part of the body or environment. What the coupling-constitution fallacy, therefore, presupposes is that it makes sense to ask of the processing that occurs in just the pencil and notebook – the shearing of graphite from the pencil onto the paper, the movements of the pages, and so forth – whether or not they are themselves cognitive processes. Without the premise that such questions make sense, the coupling-constitution fallacy cannot get off the ground. Does it make sense to ask whether a V4 neuron, for example, carries on a cognitive process? No, say Wilson and Clark.

We, however, think, in general, it does make sense to ask whether a subprocess of a cognitive process is itself cognitive. We think cognitive psychologists regularly decompose cognitive processes into further cognitive subprocesses. This is what is done in much of the "boxology" of cognitive psychology, where cognitive processes are decomposed into a kind of flow chart of cognitive subprocesses. Think about what cognitive psychologists say about, for example, the auditory perception of language. Maybe a first cognitive step in the process is the separation of specifically linguistic sounds that correspond to phonemes from other ambient sounds, such as whistles, bells, and hums. Think about multimodal sensory processing of the sort found in the McGurk effect. In these kinds of cases, we apparently have visual processing of facial movements being integrated with auditory processing of speech to determine a linguistic perceptual experience. The reason, we hypothesize, that the causal process that begins in the eye and the causal process that begins in the ear are both cognitive is that they bear the mark of the cognitive. They both involve more or less idiosyncratic kinds of processing on non-derived representations.

We should add that we do not suppose that *every* subprocess of a cognitive process must itself be cognitive or that every subprocess of a cognitive process must bear the mark of the cognitive.[14] That would be too strong a presupposition. Think of the passage of a particular sodium ion through a sodium channel in a neuron in the primary visual cortex. Let this ion flux be part of the realization base of a cognitive process; say, the perception of an oriented line. We do not think that this ion's movement must bear the mark of the cognitive in order for the perception of an oriented line to count as a cognitive process. Our presupposition is merely that every *cognitive* subprocess of a cognitive process must bear the mark of the cognitive.

[14] Cf., Wilson and Clark (forthcoming).

This is the kind of presupposition that one appears to need in order to do justice to cognitive psychology. It allows us to recognize the cognitive subprocesses involved in the McGurk effect as genuine cognitive processes, while rejecting ion fluxes as non-cognitive. It also is enough to see the problem with the coupling-constitution fallacy.

Clark's strategy in replying to our assumptions about subprocesses of cognitive processes is to pin on us an implausibly strong hypothesis. He and Wilson (forthcoming) adopt the same strategy in attributing to us the assumption that there are objects that are intrinsically non-cognitive.[15] They pin on us what they call the Dogma of Intrinsic Unsuitability: "Certain kinds of encoding or processing are intrinsically unsuitable to act as parts of the material or computational substrate of any genuinely cognitive state or process" (Wilson and Clark, forthcoming). This, they note, conflicts with a fundamental tenet of computationally inspired cognitive science, what they call the Tenet of Computational Promiscuity, according to which "pretty much anything, including any kind of processing or encoding, *provided that it is properly located in some ongoing web of computational activity*, can contribute to the nature and unfolding of the cognitively relevant computations, and hence emerge as a proper part of the material substrate of some target cognitive process or activity" (ibid., italics in original). Given the choice between the Dogma of Intrinsic Unsuitability and the Tenet of Computational Promiscuity, Wilson and Clark claim that we must stick with the latter.

As we just hinted, the problem with Wilson and Clark's reply is that we are not committed to the Doctrine of Intrinsic Unsuitability. We do not need to rely upon this doctrine to press the coupling-constitution fallacy. We do not need this doctrine in order to make the case that the cognitive does not extend under the conditions that are invoked in coupling arguments. Nor do we need to adopt the doctrine in the articulation or defense of our view that, as a matter of contingent empirical fact, cognitive processes typically occur within the brain. Our view has always been that, as a matter of contingent empirical fact, pencils, paper, eyeglasses, Rolodexes, and so forth happen not to be parts of any currently existing cognitive economy. It is, in principle, possible that, say, a pencil or notebook could be so employed as to be a contributor to a cognitive process. This would happen if the pencil and notebook were, in whole or in part, to satisfy

---

[15] Much the same idea crops up in Clark (forthcoming b).

conditions on the possession of non-derived content and participate in the kinds of causal relations that we theorize are distinctive of cognitive processes. This is just to say that portions of the body and tools in the extra-corporeal environment could be parts of cognitive processes, if only they were to bear the mark of the cognitive. It is because of our commitment to this principle that, in order to resist the extension of cognitive processes into environmental objects, we argued in Adams and Aizawa (2001), and will argue in more detail in Chapter 8, that, in fact, cognitive processes do not extend, because they do not bear what we take to be the mark of the cognitive.

How can we run the coupling-constitution fallacy without recourse to the Doctrine of Intrinsic Unsuitability? Put very simply, the idea is that coupling to a pencil and notebook is not sufficient to get the pencil and notebook to bear the mark of the cognitive. The point can be made in terms more familiar from Wilson and Clark's Tenet of Computational Promiscuity: Otto's coupling to a pencil and notebook is not sufficient to properly locate the pencil and paper in an ongoing web of computational activity that constitutes cognitive processing. Wilson and Clark apparently think they can make a concession sufficient to get around this observation when they claim that

> Computational Promiscuity is, it is important to notice, fully compatible with the thought that certain kinds of computational structure may be *necessary* for fluid, real-world intelligence. It is even compatible with the thought that such necessary computational structures (if such there be) may all be located, at present at least, inside the heads of biological agents. It asserts only that *once any such necessary structuring conditions have been met*, there is then no limit on the kinds of additional resource that may then be co-opted as proper parts of an extended cognitive process. (Wilson and Clark, forthcoming)

We can agree that there are necessary structuring conditions in the brain and that there is then no limit on the kinds of additional resource that can then be co-opted as proper parts of an extended cognitive process. Our claim is not that additional resources cannot be co-opted; it is that in the kinds of scenarios described by Clark and Chalmers, they are not. What would enable them to be co-opted into the cognitive would, of course, be their bearing the mark of the cognitive. Just as you cannot get computation to extend outside a computer simply by affixing a green "on" light to it, so you cannot get cognition to extend outside of a brain by simply by using a pencil and notebook a lot.

Here is yet another way of making the point. Take a bowling ball. Perhaps if this bowling ball were in a larger causal order in which its being "holes up" were a "1" and "holes down" were a "0," and this bowling ball somehow satisfied a set of sufficiency conditions on non-derived representations, and there were enough other surrounding hardware, such as ball returning and ball moving apparatus, configured into a computer, and this entire system had something corresponding to a program that realizes some cognitive function, then one would be on the road to having this bowling ball fit for cognitive duty. Our point in the coupling-constitution fallacy is that merely having a person coupled to the bowling ball, in either Clark's sense, or Haugeland's sense, or in the dynamical systems theory sense, or in any pedestrian sense, is not sufficient to place the bowing ball into the right kind of ongoing web of computational activity that might constitute cognitive processing.

7.4   Conclusion

For most of this chapter, we have argued that, insofar as the hypothesis of extended cognitive systems is not stipulated to be logically or conceptually equivalent to the hypothesis of extended cognitive processing, the hypothesis of extended cognitive systems does not support the hypothesis of extended cognitive processes. The problem is that the process by which we pick out a kind of system, such as air conditioning or computing, need not pervade the whole of the system. Perhaps there are systems in which the individuating process does takes place in every component of the system, but at the very least not all systems are like this. This being the case, further argumentation would have to be provided in order to validate the move from the extended cognitive system hypothesis to the extended cognition hypothesis.

To conclude this chapter, we want to draw attention to one way in which the extended cognitive system hypothesis threatens to undermine the extended cognition hypothesis. Not only does the first hypothesis not support the second; the first challenges the second. To see this, let us return to Haugeland's idea that the way to understand a system is to decompose it into its components, by which he means that we should find out what is connected to what via interfaces. Yet we noted that, in general, knowing how a set of components interfaces is not sufficient to enable us to understand how a complex system works. In addition, one typically needs to know the principles by which the components operate. In the beautifully illustrated and clearly and cleverly written *The New Way Things Work*, David Macaulay introduces his readers to his book with the following:

> To any machine, work is a matter of principle, because everything a machine does is in accordance with a set of principles or scientific laws. To see the way a machine works, you can take the covers off and look inside. But to understand what goes on, you need to get to know the principles that govern its actions. The machines in this and the following parts of *The New Way Things Work* are therefore grouped by their principles rather than by their uses. This produces some interesting neighbors: The plow rubs shoulders with the zipper, for example, and the hydroelectric power station with the dentist's drill. They may look different, be vastly different in scale, and have different purposes, but when seen in terms of principles, they work in the same way. (Macaulay, 1998, p. 8)

Macaulay nicely articulates the theory of understanding systems that we embrace. To understand an air conditioner, you need to know more than how the parts are put together. You need to know what evaporative cooling is. If you don't know that Freon™ is a highly volatile liquid that evaporates at room temperature, and that as it evaporates, it cools its environment, then you won't understand how an air conditioner works. If you don't understand how the pressure of a gas is related to condensation, then again you won't understand how an air conditioner works. To take another example, if you don't understand refraction, you won't understand how a set of lens arranged in a tubular structure would enable one to resolve the stars of the Milky Way.

Apply the foregoing to our understanding of the cognitive system consisting of Otto, his pencil, and his notebook. In order to understand this cognitive system, it will not be enough to know that Otto, his pencil, and his notebook causally interact. We will also need to know the principles at work in the components. We will need to know how pencils work, how paper works, how the binding works, and we will need to know how Otto works. We will need to know how his bones, muscles, and nerves work. We will need to know how the fact that light enters his eyes influences his behavior and what happens once the light strikes his retinas. We will need to know what many of those anatomical brain structures, such as V1, V2, and so on, do. We will want to know more than just the biology and chemistry of the brain. We will want to know something that looks like good old-fashioned cognitive psychology. If we accept the idea that humans form cognitive systems with their environments, that still seems to support the idea that we want to pursue an intracranial research program that we might as well call cognitive psychology. This, however, appears to be just the old-fashioned locus of cognition. So, it looks as though a fair appreciation of the extended cognitive system hypothesis actually challenges the motivation for extended cognition.

Chapter 8

Cognitive Equivalence, Complementarity, and Evolution

In this chapter, we will review the cognitive equivalence and complementarity arguments. We put them together, in part, to highlight just how uneasily they sit together. The cognitive equivalence argument is inspired by the presupposition that what is traditionally conceived to be cognitive processing also takes place in larger collections of brain, body, and environment. The complementarity argument begins with the observation that what is traditionally conceived to be cognitive processing is unlike what is found in external biological and physical objects. These considerations are not strictly inconsistent, but they are an odd couple. The third argument, the argument based on evolution, is included in this chapter, in part, because we couldn't think of a better place to consider it. More importantly, however, what ties all three of these arguments together is that, as we shall argue, they are all enabled by inattention to the issue of what differentiates cognitive processes from non-cognitive processes.

8.1 Cognitive Equivalence

The cognitive equivalence argument has the form of a quasi-syllogism whose major premise strikes us as something like a logical or conceptual truth, namely, that any process that is cognitively equivalent to a cognitive process is itself a cognitive process. The minor premise maintains that this or that process spanning the brain, body, and perhaps environment is cognitively equivalent to a cognitive process. Given the status of the major premise as something close to a conceptual truth, the way to resist any application of this argument is surely to show that the minor premise is false. Although we believe that, in principle, it is possible for transcranial processes to be cognitive processes, we will argue that this does not happen in the cases that advocates of extended cognition have brought forth to date.

Of course, the argument form we have just sketched is a generalization of what is sometimes called a functional isomorphism argument.[1] One way to argue that cognition extends into the body and physical surroundings of an organism would begin with the supposition that cognitive processing is a type of functional processing. Clark (forthcoming a) explicitly endorses this view. On this assumption, if one finds that some transcranial process is functionally isomorphic to the functional organization of a cognitive process, then one has some basis for maintaining that that cognitive process is transcranial. The functional isomorphism argument is inspired by one reading of what has been called the "parity principle." According to this principle, "If as we confront some task, a part of the world functions as a process which, *were it done in the head*, we would have no hesitation in recognizing as part of the cognitive process, then that part of the world *is* (so we claim) part of the cognitive process" (Clark and Chalmers, 1998, p. 8). A common way of interpreting this passage is as saying that if something functions like a cognitive process, then it is a cognitive process. We prefer our generalization of the functional isomorphism argument to a cognitive equivalence argument for two reasons. First, it does not rely on the assumption that it is functional organization that makes a cognitive process a cognitive process. It allows this, but does not presuppose it. Second, it makes explicit the kind of equivalence that is relevant, namely, sameness of cognitive process. It is one thing for Otto's notebook to play the same functional role, *in some sense of same functional role*, as does Inga's biological memory. It is another to say that Inga's biological memory and Otto's pencil and notebook realize the same cognitive processes, that they are cognitively equivalent. Why would it matter to the hypothesis of extended cognition if both Inga's memory and Otto's pencil and notebook were only functionally equivalent in being, say, semantically evaluable triggers to action, if they were not actually cognitively equivalent? Being a semantically evaluable trigger to action is something less than being a belief. Why care about the sameness of "functional poise," unless that is simply a vague way of speaking of sameness of cognitive process? To put the point one other

---

[1]   Cf., e.g., Weiskopf (unpublished). Sutton (forthcoming) claims that "first wave" extended cognition theories invoked functional isomorphism arguments for extended cognition.

way, not just any functional equivalence is cognitive equivalence; what we should care about in extended cognition is cognitive equivalence.

In the remainder of this section, we will review cases in which one might think that there is a cognitive equivalence between an intracranial cognitive process and a transcranial process. This will involve revisiting the Inga–Otto example and the Tetris example.[2]

8.1.1   Inga and Otto revisited

Although the relevant texts may not be perfectly unambiguous, there is reason to read the Inga–Otto example as a case of putative cognitive equivalence. After introducing the example, Clark and Chalmers (1998) write,

> For in relevant respects the cases are entirely analogous: the notebook plays for Otto the same role that memory plays for Inga. The information in the notebook functions just like the information constituting an ordinary non-occurrent belief; it just happens that this information lies beyond the skin. (p. 13)

Then, later,

> Certainly, insofar as beliefs and desires are characterized by their explanatory roles, Otto's and Inga's cases seem to be on a par: the essential causal dynamics of the two cases mirror each other precisely. (ibid.)

Then, still later,

> What makes some information count as a belief is the role it plays, and there is no reason why the relevant role can be played only from inside the body. (ibid., p. 14)

This last sentence readily admits of being interpreted as the argument that beliefs are defined in terms of functional roles, so that anything that has that functional role, even something outside of the brain, will count as a

---

[2]   Hurley (forthcoming) provides two cases of the cognitive equivalence argument: an example of acallosal patients and Esther Thelen and Linda Smith's dynamical systems theory analysis of infants' "A-not-B" error (cf., Thelen and Smith, 1994). Lack of space prevents us from addressing these cases.

belief. This, however, is just a special case of the cognitive equivalence argument. In a later paper, Clark seems to say much the same thing:

> Inga's biological memory systems, working together, govern *her* behaviors in the functional ways distinctive of believing. Otto's bio-technological matrix (the organism and the notebook) governs his behavior in the same sort of way. So the explanatory apparatus of mental state ascription gets an equal grip in each case, and what looks at first like Otto's action (looking up the notebook) emerges as part of Otto's thought. Mind, we conclude, is congenitally predisposed to seep out into the world. (Clark, forthcoming a)

And Clark even goes so far as to subscribe to a species of functionalism about belief:

> To repeat, our claim is not that the processes in Otto and Inga are identical, or even similar, in terms of their detailed implementation. It is simply that, in respect of the role that the long-term encodings play in guiding current response, both modes of storage can be seen as supporting dispositional belief. It is the way the information is poised to guide reasoning (such as conscious inferences that nonetheless result in no overt actions) and behavior that counts. This is not behaviorism but functionalism. It is systematic role that matters, not brute similarities in public behavior (though the two are of course related). (ibid.)

So, to reiterate, there seems to us to be an abundance of text suggesting that we should explore the Inga–Otto example as a putative case of cognitive equivalence.

The thrust of our reply will be to draw attention to the numerous psychological differences between Inga and Otto. The point will not be that there are "implementation-level," fine-grained differences between Inga and Otto, as for example that Inga's memory is realized with sodium and potassium ion channels, where Otto's are realized with cellulose and graphite. Our point will be that there are differences between Inga and Otto that are of a kind that have traditionally interested cognitive psychologists. These differences, we contend, provide a principled, non-question-begging reason to believe that there are intracranial cognitive processes in Inga that are unlike the causal processes involved in Otto's interactions with his notebook. These are differences of the sort described briefly in Chapter 4.

Consider a free recall task in which subjects hear a list of 20 words at a fixed rate of one word every two seconds and in which they are asked to recall those words in any order. In normal human memory, such as Inga's, one finds recency and primacy effects. If we plot the probability of correct recall of words against position, averaging across subjects and lists, we find that it varies with the position of the words in the list. Recall is better at the beginning of the list and at the end of the list. This seems to be a fact about at least one kind of human memory that scientific theories of memory should care about and should be able to explain. *Ex hypothesi* Inga has normal human memory, so we expect that her recall will be correctly described by a curve of this familiar sort. Now suppose that Otto takes this same free recall task and that when he does so, he quickly writes each word he hears into his notebook. If he can write as fast as the words come, then we suppose that his recall will be astonishingly good. He will recall all 20 words he hears. The probability for recall will be high for all words on the list. The point, of course, is that Otto's performance will not be like Inga's. Where Inga's recall will display both primacy and recency effects, Otto's will not. This is the kind of evidence that psychologists can use to draw a principled distinction between the processes and mechanisms in Inga and those in Otto.

But, the advocate of extended cognition may interject, suppose that Otto cannot write the words down as quickly as the experimenter utters them. In such a case, Otto's recall might be quite good for the first few items, but then falter at subsequent points where he gets behind, then recover somewhat near the end as he catches every second or third word, perhaps. Maybe in that case, Otto's performance, averaged over several lists, could turn out to display both primacy and recency effects. So, there would be some similarities between Otto and Inga, suggesting that they possess the same cognitive mechanisms and perform the same sorts of memory processes.

This is an apt and important point, which we think, ultimately, reinforces our view. In the first place, even in this case, there will likely remain differences between Inga's performance and Otto's performance. In Inga's case, the recency effect is stronger than the primacy effect. Words near the end of the list are even more memorable than words at the front of the list. For Otto, in the kind of scenario described above, however, it sounds as though the primacy effect would be stronger than the recency effect. This would still give psychologists some basis for distinguishing the processes and mechanisms in Otto from the processes and mechanisms in Inga, saying that the former are cognitive, where the latter are not. Further, cognitive psychologists will likely not rest with finding a single point of similarity between Otto and Inga. Even in the event that Otto and Inga have identical primacy and recency effects, this would not stop psychologists from probing deeper into the possible differences between them. For example, given the scenario described, psychologists would probe to see why Otto displays the primacy and recency effects. Psychologists might try slowing the rate of presentation of words in the list from one every two seconds to one every three seconds. Inga may then still show primacy and recency effects in her recall, where Otto, freed from the constraints of having to write fast enough, might then recall at near perfect rates. These are the kinds of variations that psychologists explore in attempting to discern the causes of measurable behavior. They are the kinds of steps cognitive psychologists take in order to discover cognitive mechanisms giving rise to behavior.

Primacy and recency effects are, of course, not the only points of difference between Inga's memory and Otto's "memory." Consider the effects of practice on memory. Recall from Chapter 4 that Anderson (1981) presented subjects with paired associates of words, such as *dog-3*, then later asked them to recall the target word "3" given the cue word "dog." What Anderson found was that with practice, subjects were better able to recall the target words when given the cue words. So, this is the kind of result one expects with Inga. But what should we expect with Otto and his notebook "memory"? When Otto is presented with a pair of words, he writes both on a page in his notebook. When cued with a target word, he finds the page in his notebook, then scans down the list until he finds the cue word, then recites the target word. If Otto is proficient in his use of his notebook, he will somehow have the means to find the correct page of the book and find the correct cue word in his list. So, we expect that his performance on this task will be excellent from the start. He will correctly recall target words with better than, say, 95 percent accuracy. Further, since he is already proficient in the skills needed to open the notebook and search lists in it, there will be little improvement over successive trials. So, Inga and Otto will likely differ in the effects of practice.

Inga is also likely to have depth of processing effects that Otto does not. In the Craik and Tulving (1975) experiment, for example, subjects were given words, then asked to report either the case of the word, a rhyme for the word, or whether the word could be used in a given incomplete sentence. So, when the target word was "table," a subject might be asked whether it was written with large case or small case letters, whether it rhymed with "cable," or whether it could be used to complete the sentence "He left the book on the _____." Subjects were then later asked whether they had seen the target word. Averaged over a large set of words, the rhyming question was more helpful in fostering recall than was the question of case, and the sentence completion question was more helpful than the rhyming question. Presumably, this regularity holds true of Inga, but what should we expect of Otto? Given the target word, Otto simply writes this in his book, then answers the questions put to him. When later asked if he "recalls" a given word, he turns to the appropriate page in his notebook, and then searches his list for the word. Again, it seems highly likely that his "recall" will be high, no matter what kind of question was subsequently asked of him. Otto's "recall" will be nearly perfect, where Inga's will be far from perfect. This is why it is eminently plausible to suppose that Inga will have a depth of processing effect that Otto does not have and that Inga's memory differs from Otto's "memory." These differences give the orthodox cognitive psychologist a principled reason to maintain that Inga has memory in a sense in which Otto does not. Indeed, spacing effects in practice and generation effects in training are just as likely to provide principled ground for maintaining that Inga has a kind of cognitive processing not found in Otto.

Our best guess is that were psychologists to apply many of their familiar experimental protocols for testing memory to Otto and his notebook, they would find vast differences between Inga and Otto. Test after test, we conjecture, would reveal significant divergences. It is not that Inga and Otto will differ only in, say, the strength of their primacy effect. If this is the way things turn out, then there will be a perfectly good sense in which we can discriminate between Inga's memory and Otto's use of his notebook. We know, of course, that we are merely conjecturing how Otto would fare in the standard tests of his memory capacities. We have not actually gotten a set of human subjects matching Otto's personal history and performed these tests. We are not cognitive psychologists. So, in principle, we could be surprisingly wide of the mark in our suspicions about what experiments will reveal. At this point, we have to leave it to the cognitive psychologists to test our predictions. They have to decide if such predictions are sufficiently plausible to be worth their time and effort to bother checking.

In analyzing these cases, one might notice a kind of symmetry between our position and Clark and Chalmers's position on the level of detail. Clark and Chalmers might charge us with looking at too fine a level of detail in comparing Otto and Inga, where we charge Clark and Chalmers with looking at too coarse a level of detail in comparing Otto and Inga. Given this kind of symmetry, how can the dispute be resolved? Our proposal, of course, is that we let the empirical facts fall where they may. We let cognitive psychologists tell us what to count as cognitively relevant differences. We let cognitive psychologists tell us what to count as the right level of detail. We think that current cognitive psychology already speaks to the issue of the correct grain of analysis and that we appeal to that grain. Cognitive psychology could take a radical shift toward a more coarse-grained level of analysis, but until it does we have some principled reason to think that there is a level of detail of scientific study that provides a non-question-begging reason to hypothesize an intracranial cognitive psychology.

However, consider yet another way of challenging our appeal to the results of current cognitive psychology. Surely it is too stringent to require that there be no statistically significant differences between Inga and Otto on standard memory tests. The extended cognition hypothesis might be taken to say that cognitive psychologists will find some new more general category of memory that accurately describes Inga and Otto. There will be some family resemblances between Inga's memory processes and Otto's "memory" processes.

To meet this reply, we admit that there are no hard and fast rules as to how different the processing can be, while still being memory processing. As we have noted before, were an otherwise normal human to follow Miller's short-term protocols and prove to have a "magic number five," plus or minus two, then surely this person would count as having human short-term memory. And, of course, our point is not to make linguistic stipulations about what to call memory and what not to call memory. However, there seem to us to be any number of differences between Inga and Otto, not just one, and they are of the sorts that cognitive psychologists have cared about for decades. Surely the admission by advocates of extended cognition that there is a distinctly human kind of memory processing that Inga has, but that Otto does not, warrants cognitive psychologists in pursuing an intracranial human cognitive psychology that is not based on mere prejudice. Surely any such concession undermines much of the radical revolutionary rhetoric of extended cognition. That is, if Inga and Otto differ in ways that cognitive psychologists have taken to be important, that provides principled reasons to think that there is something interesting and answers at least very roughly to what has normally been taken to be cognitive processing that is going on in Inga's brain, which is not very much like what is going on with Otto and his notebook. The existence of what we might call normal human cognition in Inga, but not in Otto, is enough to vindicate orthodox cognitive psychology and adequately reply to charges of mere (Cartesian) prejudice.

Advocates of extended cognition are, of course, free to propose that we reject the putative discoveries of cognitive psychologists. Perhaps they will contend that it is these putative results or methods of cognitive psychologists that have held them back from a better understanding of the mind. In reply, we think that to dismiss the familiar methods cognitive psychologists use to discriminate among cognitive mechanisms brings about other problems. It threatens merely to change the subject from something not so clearly understood (human cognition) to something even less well understood (general cognition). In Chapter 4, we claimed that the advocates of extended cognition do not have a plausible theory of cognition; we provided a defense of this claim in Chapter 5. Without a plausible theory of cognition, one cannot have a plausible theory of "general cognition." So, what appears to be going on when the advocates of extended cognition offer a new theory of memory or cognition is that there is a threat of changing the subject, only we do not yet really know what this new subject is. We also noted in Chapter 4 that the development of such a more general theory of cognition would be complicated by the fact that it is meant to cover such a broad range of phenomena. We now have to find something that unifies human memory, canine memory, mollusk memory, humans and computers, humans and books, humans and personal digital assistants, and who knows what else? Or if there is nothing that unifies the distinct kinds of processes that are grouped under the heading of "memory processing" or "cognitive processing," it would be good to have some explanation of what scientific advance there is to be had in using these terms so liberally.

8.1.2   Three modes of Tetris play

Consider now a second putative example of cognitive equivalence between the intracranial and the transcranial. Clark and Chalmers propose a simple thought experiment involving three hypothetical modes in which one might play the computer game Tetris. In this game, blocks of various shapes descend from the top of the screen to a kind of wall of blocks. The aim is to rotate the oddly shaped, falling blocks in such a way as to form a complete horizontal row of blocks, which can then be eliminated from the rising wall of bricks. Because we think the example somewhat underdescribed, we want to quote Clark and Chalmers at length:

(1) A person sits in front of a computer screen which displays images of various two-dimensional geometric shapes and is asked to answer questions concerning the potential fit of such shapes into depicted 'sockets'. To assess fit, the person must mentally rotate the shapes to align them with the sockets.

(2) A person sits in front of a similar computer screen, but this time can choose either to physically rotate the image on the screen, by pressing a rotate button, or to mentally rotate the image as before. We can also suppose, not unrealistically, that some speed advantage accrues to the physical rotation operation.

(3) Sometime in the cyberpunk future, a person sits in front of a similar computer screen. This agent, however, has the benefit of a neural implant which can perform the rotation operation as fast as the computer in the previous example. The agent must still choose which internal resource to use (the implant or the good old fashioned mental rotation), as each resource makes different demands on attention and other concurrent brain activity.

How much *cognition* is present in these cases? We suggest that all three cases are similar. Case (3) with the neural implant seems clearly to be on a par with case (1). And case (2) with the rotation button displays the same sort of computational structure as case (3), distributed across agent and computer instead of internalized within the agent. If the rotation in case (3) is cognitive, by what right do we count case (2) as fundamentally different? We cannot simply point to the skin/skull boundary as justification, since the legitimacy of that boundary is what is at issue. But nothing else seems different. (Clark and Chalmers, 1998, p. 1)

We take the point here to be that there is no principled difference among these cases, hence that there is a cognitive equivalence between the three cases, so that we have an instance of extended cognition in case (2). The way to meet such "no principled difference arguments" is to provide a principled difference; it is to show that the cases are not cognitively equivalent.

Consider the ways in which the processes in (1) and (2) differ at what appears to be a cognitive level. In case (1), the agent presumably uses mental representations, mental images, of the blocks and their on-screen rotations as part of the method by which he determines the best way to try to place a given block in the rising array of blocks. These mental representations, we presume, have non-derived content. By contrast, in case (2), the blocks on the screen that are physically rotated by pushing the button are not representations at all, either derived or non-derived. They do not *represent* blocks to be fitted together; they *are* the blocks to be fitted together. Cases (1) and (2) also differ in the kinds of causal processes that are deployed. Some of these will be processes that have traditionally been taken to be cognitive, where the others have not. The process that physically rotates the image on the screen at the push of the button as described in case (2) is not the same as the cognitive process that occurs in the brain. Pushing the button closes an electrical circuit that, at some extremely short time delay, changes the way electrons are fired at the phosphorescent screen of a cathode ray tube. This sort of causal process is surely not the same as any cognitive process, or any fragment of a causal process, in the brain. The point is not that the electronic processes in the computer could not be so organized as to constitute a cognitive process; it is merely that as a matter of contingent empirical fact they are not. In case (2), but not case (1), there is muscular activity, and the attendant cognitive processing associated with it, that is involved in pushing the button. The fact that, in case (2), the agent must decide between the two available methods of checking for fit – the method of mental rotation and the method of button pushing – entails numerous other cognitive differences in cases (1) and (2). In case (2) one must actually use the cognitive decision mechanisms. There must be attentional mechanisms that bring the decision mechanisms into play and there must be memory mechanisms that store for the agent the information about the existence of the button and its use. So, even within the brain where the cognitive action is, there are cognitive differences in processing. Recognizing and controlling for these diverse cognitive factors under experimental conditions is absolutely foundational for psychology. Is it too much to say that the science of cognitive psychology as we know it would cease to exist without attention to such differences?

8.2   The Complementarity Argument

In an elaborate theory of the evolution of the human mind, Donald (1991) argues that the last dramatic transition in the cognitive evolution from australopithecines to *Homo sapiens sapiens* occurred with our use of "external symbol storage." This began some 40,000 years ago with the first uses of visuographic representations in the form of body decoration, grave decoration, and object arrangement, and continues today with the vast array of representational possibilities opened up with multimedia productions. Donald claims that these "exograms" (to be contrasted with Karl Lashley's "engrams") constitute a vast memory store that has radically changed the architecture of human cognition. More specifically, exograms enable humans to engage in analytic thought not found in prior cultures:

> The major products of analytic thought . . . are generally absent from purely mythic cultures. A partial list of features that are absent includes: formal arguments, systematic taxonomies, induction, deduction, verification, differentiation, quantification, idealization, and formal methods of measurement. Argument, discovery, proof, and theoretical synthesis are part of the legacy of this kind of thought. The highest product of analytic thought, and its governing construct, is the formal *theory*, an integrative device that is much more than a symbolic invention; it is a system of thought and argument that predicts and explains. (Donald, 1991, pp. 273–4)

Donald illustrates his view with a detailed account of the development of all manner of external representations, including body decoration, grave decoration, sculpture, Stonehenge, hieroglyphics, cuneiform, maps, graphs, and musical scores. What makes exograms so important and valuable are the ways in which they differ from normal human engrams. Engrams are limited to a relatively fixed quantity of one type of biological storage material, namely, neurons. Exograms, however, provide a wide range of different media in virtually unlimited quantities. We can store information in drawings, graphs, photographs, and books, which can be stored on magnetic and optical disks, flash drives, paper, and microfilm. Where human engrams fade relatively quickly over time, exograms can persist for vast periods of time, largely unaffected. Paper, microfilm, magnetic disks, and stone all fade away with time, but they are far more durable than are collections of neurons.

We think that Donald is exactly right to observe the various ways in which his exograms differ from human engrams and how exograms enable us to do things better and more efficiently. Exograms may enable us to do things we might not be able to without them. Making a list with pencil and paper surely facilitates recalling what to buy at the grocery store. Perhaps

Andrew Wiles could not have proved Fermat's last theorem without the use of pencil and paper. Indeed, what holds for exograms holds for any number of tools we use. Eyeglasses enable us to see better than we might otherwise. Stethoscopes enable doctors to hear the heartbeat better than they could without them. Timers on cook stoves and warning lights on gas gauges compensate for our potential lapses of attention.

Some advocates of extended cognition have seen these observations as providing a basis for saying that cognitive processes extend into these tools. Clark (1998), for example, writes,

> The argument for extended mind thus turns primarily on the way disparate inner and outer components may co-operate so as to yield integrated larger systems capable of supporting various (often quite advanced) forms of adaptive success. (p. 99)

Sutton (forthcoming) has perhaps most enthusiastically embraced this idea. His view is that there is "first-wave" extended cognition based on some version of the "parity principle." This kind of extended cognition is supported by some version of the cognitive equivalence argument we have just explored. "Second-wave" extended cognition, however, is based on what Sutton calls a "complementarity principle":

> in extended cognitive systems, external states and processes need not mimic or replicate the formats, dynamics, or functions of inner states and processes. Rather, different components of the overall (enduring or temporary) system can play quite different roles and have different properties while coupling in collective and complementary contributions to flexible thinking and acting. (Sutton, forthcoming)

We agree with this completely. Only, we do not think this in any way supports the hypothesis that cognitive processes extend from the brain into the body and environment. Many of the ideas we have developed in previous chapters should make it clear why.

Notice that both Clark and Sutton use complementarity to argue for the existence of an extended cognitive system. The brain is one component in this system, but the sundry tools are others. As we noted in Chapter 7, this view has considerable plausibility, but as we also argued in Chapter 7, the extended cognitive system hypothesis does not, at least without further argumentation, support the extended cognition hypothesis. On an informal notion of a system, cognitive processing need not pervade the whole of a cognitive system. This is the kind of thing we observe in an air conditioning system and a computing system. Air conditioning does not take place in every component of an air conditioning system and computing does not take place in every component of a computing system. We have proposed that cognitive processing involves specific forms of information processing operations on non-derived representations. By our lights, the only cognitive processes in these cognitive systems are those found in the brain. As far as we can tell, the observation of complementary relations between brain and body provides no reason at all to doubt this.

In addition, we also observed near the end of Chapter 7 that the extended cognitive system hypothesis can still be used to make a case for an intracranial cognitive psychology. One of the points we observed in connection with Haugeland's theory of systems was that he understated, if not entirely omitted, the importance of understanding how the components of a complex system work. Haugeland's picture suggested that understanding a system was merely a matter of knowing what interfaced with what or what was coupled with what. By our lights, this is only part of the story of what is involved in understanding complex systems. One also needs to understand what the components are doing. So, apply this idea to the extended cognitive system consisting of, say, a person using pencil and paper or a person and her PDA. To understand this complex extended cognitive system, we need to understand, among other things, how the components work. One of these components will, of course, be the brain. But, old-fashioned intracranial cognitive psychology in the "Cartesian" tradition has told us a fair amount about the kinds of processes that take place in the brain. It seems to us that, even embracing the hypothesis of extended cognitive systems, the study of these intracranial processes will remain a scientifically valid and important subject, a subject that we might fairly call "cognitive psychology." So, even embracing the extended cognitive system hypothesis does not seem to overturn the scientific orthodoxy concerning the bounds of cognition.

Let us return now to the distinction between human cognition and some more general kind of cognition. Perhaps a person and a PDA form an entirely new kind of cognitive agent. What might be said about this? To begin with, this new enterprise would not appear to have the revolutionary consequences of denying intracranial cognition. It would simply be a new enterprise that might complement old-fashioned cognitive psychology. Or it might not. What, if anything, is supposed to unify these open-ended combinations of brains and tools into a single science of cognitive psychology? As we have noted repeatedly, the advocates of extended cognition do not have a theory of human cognition, much less a theory of this open-ended category of brains plus tools. Moreover, it is not likely that this open-ended category of objects would conform to a natural science, since tools are not natural kinds. They are artifacts. But, then it could be that the extended cognition movement is not really about developing a new science of the mind, but some other sort of intellectual activity. But what intellectual activity is this? At this point, the hypothesis of extended general cognition seems to raise more questions about scientific methodology and actual scientific practice than it answers about cognition. It is more about the philosophy of science than about cognition.

8.3 Evolutionary Arguments

The final "philosophical" argument for extended cognition is Mark Rowlands's argument based on evolutionary theory. One might be surprised to find a biological theory invoked as a means to delimit where cognitive processes are found, but he is not alone in thinking it relevant.[3] In soft focus, Rowlands's evolutionary argument has the form of *modus ponens*:

1 Development of our cognitive capacities has followed the most efficient evolutionary path.
2 If development of our cognitive capacities has followed the most efficient evolutionary path, then cognitive processes are an essentially hybrid combination of internal and external processes (cf., Rowlands, 1999, p. 25).

Therefore, cognitive processes are an essentially hybrid combination of internal and external processes.

Matters would have been simpler had Rowlands just presented this argument and stood by it. At least this argument has the virtue of having a conclusion that is inconsistent with intracranialism. Unfortunately, various reasons move Rowlands to depart from this. In running the argument,

---

[3] Cf., Gibbs (2006, p. 12).

Rowlands wants to mark the conclusion as a defeasible inference. Thus, in his version of the consequent and the conclusion, we are told that *we should expect* our cognitive processes to be an essentially hybrid combination of internal and external processes. Yet, the conclusion of this argument is logically consistent with the hypothesis that cognitive processes are found only in nervous systems, so technically irrelevant. So, to make its relevance clearer, we should probably interpret Rowlands in the way presented above. Second, in a desire not to rely too heavily on empirical assumptions about evolutionary history, Rowlands asserts only something like the second premise. Yet, premise 2 is logically consistent with intracranialism, so not particularly germane to the debate. Third, it should be noted that essentially all of Rowlands's discussion in chapter 4 of his book is directed toward the exposition and defense of something like premise 1, where nothing at all is said in defense of premise 2. Reading Rowlands as interested only in premise 2 is, in this regard, a distortion of the argumentation of his book. We propose not to be a party to this distortion and instead hold Rowlands to the argument above.

So, what are we to make of the foregoing argument? Aside from the fact that Rowlands provides no evidence or argument for premise 2, we think that premise 2 is clearly false.[4] In general, an inference of this form is no good, since the second premise is false:

1   Development of our capacities for X has followed the most efficient evolutionary path.
2   If development of our capacities for X has followed the most efficient evolutionary path, then processes for X are an essentially hybrid combination of internal and external processes (cf., Rowlands, 1999, p. 25).

Therefore, processes for X are an essentially hybrid combination of internal and external processes.

Consider human spermatogenesis. Even if the development of this capacity had followed the most efficient evolutionary path, it is evidently not a process that extends into the external world. Consider the phosphorylation of ADP to form ATP. Even if the phylogenetic development of this capacity

---

[4]   Clearly the truth value of premise 2 is a primary concern whether Rowlands wants to assert just premise 2 or run the whole *modus ponens* sketched above.

had followed the most efficient evolutionary pathway, it is pretty clearly an intracellular process, if anything is. Consider transcription of DNA into RNA, meiosis, the phases of mitosis (prophase, metaphase, anaphase, and telophase), the secretion of bile, filtration of the blood in the kidneys, and pumping of blood. All are intraorganismal processes. What does it matter how efficiently they evolved?

Nor are counterexamples to the above form of argument limited to processes that are clearly internal to the body's functions. Even processes that have presumably been selected for their role in aiding an organism in responding to its environment have their easily recognized internal sub-processes.[5] Presumably the patellar reflex was selected for, in part, to prevent injury to the patellar tendon. Still, we recognize that the process of extending the lower leg involves sub-processes of distinct kinds that are internal to the leg. There is the stretching of the proprioceptive cells in the tendon, the firing of the proprioceptive cells, the propagation of the action potentials to the spinal cord, the release of neurotransmitters in the spinal cord, the firing of motor neurons in the spinal cord, the propagation of the action potentials to the sundry muscles of the thigh, the release of neurotransmitters at the neuromuscular junction, and the contractions of the muscles, just to name a few. None of these processes extends into the environment, despite their interaction with the environment.

Rowlands may well wish to say that these counterexamples merely clarify what he had already conceded, namely, that the inference he is making is defeasible. His idea is really that, if the development of a capacity has followed the most efficient evolutionary path, then this gives us some defeasible reason to think that the process is a hybrid combination of internal and external processes. This, however, misses what should be the moral of the counterexamples. The point is that there is no reason to link the property of being a product of natural selection with the property of extending into the environment. They appear to be entirely orthogonal concerns.

---

[5] Rowlands (1999, p. 25) adds another small wrinkle to his argument: "if we have adopted the most efficient strategy for accomplishing tasks, then the cognitive mechanisms we have evolved should be designed to function in conjunction with environmental structures. Then, the cognitive processes realized by these mechanisms would have to be understood as straddling both internal processes and those external processes whereby the organism interacts with these environmental structures." The consequent in the second sentence motivates the present paragraph. Note as well that it is the move from the second sentence to the third in this passage that constitutes for us the *non sequitur*.

Here is another way to make the foregoing point. Rowlands spends the bulk of chapter 4 of *The Body in Mind* making a kind of plausibility argument for the view that tool use makes for greater fitness than not using tools. We concede, just for the sake of running another argument more simply, that this is so. Our objection to Rowlands's evolutionary argument is that even if organisms that use tools are more fit than organisms that do not, this has nothing to do with how we discriminate among types of processes and their subcomponents. Surely, the most reasonable thing to expect evolutionary theory to provide is a theoretical taxonomy of processes based on evolutionary theory, not a theoretical taxonomy of processes based on cognitive theory, whether this be a theory of human cognition or a theory of some other more generic cognition. Evolutionary theory parses the world up into units that are significant in terms of evolution, not in terms of cognition. So, one should expect that appeals to evolutionary theory are entirely orthogonal to the extended cognition debate.

8.4   Conclusion: The Importance of the Mark of the Cognitive

In Chapter 1, we alleged that one of the leading enabling conditions of the hypothesis of extended cognition is insufficient attention to the difference between cognitive and non-cognitive processes. In Chapter 5, we drew attention to some of the implausible theories of the cognitive that have appeared in the extended cognition literature. We also noted in Chapter 1 that this inattention has both obvious and subtle consequences for the hypothesis of extended cognition. Finally, we promised to elaborate on this charge at a later point. We can now try to make good on that promise.

In the cognitive equivalence arguments, one never finds an explicit assertion that the processes spanning the brain, body, and environment are *cognitively* just like familiar intracranial cognitive processes. Instead, we are told such things as that Inga and Otto are on a par, that their causal dynamics mirror each other precisely, that they are in all relevant respects entirely analogous, or that Inga's brain and Otto's notebook have the same "functional poise." Instead of a plausible theory of what cognitive processes are and how certain brain–body–environment interactions meet the profile of a cognitive process, we have these vague proposals. By setting aside hypotheses, theories, and empirical results concerning memory and cognition drawn from cognitive psychology, it is much easier to get by with ill-defined notions, such as sameness of "functional poise." It seems much more plausible to say that Inga's brainy memory and Otto's notebook share something like the same "functional poise" than it is to say that the two kinds of "memory" are cognitively the same, that they involve the same cognitive process.

Regarding the complementarity arguments, one has to wonder how it is supposed to be that the combination of processes in brain, body, pencil and paper constitutes a cognitive process. Why is it the whole of the larger constellation, rather than what is merely internal to the brain, that is supposed to constitute a cognitive process? If there are distinctive kinds of processes in one's brain and in the combination of one's brain and tools, why suppose that it is the combination of brains and tools that realizes cognitive processes, rather than just the brain? Or, to put the matter in another way, if one has a cognitive system that spans brain, body, and environment, why say that cognitive processing pervades the whole of system, rather than just one component, namely, the brain? Inattention to what distinguishes cognitive processes from non-cognitive processes helps these kinds of apparently embarrassing questions fade from view.

Finally, regarding the evolutionary argument, we return to the point we made in the last section above. Evolutionary theory might well encourage cognitive psychologists to investigate the relations between cognitive processes, bodily processes, and environmental processes. However, the hypothesis of extended cognition is concerned with more than just the causal dependencies between cognitive processes and bodily and environmental processes. The hypothesis of extended cognition maintains that brain, body, and environment realize or constitute cognitive processes. It conjectures that certain processes in the world are of a kind, a cognitive kind. But, why would one think that evolutionary theory would specify how one is to distinguish cognitive processes and non-cognitive processes and where they are to be found? Our conjecture is that it is inattention to the mark of the cognitive that enables this oversight.

Chapter 9

Inference to the Best Explanation and Extended Cognition

In the preceding three chapters, we have examined a series of more philosophical arguments for the view that, under certain circumstances, cognitive processes extend into the body and environment. These were the coupling arguments of various stripes, the equivalence argument, the complementarity argument, and the evolutionary argument. Yet there is another approach. The usual way to evaluate empirical scientific hypotheses is through some form of what is often loosely described as inference to the best explanation. The way to support the hypothesis of extended cognition, therefore, is by appeal to the way, or ways, in which it explains certain behavioral or cognitive phenomena. These kinds of evaluations have to be undertaken on a case-by-case basis. In this chapter, we will explore what looks to us to be one attempt to pursue this strategy. We will consider Alva Noë's (2004) case for a theory of enactive perception.

Noë's view, as we understand it, maintains that perceptual experiences are constituted, in part, by the exercise of sensorimotor skills. This view is easily connected to the hypothesis of extended cognition. Given the hypothesis that perceptual experiences are generated by cognitive processes, one has it that at least some cognitive processes – namely, the perceptual ones – are constituted, in part, by the exercise of sensorimotor skills. Given the additional assumption that sensorimotor skills are exercised, in part, through processes in the sensory and motor nerves and muscles, one has it that at least some cognitive processes – namely, the perceptual ones – are constituted, in part, by processes in the sensory and motor nerves and muscles. In other words, at least some cognitive processes extend into the body. Noë contends that a combination of empirical evidence supports this view. This evidence is based on cases of the removal of congenital cataracts in adults, the effects of distorting lenses on perception, and the fading of retinally stabilized images.

Each invocation of an inference to the best explanation argument in favor of the hypothesis of extended cognition must be evaluated on its own merits, but for simple reasons of space we cannot review all the possible invocations of this strategy. Our discussion must be more focused. Aside from reasons of space, there is reason to focus specifically on Noë's theory as an important case. Noë's view seems to us to have one of the most empirically detailed defenses of a special case of the hypothesis of extended cognition. Further, much of Noë's argumentation does not fit into any of the forms of argumentation criticized in previous chapters, but does readily fit something like a model of inference to the best explanation. In opposition to Noë's analysis, we will argue that the sources of scientific evidence Noë brings forth do not in fact support his hypothesis of enactive perception over the hypothesis that cognitive processes are causally influenced by bodily processes. Further, we will draw attention to another source of evidence, the existence of perception in the face of paralysis, which seems to us to tell strongly against the enactive theory. The upshot, we believe, is that the current weight of evidence tells against Noë's enactive theory.

9.1   What is the Theory of Enactive Perception?

The scientific case for enactive perception is given in chapter 1 of Noë's book.[1] What attracts our attention here are the following claims:

> The central claim of what I call *the enactive approach* is that our ability to perceive not only depends on, but is constituted by, our possession of this sort of sensorimotor knowledge. (Noë, 2004, p. 2)

> What perception is, however, is not a process in the brain, but a kind of skillful activity on the part of the animal as a whole. (Noë, 2004, p. 2)

> For mere sensory stimulation to constitute perceptual experience – that is, for it to have genuine world-presenting content – the perceiver must possess and make use of *sensorimotor knowledge*. (Noë, 2004, p. 10)

[1]   As we noted in Chapter 6, Noë actually has what seems to us to be two discussions of extended cognition. The first of these, the one that will concern us in this chapter, comes in Noë's chapter 1. The second of these, reviewed earlier, comes in his chapter 7, where he runs familiar sorts of coupling arguments.

The basic claim of the enactive approach is that the perceiver's ability to perceive is constituted (in part) by sensorimotor knowledge (i.e., by practical grasp of the way sensory stimulation varies as the perceiver moves). (Noë, 2004, p. 12)

Most recent work on the relation of perception and action stops short of making the constitutive claim that defines the enactive standpoint. (Noë, 2004, p. 18)[2]

It seems to us that these sorts of claims, in conjunction with the auxiliary hypotheses mentioned above, can easily lead to a special case of the extended cognition hypothesis according to which perceptual processes are constituted, in part, by bodily processes.

Five features of Noë's theory bear comment. First, in investigating this theory, we assume that perceptual experience is, in some sense, other than mere peripheral stimulation of the sense organs and something more than sensation. Perceiving is more than a "blooming, buzzing confusion." Perceiving might, thus, involve computational processes generating conceptual representations based on sensory, and perhaps motoric or higher-level cognitive, inputs.

Second, we assume that in asking whether perceptual experiences are constituted, in part, by the deployment of sensorimotor skills, we are asking an empirical question. Thus, to make this an interesting empirical question, rather than a matter of stipulation, we will want some characterization of "perceptual experience" that is conceptually independent of sensorimotor skills. In other words, it would be uninteresting to find that perceptual experiences are constituted, in part, by the exercise of sensorimotor skills if one simply means by "perceptual experiences" those experiences that are constituted, in part, by the exercise of sensorimotor skills. That is, we presuppose that it is conceptually possible to have perceptual experiences that are not constituted, in part, by the exercise of sensorimotor skills, even if as a matter of empirical fact this is (nomologically?) impossible on the grounds that perceptual experiences are constituted, in part, by the exercise of sensorimotor skills.[3]

---

[2] Cf., Noë (2004, p. 215).

[3] Our assumption is perhaps not entirely unproblematic, since in an earlier paper we find the claim, "We suggest that *perception* could be considered to be the exercise of mastery of this kind of object-related sensorimotor contingency" (O'Regan and Noë, 2001, p. 88).

The third refinement is more complicated. It concerns what a sensorimotor skill is. To begin, a sensorimotor skill is a capacity to perform in a certain way. It is not merely possessing some theoretical understanding. It is one thing to know what a poker face is, to have a theoretical understanding of what it is; it is another to have the skill to keep a poker face during a poker hand. Noë also believes that perception involves a kind of theoretical understanding, that perception involves the application of concepts. Thus, he also thinks that perception is, in part, constituted by theoretical understanding. This dimension of Noë's view, however, is not germane to present concerns, since it is a component of Noë's view that is independent of the embodiment of perception and theories of extended cognition. If theoretical knowledge resides wholly in the brain, and Noë gives us no reason to think otherwise, then perception's theoretical component doesn't require either embodiment in or extension into peripheral nerves and muscles. So, this component of Noë's view will be set aside for present purposes.

Fourth, it should be emphasized that the version of extended cognition – that is, extended perception – that we are concerned with centers on synchronic, rather than diachronic evolutionary or developmental claims. More specifically, the issue is how, at a given time, perception involves sensorimotor knowledge, if at all. Does perceptual experience at a given time causally depend on sensorimotor skills? Does perceptual experience at a given time constitutively depend on sensorimotor skills? It is a separate matter whether the evolution of an organism's perceptual abilities requires that the organism possess sensorimotor skills. Perhaps an organism could evolve perceptual capacities in the absence of sensorimotor skills; perhaps not. This evolutionary issue, however, is not the present concern. It is also a separate matter whether the (normal or proper) ontogenetic development of an individual organism's perceptual abilities depends on the possession of sensorimotor skills. There appears to be considerable experimental evidence to suggest that they do so depend, but that is not at issue for the present.

Fifth, we are taking Noë to be claiming that perception is constituted, in part, by bodily processes. Yet, Noë writes that "The central claim of what I call *the enactive approach* is that our ability to perceive not only depends on, but is constituted by, our possession of this sort of sensorimotor knowledge" (Noë, 2004, p. 2). Perhaps it is not *perceptual experience* that is constituted, in part, by the exercise of sensorimotor skills, but only *perceptual abilities* that are. This might raise the suspicion that we are misinterpreting Noë. In reply, we don't think that Noë should be viewed as defending the perceptual abilities claim over the perception claim. The reason is that the abilities claim does not represent a theoretical innovation of the sort that Noë seems to be after. On any orthodox view, human perceptual experiences are constituted by something entirely neural in nature. There are neural correlates of perceptual experience. Perhaps visual experiences are constituted entirely by processes in V1, V2, and a few other visual processing areas. This is the kind of theory Noë wishes to reject. By contrast, even on the view that there are neural correlates of perceptual experience, one can say that our perceptual abilities are constituted, in part, by the capacities of our corneas. Our *ability* to perceive depends upon the ability or capacity of the cornea to refract light to just the degree needed to enable the lens to focus light more or less precisely on the retina. The human capacity to perceive is constituted in part, by a subcapacity of the cornea, as well as many other subcapacities. The subcapacities of the cornea, individual neurons, and so forth play no mere causal role in human perceptual capacities; they play a constitutive role in those perceptual capacities. Given this, the way is open to say that certain perceptual abilities are constituted, in part, by sensorimotor skills. For example, it would appear to be completely standard to suppose that the human ability to perceive an object moving through space via smooth tracking is constituted, in part, by sensorimotor skills involving the rectus and oblique muscles of the eye. This reading of the theory of enactive perception appears to be true, but entirely commonplace. So, to keep to the radical spirit of Noë's theory, we do not adopt this reading.

9.2   Noë's Evidence for Enactive Perception

A thorough evaluation of the theory of enactive perception would require looking at evidence bearing on each sense modality. As a bit of *a priori* scientific methodology, we should not simply assume that all sense modalities involve sensorimotor skills or that they all involve sensorimotor skills in the same way. Be this as it may, much of our discussion will, following Noë's lead, center on visual perception. The upshot of our critique of Noë's evidence is that the hypothesis of extended perception does not offer a better explanation of the phenomena than does the standard view we maintain, according to which perception is causally influenced by sensori-motor processes.[4]

9.2.1   Cases of congenital cataracts

The first source of evidence Noë cites involves the consequences of removing congenital cataracts in adult patients. Consider some of the reports to which Noë draws our attention. One is Gregory and Wallace's description of patient, S. B.:

> S. B.'s first visual experience, when the bandages were removed, was of the surgeon's face. He described the experience as follows: He heard a voice coming from in front of him and to one side: he turned to the source of the sound and saw a "blur." He realized that this must be a face. Upon careful questioning, he seemed to think that he would not have known that this was a face if he had not previously heard the voice and known that voices came from faces. (Gregory and Wallace, 1963, p. 366; cited in Noë, 2004, p. 5)[5]

Oliver Sacks provides another example that Noë cites:

> Virgil told me later that in this first moment he had no idea what he was seeing. There was light, there was movement, there was color, all mixed up, all meaningless, a blur. Then out of the blur came a voice that said, "Well?" Then, and only then, he said, did he finally realize that this chaos of light and shadow was a face – and, indeed, the face of his surgeon. (Sacks, 1995, p. 114; cited in Noë, 2004, p. 5)

Clearly, immediately after surgery, the adult patients continue to have some sort of visual deficit. It is not as though they have been transformed from being completely blind to having completely normal vision.

The existence of this deficit does not, of course, tell us about its nature. The cataract patients have visual sensations, as indeed they did before their operations, but there still appears to be something missing. What's missing? The hypothesis Noë favors is that the deficit arises because these patients

---

[4]   This general point is also made in Block (2005) and Prinz (2006). In other words, they draw attention to what we have called the "coupling-constitution fallacy."

[5]   Technically, S. B. did not suffer from congenital cataracts, but from corneal occlusions (Gregory and Wallace, 1963, p. 2). This, however, does not affect any of the philosophical or scientific points to be made here.

have not integrated their sensations with their sensorimotor skills. The patients are what Noë describes as "experientially blind" (Noë, 2004, p. 4). Another hypothesis is that growing up with cataracts in place disrupts normal developmental processes, hence producing deficits in sensory processing. Sensory processes are distorted, hence so are the perceptual processes based on them. These possibilities are, of course, not mutually exclusive. Growing up with cataracts may well cause both deficits in the production of sensations and in the integration of sensations with the normal sensorimotor apparatus. Indeed, this suggests yet another possibility. Improper development of either sensation or improper integration of sensation and motor skills could lead to deficits in the sensorimotor apparatus itself.

Unless Noë can rule out sensory deficits as the explanation for the behavior of the cataract patients, his argument for enactive perception collapses. Yet, after providing an articulate statement of this problem, Noë offers the following comments: "This objection has some force. In section 1.3 I turn to an example of putative experiential blindness [that of distorting lenses] that is not vulnerable to this criticism. Taken together the two examples make a strong case for experiential blindness and so for the enactive approach" (Noë, 2004, p. 7). Noë's idea here is that, while the cases of congenital cataracts alone might not (do not?) make a strong case for experiential blindness, there is an explanatory or evidential synergy between the cases of congenital cataracts and distorting lenses that makes for a strong case. The synergy arises because the enactive theory explains both phenomena in a unified way.[6] Although we are skeptical that Noë can flesh out this claim of explanatory synergy in a plausible way, we will limit ourselves to making the point that neither the cases of congenital cataracts nor the cases of distorting lenses in isolation provide any evidence in favor of the enactive hypothesis that perception is constituted, in part, by sensorimotor skills over the rival hypothesis that perception is causally influenced by sensorimotor skills. So, our principal point mentioned above stands. Insofar as Noë cannot rule out the hypothesis that congenital cataracts lead to sensory deficits, he does not have a clear case of what he calls experiential blindness.

To begin our critique, we point out that the situation here is worse for Noë than just the logic of the situation indicates. It is not just that sensory processing deficits are logically possible in cases of congenital cataracts.

---

[6] This interpretation was provided by Noë in personal communication.

There is, in fact, abundant experimental evidence indicating that congenital cataracts do lead to deficits in sensory processing. Perhaps there are sensorimotor integration problems and sensorimotor problems as well, but there is evidence for sensory deficits. Consider, for instance, two of the very cases Noë cites. This is valuable insofar as the source might be assumed to be common ground for us and for Noë. According to Gregory and Wallace, even weeks after his cataract surgery, their subject, S. B., showed abnormal performance on the Hering illusion, the Zölner illusion, the Poggendorf illusion, and the Müller–Lyer illusion. None of these illusions makes any obvious sorts of demands on the coordination of sensation with sensorimotor skills. They appear to be deficits in the processing of sensory information into perceptions. In addition, the case of Virgil is highly problematic for a number of reasons that might well be unrelated to his congenital cataracts. In the first place, the passage cited by Noë was a report following the removal of the cataract in Virgil's right eye, with the cataract in his left eye untreated.[7] Thus, even if the visual apparatus of the right eye had been completely restored, Virgil would have had not had normal use of his left eye. This means that Virgil would not have had normal use of binocular disparity, and hence would have lacked the use of an important depth cue. Loss of an important depth cue, however, might go some distance to explaining, in purely sensory terms, some of Virgil's difficulties in coordinating such sensory input as he was receiving with motor actions. In the second place, Virgil appears to have had difficulties synthesizing parts into wholes; for example, the parts of a cat into a whole cat.[8] It would not, therefore, be surprising to find that this was both a sensory deficit and that it had consequences for his abilities to handle objects. Finally, there was clear damage to Virgil's retina, perhaps as a result of disease during childhood:

> It was evident that the central, or macular, part of the retina . . . was scarcely functioning, and that it was only the surrounding *para*macular area that was making possible such vision as he had. The retina itself presented a moth-eaten or piebald appearance, with areas of increased and decreased pigmentation – islets of intact or relatively intact retina alternating with areas of atrophy. The macula was degenerated and pale, and the blood vessels of the entire retina appeared narrowed. (Sacks, 1995, p. 115)

[7]   Cf., Sacks (1995, pp. 113–14).
[8]   Cf., Sacks (1995, p. 124).

This last point emphasizes how problematic clinical data can be, but also that Virgil's case is hardly usable for Noë's purposes.

Recent literature supports the view that congenital cataracts lead to deficits in adult sensory processing after corrective surgery. These included deficits in grating acuity, spatial contrast sensitivity, temporal contrast sensitivity, peripheral vision, stereo vision, perception of global form, and perception of global motion (Mioche and Perenin, 1986; Tytla et al., 1988, 1993; Bowering et al., 1993; Lewis et al., 1995, 2002; Birch et al., 1998; Ellemberg et al., 1999, 2000, 2002). None of these deficits have been described as any kind of failure to coordinate vision with sensorimotor skills. While many of these studies, of course, have appeared too recently to have been incorporated into Noë's book, there is another source of evidence bearing on the nature of the deficits in patients with congenital cataracts.

For over 40 years, neuroscientists have been investigating the neuroanatomical and neurophysiological effects of various forms of visual sensory deprivation in non-human animals. Among the best known are classic early experiments conducted by Torsten Wiesel and David Hubel.[9] Most relevant for present purposes are studies involving bilateral eyelid suture. These experimental interventions, like large dense congenital cataracts, allow the projection of diffuse light onto the retina, while blocking the highest frequency spatial patterns in the stimuli. That is, eyelid suture and large dense congenital cataracts allow only broad patterns of light and dark to play upon the retina. Even this restricted type of sensory deprivation has a substantial literature. In a 1982 review, Murray Sherman and Peter Spear reported that the striate cortex of binocularly lid-sutured cats shows any number of abnormalities.[10] The visually deprived striate cortex is less responsive than normal striate cortex to visual stimulation. In deprived cats, fewer cells respond to standard stimuli and even those cells that do respond have lower peak response rates. In addition, among cells that remain responsive, a large proportion have abnormal receptive fields. In normal cats, a large fraction of cortical cells have excitatory and inhibitory regions that make them sensitive to the orientations of edges, bars, and lines. In bilaterally lid-sutured cats, however, the inhibitory portions of the receptive fields of these cortical cells are weak or absent. This will likely

---

[9]   Hubel and Wiesel (1963, 1965).
[10]   Sherman and Spear (1982). There are, in addition, abnormalities in the lateral geniculate nucleus.

make the perceptual experience of borders faint or fuzzy, suggesting a sensory component to some of the perceptual deficits found in Gregory and Wallace's patient, S. B., and Sacks's patient, Virgil. Further, in normal cats, many of the cells in striate cortex are sensitive to the direction of motion of edges, bars, and lines. In bilaterally lid-sutured cats, many of the responsive cortical cells lose their sensitivity to the direction of motion. This might explain any failure of sensorimotor coordination found in patients after bilateral congenital cataract removal. Finally, bilaterally lid-sutured cats also lose sensitivity to binocular disparity, thereby losing an important depth cue. Again, this purely sensory deficit might explain any difficulties patients might have in negotiating the three-dimensional world.

The point is not that the current clinical and experimental results definitively establish a purely sensory explanation for patient deficits. There are clear differences between the human cases and the animal experiments. For example, in the animal experiments, the eyelids are sutured before the animal's eyes open. In human patients, the opacification of the cataracts can take time, thereby allowing some amount of visual experience. Further, the cataracts need not cover the entire pupil, thereby allowing "slits" of relatively normal visual stimulation around the edges of the cataract. Still further, the presence of cataracts in humans can induce behavioral abnormalities, such as squinting, that are not found in the animal.[11] The point is that the possibility of congenital cataracts giving rise to sensory deficits is not a mere logical or conceptual possibility; it is an empirical possibility supported by a serious body of evidence that challenges Noë's interpretation of the data.

The foregoing empirical problems are, however, just the beginning of the difficulties in Noë's reliance on observations of post-operative cataract patients to argue for enactive perception. Suppose, for the sake of argument, that in fact these patients are experientially blind in Noë's sense. That is, suppose that these patients do not or cannot integrate their sensations with patterns of movement and thought. Does this suffice to establish the hypothesis of enactive perception? No. There still remain two ways in which the existence of experiential blindness fails to support the hypothesis of extended cognition. Noë takes experiential blindness to be a kind of perceptual deficit in some respects comparable to sensory blindness.

---

[11] Each of these possibilities is described in a case study in Fine et al. (2002).

Experiential blindness is an inability to integrate sensations with patterns of movement and thought. But, there are, of course, many kinds of perceptual blindness. There is achromotopsia (color blindness) and this of several types. There is akinetopsia, motion blindness. There is face agnosia and form agnosia. But, of course, a person who is color blind is not entirely lacking in perceptual capacities, only the capacity to discriminate some colors. A person who is color blind is not entirely without perceptual experiences, only without perceptual experiences of some colors. A person who is motion blind is not completely blind, only blind to motion – and similarly for face and form agnosia, as well as Noë's experiential blindness. As a conceptual possibility, it appears to be possible that some humans might perceive things, only without these perceptions being integrated into patterns of personal movement and thought. The only thing that would preclude this conceptual possibility is if Noë's concept of perceptual experience simply includes being constituted, in part, by exercise of sensorimotor skills. But, then, Noë's enactive hypothesis just becomes some sort of logical truth, rather than an empirical hypothesis. The empirical examples of cataract patients are then irrelevant to this logical hypothesis.

Even if we concede that the cataract patients are experientially blind, there still remains one more problem in using this to support the hypothesis of enactive perception. One must ask what is responsible for a patient's failure to integrate sensory stimulation with sensorimotor skills. What explains this failure? Noë concludes that the failure is due to the loss of a constituent of perception, namely, sensorimotor skills – no sensorimotor skills, no perceptual experience. That is, he thinks that the hypothesis of enactive perception explains the failure of integration; he thinks that enactive perception explains the experiential blindness. But the hypothesis that sensorimotor skills causally influence perception seems to offer just as good an explanation of the putative experiential blindness as does Noë's hypothesis. We might suppose that, even granting experiential blindness, the reason post-operative cataract patients are experientially blind is that their sensorimotor skills are not yet causally connected to their sensory apparatus in the proper way. It is not that these sensorimotor skills are essential to perception because they are constitutive, in part, of perception; it is that these sensorimotor skills are essential to perception because they have an essential causal role in shaping perceptions and the normal causal connections have been disrupted.

So, it appears that Noë's appeal to post-operative congenital cataract patients fails to establish enactive perception in three ways. First, the cataract patients may well suffer from sensory deficits of one or more types that could entirely account for any perceptual or sensorimotor deficits. Second, even if cataract patients are experientially blind in Noë's sense, this still fails to establish enactive perception for two reasons. First, these patients might be experientially blind, but this does not imply that they must be totally blind as enactive perception requires. Second, enactive perception provides no better explanation of experiential blindness than does the view that perception is causally influenced by sensorimotor skills.

9.2.2   Distorting lenses

Since the late nineteenth century experiments by George Malcolm Stratton, psychologists have been interested in the effects of long-term use of distorting lenses of one sort or another.[12] Noë appeals to them in support of enactive perception. Noë is correct in his claim that these experiments provide cases of experiential blindness that overcome the problem of possible sensory deficits in cataract patients.[13] Nevertheless, he fails to recognize the gap between the discovery of experiential blindness and the confirmation of enactive perception that we just rehearsed above. Consider, then, a description of the effects of wearing spherical prism lenses:

> During visual fixations, every movement of my head gives rise to the most unexpected and peculiar transformations of objects in the visual field. The most familiar forms seem to dissolve and reintegrate in ways never before seen. At times, parts of figures run together, the spaces between disappearing from view: at other times, they run apart, as if intent on deceiving the observer. Countless times I was fooled by these extreme distortions and taken by surprise when a wall, for instance, suddenly appeared to slant down the road, when a truck I was following with my eyes started to bend, when the road began to arch like a wave, when houses and trees seems to topple down, and so forth. I felt as if I were living in a topsy-turvy world of houses crashing down on you, of heaving roads, and of jellylike people. (Kohler, 1964, p. 64; cited in Noë, 2004, p. 8)

[12]   Stratton (1896, 1897a,b).
[13]   Cf., Noë (2004, p. 7), and noted in the previous section.

What appears to be going on here is a failure to integrate sensations into sensorimotor skills; that is, we appear to have experiential blindness. This is the point of Noë's example.

Nevertheless, as we saw in the previous section, the existence of experiential blindness does not suffice to establish enactive perception for two types of reasons. Recall that experiential blindness, as Noë defines it, is just a particular kind of perceptual deficit in just the way achromotopsia and akinetopsia are. Importantly, one can have this deficit without being entirely without perception. In the case of the subject K, even Noë admits that "K is not completely blind, to be sure; he recognizes the trucks, the trees, and so forth. But nor is he completely able to see. His visual world is distorted, made unpredictable, and topsy-turvy" (Noë, 2004, p. 8; cf. p. 9). If K is able to synthesize the sensations caused by trucks, trees, people and so forth into forms that enable him to recognize them as trucks, trees, and people, then there seems to be some reasonable basis for saying that he perceives the trucks, trees, people, and so forth. Thus, K perceives things, even though experientially blind. K perceives things despite the misalignment between his vision and his sensorimotor skills. So, Noë does not give us a case in which there are no sensorimotor skills, and hence no perception. Thus, the observations regarding K do not support the theory of enactive perception.

Noë is evidently aware of the force of this objection and subsequently tries to blunt it. Noë observes that the left–right distorting lenses only affect one's perceptions involving motions to the left or right, not those involving motions up and down. Indeed, the left–right goggles do not influence perceptions of colors or light and dark. In drawing attention to this point, Noë appears to be suggesting a refinement, or perhaps a clarification, of the enactive theory. It is not that perceptual experiences are constituted, in part, by the exercise of sensorimotor skills. Instead, the refinement appears to be a shift in the direction of a set of constitutive relations between particular types of perceptual experiences and particular types of sensorimotor skills. One such hypothesis might be that perceptual experiences involving left and right motion are constituted, in part, by the sensorimotor skills involved in moving the eyes right and left. In such a case, these perceptual experiences would extend into, say, the lateral and medial rectus muscles of the eyes. Another might be that perceptual experiences involving up and down motion are constituted, in part, by the sensorimotor skills involved in moving the eyes up and down. In such a case, these perceptual experiences would extend into, say, the superior and inferior rectus muscles of the eyes. The exact details of this refinement are unclear, but schematically the idea appears to be that perceptual experiences of type ψ are constituted, in part, by the exercise of sensorimotor skills of type Σ.[14]

Whether or not Noë accepts this refinement/clarification, this theory is still no better off regarding the role of sensorimotor skills in perception. Suppose that the example of K and the spherically distorting lenses is supposed to show something to the effect that perceptual experiences during head and eye motions are constituted, in part, by the exercise of sensorimotor skills involved in head and eye motions. The standard kind of view that we defend is something to the effect that perceptual experiences during head and eye motions are causally influenced by the sensorimotor skills involved in head and eye motions. We can now ask why one should believe that the constitutive account that Noë proposes provides a better explanation of K's deficits than does the causal account that we prefer. Visual perceptions are influenced by two types of factors, input from the retina and input from the sensorimotor mechanisms, such as those in the vestibular system, that compensate for bodily motions. The distorting lenses disrupt the relationship that normally exists between the retinal input and the motion-compensating mechanisms. Thus, the lenses distort the coordination of retinal signals and bodily signals. There is, therefore, no need to adopt even the (refined/clarified) enactive theory of perception for this explanation. In view of this last point, the observations on the effects of distorting lenses provide no reason to think that any perceptual capacities are constituted, even in part, by the exercise of sensorimotor skills.

9.2.3   Visual fading of retinally stabilized images

It has long been known that images projected to a fixed location on the retina fade due to sensory adaptation.[15] Rods and cones cease to respond to a uniform pattern of illumination. Although Noë claims that visual

---

[14]   In truth, it is not completely clear to us that Noë would endorse this proposal as either a refinement or clarification of his view. In presenting an objection to the enactive view based on optic ataxia (the inability to use vision to guide action), Noë concludes with the following: "The neurological evidence suggests that although some facets of vision are bound up with visuomotor skill, this is not true of vision as a whole. The enactive approach, it would seem, exaggerates the importance of action in perception" (Noë, 2004, p. 12). In replying to this challenge, Noë does not appear to accept the charge that the enactive approach exaggerates the importance of action in perception. Thus, it appears that he might not believe that we need to restrict particular perceptual deficits to particular losses of sensorimotor skills.

[15]   Riggs and Ratliff (1952) and Ditchburn and Ginsborg (1952) are sometimes cited as the classic papers on the topic.

fading "suggests that some minimal amount of eye and body movement is necessary for perceptual sensation" (Noë, 2004, p. 13), this suggestion does nothing to support enactive perception. In the first place, this provides no grounds for extrapolating from a putative need for motion in vision to a need for motion in other sense modalities, such as olfaction. Second, it is simply not true that some minimal amount of eye or body movement is necessary even for visual perception. Even if the eye and body are entirely stationary, the fading can be prevented simply by moving images across the retina or changing the pattern of light projected onto the retina. Third, even if eye or body motions were necessary to prevent visual fading, that would not show that the exercise of sensorimotor skills is necessary to prevent visual fading. Parkinsonian tremors, for example, might induce sufficiently large motions of the eye and body to prevent visual fading, but the tremors are not the exercise of sensorimotor skills. One cannot simply identify eye and bodily motions with the exercise of sensorimotor skills. Fourth, suppose that the exercise of sensorimotor skills really is necessary for visual perception. As we have noted twice above, even that would not show that sensorimotor skills are constitutive of visual perception, rather than that they are items that are causally necessary for the production of visual perception. The hypothesis that sensorimotor skills causally influence perception provides as good an explanation of the necessity as does the hypothesis that perception is constituted, in part, by sensorimotor skills. So, Noë provides no evidence that even some perceptual abilities ψ are constituted, in part, by sensorimotor skills Σ. There really is a surprising gap between the actual empirical data and the interpretation Noë wishes to place on them.

9.3   The Case against Enactive Perception: Paralysis

We now wish to consider what appear to be some falsified predictions of the enactive theory of perception. Noë writes,

> Genuine perceptual experience depends not only on the character and quality of stimulation, but on our exercise of sensorimotor knowledge. The disruption of this knowledge does not leave us with experiences we are unable to put to use. It leaves us without experience. For mere stimulation to constitute perceptual experience – that is, for it to have genuine

world-presenting content – the perceiver must possess and make use of *sensorimotor knowledge*. (Noë, 2004, p. 10)

Cases of paralysis seem to be a problem for the theory of enactive perception. If perceptual experience requires a perceiver to make use of sensorimotor knowledge, then any form of paralysis that prevents a subject from making use of her sensorimotor knowledge would seem, thereby, to prevent her from having perceptual experiences. If perceptual experience is constituted, in part, by the use of sensorimotor skills, then loss of those skills in paralysis should produce loss of perceptual experience. This is the kind of thing that appears to occur in cases of, say, face agnosia. One explanation of this type of agnosia, like other types of agnosia, is that lesions to particular regions of the brain are lesions to parts of the brain that constitute those experiences. Paralysis of striate muscles does not have this effect. There are cases in which an individual loses sensorimotor skills through paralysis, but retains perceptual capacities.

Noë, aware of the challenge posed by these cases, hints at two strategies that might be applied to the problem of paralysis. The first is by appeal to sensorimotor knowledge as theoretical and the other by appeal to the incompleteness of paralysis. The first approach does nothing to save the embodiment of perception; the second only works for a limited range of types of paralysis. We will consider these strategies in order.

Noë comments on cases of motor paralysis and optic ataxia (the inability to coordinate motor actions with sensations) in ways that suggest that perception requires either sensorimotor skills *or* sensorimotor knowledge. Paralysis could remove sensorimotor skills, but not sensorimotor knowledge, since sensorimotor knowledge is a species of theoretical knowledge. Here is the relevant passage:

> The existence of optic ataxia, therefore, does not undercut the enactive view, for from the fact that a patient suffers optic ataxia, it doesn't follow that he or she lacks the relevant sensorimotor knowledge. What would undercut the enactive approach would be the existence of perception in the absence of bodily skills and sensorimotor knowledge which, on the enactive view, are constitutive of the ability to perceive. Could there be an entirely inactive, *inert* perceiver? (Noë, 2004, p. 12)

What Noë suggests in the second sentence is that perceptual abilities must constitutively involve either bodily skills or (theoretical) sensorimotor knowledge. In optic ataxia one loses the bodily skills but retains the theoretical sensorimotor knowledge. Therefore, the enactive view predicts that those suffering from optic ataxia should not be completely without perception. Noë could, in principle, apply the same strategy to dealing with cases of paralysis. Perhaps possessing the theoretical knowledge that turning one's head to the left will cause visual changes as of objects moving to the right is sufficient for perception. In that case, paralysis would not undermine perception. This reading of this text is, however, strained, first, by the claim made in the previous citation, namely, that perceivers must possess *and* make use of sensorimotor knowledge. How is having theoretical knowledge a matter of making use of sensorimotor knowledge? This reading is also strained by the concluding question. An entirely inactive, inert perceiver would be without bodily skills, not one necessarily lacking theoretical sensorimotor knowledge. So, in this passage it still looks as though Noë is committed to bodily skills found in muscles and peripheral nerves being constitutive of perception. But, then again, just a paragraph later, Noë writes the following:

> More important, paralysis does not undermine the paralyzed person's practical understanding of the ways movement and sensory stimulation depend on each other. Even the paralyzed, whose range of movement is restricted, understand, implicitly and practically, the significance of movement for stimulation. They understand, no less than those who are not disabled, that movement of the eyes to the left produces rightward movement across the visual field, and so forth. Paralyzed people can't do as much as people who are not paralyzed, but they can do a great deal; whatever the scope of their limitations, they draw on a wealth of sensorimotor skill that informs and enables them to perceive. (ibid.)

Again, the first three sentences of this passage could be taken to mean that practical understanding or theoretical knowledge of the relations between bodily motions is sufficient for preserving perception. But, of course, there are the closing comments on what paralyzed people can and cannot do, which at least suggests that Noë is sticking by the idea that perception requires the exercise of bodily sensorimotor skills.

Noë can, of course, define the theory of enactive perception as he wishes, either allowing theoretical knowledge to preserve perception or not. Our point, then, is that Noë faces a dilemma. Suppose that his view is that theoretical knowledge is sufficient unto preserving perceptual abilities. In this case, an appeal to brain-based theoretical knowledge will not support the embodiment of perception in nerves and peripheral muscles. It will fail to support the hypothesis of extended perception. Suppose, then, that his view is that theoretical knowledge is not sufficient for preserving the perceptual abilities of totally paralyzed individuals. In that case, instances of total paralysis would be a challenge to the hypothesis of enactive perception and the hypothesis of extended perception. And, as we shall see, there are cases of total paralysis that do not lead to a loss of perception.

Noë's second strategy in dealing with paralysis is to note that in the case of quadriplegics, paralysis is not complete. Here is the relevant text:

> Paralysis is certainly not a form of blindness. But isn't that precisely what the enactive theory requires, that the paralyzed be experientially blind? No. The enactive theory requires that perceivers possess a range of sensorimotor skills. It seems clear that quadriplegics have the pertinent skills. Quadriplegics can move their eyes and head, and to some extent, at least with help from technology, they can move their bodies with respect to the environment (e.g., by using a wheelchair). (Noë, 2004, p. 12)

Noë is apparently equating paralysis with quadriplegia. Quadriplegia, however, is not the only source of paralysis. In particular, there are forms of paralysis that arise from interference with the neuromuscular junction. These, we believe, make for a very serious challenge to the theory of enactive perception.

There is a broad class of neuromuscular blockers that inhibit neuromuscular function by binding to the muscle receptors for the neuromuscular transmitter acetyl choline. Acetyl choline cannot cause normal neuromuscular contraction, since the muscle relaxer blocks its binding sites on muscles. For decades, the use of neuromuscular blockade has widely been recognized to induce paralysis, but not loss of consciousness or perception or awareness. Muscle relaxers are, thus, quite different from general anesthetics. A number of studies have explored perceptions under various forms of muscular blockade, but we shall review one especially clear report.[16] Topulos et al. (1993) gave subjects the neuromuscular blocker vecuronium. The investigators applied a tourniquet to one arm, which slowed the transmission of the vecuronium from the bloodstream to the

---

[16]   Studies of perception during neuromuscular blockade include Smith et al. (1947), Campbell et al. (1967, 1969), Froese and Bryan (1974), and Stevens et al. (1976).

neuromuscular junctions, so that the arm remained functional. This allowed the immobilized subjects to communicate with the investigators using a pre-established system of finger gestures until, after anywhere from 21 to 42 minutes, the tourniquet itself led to the paralysis of the fingers. During this period, the experimenters asked subjects questions requiring yes or no answers. After the experiment, subjects could also recall events that took place during the paralysis. The results seem to be striking challenges to the need to exercise sensorimotor skills in order to have perceptions. In the first place, all subjects perceived the questions asked of them. (When they eventually did not answer with finger movements, the protocol was considered complete.) All subjects found the process of tracheal intubation, which was part of the purpose of the study, to be "extremely uncomfortable." This sounds like the perception of discomfort. In addition, all complained of the bitter taste of the lidocaine spray that was used to facilitate the intubation. At least one subject reported recollecting the accounts of his vital signs: "I had no doubt that all was well physiologically; I was told at the time that my vital signs were stable as a rock and that everything looked very good, but I hated it and I couldn't wait for the experiment to be over" (quoted in Topulos et al., 1993, p. 372). Two of the subjects also felt worried about the discomfort of the procedure. Two subjects explicitly stated that they did not know when paralysis had set in until they tried to move. Presumably, on the enactive theory, perception should fade exactly when paralysis sets in, but it did not. As a summary, the investigators report that

> Complete neuromuscular block caused no observable impairment of consciousness, sensation, memory, or the ability to think and make decisions. Objective evidence supported this assertion, as subjects responded promptly to questions. When the experimenter misunderstood their answers, subjects recognized this and made a correction. Subjects successfully used a questionnaire with many branching points to communicate their needs. Subjects also accurately recalled specific events that occurred in the room while they were paralyzed. This unimpaired mental function is consistent with the reports of previous investigators. (Topulos et al., 1993, p. 373)

It is, of course, true that the failure to paralyze one arm does not lead to complete paralysis. Yet, it is unclear why the ability to move one arm would be the kind of sensorimotor skill that would be sufficient to maintain the apparent capacity to perceive bitter tastes, the discomfort of intubation, the questions of the investigators, and the anxiety over the procedure. We know from Noë's discussion of K and his spherical distorting lenses that Noë cares about these kinds of issues. In addition, there are other studies using alternative methods that decrease the worry about the possible confounds associated with the subjects having one functional arm.

Muscle relaxers have long been an important tool in the anesthesiologist's toolkit, enabling the surgeon to better control the body position of patients. They are also exceptionally useful in suppressing involuntary motor responses, such as the gagging and coughing that occur during intubation. Unfortunately for many patients, however, combining muscle relaxers with anesthetics makes it more difficult to detect insufficient levels of anesthesia, leading to awareness during surgery. This is, in fact, such a disturbingly common phenomenon that anesthesiologists have often taken to administering drugs that increase the chances of amnesia. Patients are, thus, less likely to recall awareness during surgery, and hence (it is supposed) less likely to suffer traumatic psychological after-effects. Consider some of these reports.

In an anonymous 1979 editorial in the *British Journal of Anaesthesia*, a woman with medical experience reported in graphic detail her recollections of being aware during a Caesarian section under general anesthesia and neuromuscular blockade. Although immobilized by the anesthesiologist, she remembers feeling the pain of the incision, hearing her baby crying, and feeling the insertion of a nasogastric tube. In a more recent case study, a 74-year-old woman recalled that during her operation "1) she felt pain during the incision of the abdomen, 2) she heard the operator say, 'It is difficult to remove all tumors because the adhesion is very strong,' and 3) she remembered someone had been walking around her" (Miura et al., 2001). These post-operative recollections were independently confirmed by the surgical staff. Because of the obvious importance of this phenomenon, there have been a number of studies of its frequency in hospitals in the United States and Europe. In one study involving 45 patients, all recalled hearing sounds or voices, 33 understood and remembered conversations, 21 had visual perceptions, 29 felt being touched, six recalled moderate pain, and eight recalled severe pain (Schwender et al., 1998).

The enactive theory predicts that the more extensive the immobilization, the more likely is the loss of perception. Contrary to this prediction, one large-scale prospective study of awareness during surgery found that recollection of awareness is *more* probable when general anesthetics are used in combination with muscle relaxers than when general anesthetics are used alone. But, if, as we believe, sensorimotor skills are only a causal influence on perception, then it is not at all surprising that the use of muscle relaxers would increase the incidence of awareness during surgery. With the body incapacitated, it is much more difficult for anesthesiologists to use measures such as flinching and verbal report to detect the fact that a patient is not sufficiently anesthetized.

Cases of awareness during surgery have their methodological drawbacks as a means of challenging the theory of enactive perception. To begin with, many of the cases appear to involve problems in the administration of anesthesia, so that some individuals may not be completely immobilized. On the enactive approach, incomplete immobilization might allow for less than complete loss of perception. In addition, these studies rely on patient recollection. Sometimes these putative recollections are rather vague, such as that the patient recognized the surgeon's voice and heard the sound of instruments. Such vague recollections could be recollections of dreaming or pure confabulations. In one prospective study of awareness during surgery, participants were interviewed on multiple occasions (Sandin et al., 2000). The multiple interviews, in conjunction with the procedures used to obtain informed consent, may have increased the chances of false memories. Despite these limitations, there do appear to be cases in which completely immobilized, completely paralyzed patients perceive auditory and visual events during their operations. Moreover, unlike the method used by Topulos et al. (1993), the methodology in these studies does not leave any of part of the body in a nearly fully functional state. The experimental methods and the clinical prospective studies thus depend on the truth of different sets of auxiliary hypotheses. Therefore, they provide, in some measure, independent methods for determining the effects of paralysis on perception. Together, they provide stronger support for the view that the exercise of sensorimotor skills is not constitutively necessary for perception. This, however, weighs heavily against the enactive theory of perception.

9.4 Conclusion

In this chapter, we have tried to show that the weight of currently available scientific evidence goes against the hypothesis that bodily skills are a constitutive element in perceptual experiences. It weighs against the need to look for bodily correlates of perceptual experience, as opposed to more narrowly conceived neural correlates of perceptual experience. The facts about the removal of congenital cataracts in adult patients, distorting goggles, and retinal fading do not provide evidence for the hypothesis of enactive perception, but the evidence from paralysis due to neuromuscular blockade provides some evidence against it.

The scientific case we have made here invites any number of responses. Perhaps the theory of enactive perception could be refined in some way. Perhaps there is evidence we have overlooked or misinterpreted. Perhaps there is some way in which, even though the congenital cataract data alone and the distorting lenses data alone are not best explained by the hypothesis of extended cognition, there could be some synergy between them that could provide evidence for enactive perception. Perhaps one can even make the case that this evidence outweighs the paralysis evidence. All of these possibilities we take in stride as open to further investigation. Investigating such possibilities is just in the nature of scientific research.

Stepping back from the case of enactive perception, one can envision attempts to bring forth other cases in which the hypothesis of extended cognition might be thought to provide a better explanation of some cognitive or behavioral phenomena than the hypothesis that cognitive processing occurs within the brain. Each case must be considered on its individual merits. We don't think there is any reason in principle to suppose that all cognitive processing is, or must be, found within the brain. Exactly where cognitive processing is to be found is an empirical matter. Although we are skeptical of the prospects of the explanatory benefits of extended cognition, we have no reason to rule them out entirely.

Chapter 10

Future Directions

One way to read this book is as a guide to theorizing about extended cognition. One of our aims has been to set up a *bona fide* rival to the hypothesis of extended cognition, a view someone genuinely endorses.[1] We have tried to articulate and defend, in some small measure, a view that does justice to some of what goes on in cognitive psychology. We claim no originality for this view. We think it is a kind of generalization of the "rules and representations" view of cognition that, not so many years ago, was taken to be orthodoxy in cognitive science. This view lends support to the idea that there are processes that are reasonably construed as the traditional subject of cognitive psychology and that take place within the brain. This view supports the idea that there is a principled, non-question-begging reason for cognitive psychologists to believe that cognitive processes supervene upon, are realized by, or have their physical substrates in the brain.

We have also set up a set of three principal challenges for a theory of extended cognition. All of these may be viewed as demands for further elaboration or clarification. First and foremost, advocates of extended cognition need to have a plausible theory of cognition. Even a plausible approach to a theory of cognition would be an improvement. Cognition is more than information processing; it likely involves information processing, but not just any kind of information processing. Cognition is more than state transitions of a dynamical system; cognitive processes could only be a subspecies of the kinds of state changes that take place in dynamical systems. Cognitive processes have to be more specified than "whatever

---

[1]   Rupert (2006) comments about the lack of a well-articulated target of criticism in Gibbs (2006).

accomplishes a cognitive task." A sound theory of cognition is precisely what one needs to run a plausible cognitive equivalence argument, the only kind of argument that seems to us to be of the right form to support extended cognition. Without guidance on what cognition is, it is very hard to evaluate the hypothesis that cognition extends. If the claim is merely that there are processes that are in some respects like human cognitive processes that extend into the body and environment, this is hard to evaluate. It is certainly hard to see what scientific theory of memory and cognition would embrace the vast, open-ended array of things that falls under Merlin Donald's (1990) theory of exograms.

In the second place, the case for extended cognition has to be more sensitive to the distinction between two types of dependency relations, causal dependencies and constitutive dependencies. It is one thing for cognitive processes to causally depend on bodily and environmental processes, quite another for them to constitutively depend on bodily and environmental processes. Although the distinction is implicit in much of the extended cognition literature, the full ramifications have not been fully appreciated. Although the distinction virtually defines the hypothesis of extended cognition, arguments that begin with the existence of causal dependencies are not enough to establish the existence of constitutive dependencies. In other words, once we become sensitive to the causation–constitution distinction, we should be avoid committing any version of the coupling-constitution fallacy.

Third, more attention needs to be paid to the distinction between an extended cognitive system hypothesis and an extended cognition hypothesis. It is evidently one thing to claim that cognitive systems are spread over brain, body, and environment, but quite another to claim that cognitive processes span these regions. Barring some mere stipulation or further argumentation, conceding that there are cognitive systems that extend beyond the brain does not suffice to establish the view that cognitive processes so extend. A cognitive system can be identified by a given type of process that does not pervade the whole of the system. More significantly, it seems to us that the recognition of the distinction between cognitive systems and cognitive processes provides a means for recognizing the role of the kind of old-fashioned intracranial cognition that we think is of interest to cognitive psychologists. Systems typically consist of collections of interacting components *that work according to distinct principles*. Given this conception of systems, one will naturally want to know what the brain contributes and what principles it is governed by. This opens the door to, but does not logically require, the hypothesis that there exist distinct kinds of processes plausibly described as cognitive that take place only within the brain. Here, one can see how the complementarity arguments for extended cognition lead back to the view that one should take very seriously the standard view that there are intracranial cognitive processes.

This way of reading the book, however, suggests a stubborn adherence to extended cognition. Despite the challenges to the view, one ought to find a way to make it work. But there is an alternative to stubbornness. To see this other research strategy, let us return to some of the ideas with which we opened the book. If there is a single general idea that unifies the extended, embodied, and indeed situated approaches to cognition, it is that cognitive processes depend on the body and environment. What promotes this idea into one or another research project are the various ways in which one elaborates on this general idea. One fork in the road arises immediately when one wishes to flesh out the kind of dependence involved. The advocates of extended cognition latch onto constitution, or some kindred notion, as the relevant kind of dependence relation. They maintain that cognitive processes are constituted by, realized by, supervene upon, or have their physical substrates in processes in the brain, body, and environment. These are not necessarily equivalent formulations, but they are as precise as the literature on extended cognition allows. Cognitive psychologists should not look for neural correlates of cognitive processes; they should look for corporeal and ecological correlates. Another kind of dependence relation, however, is causation. On this kind of situated or embedded view of cognition, cognitive processes depend on the body and the environment in the sense of being causally influenced by the body and the environment. This is a much tamer hypothesis than is the hypothesis of extended cognition.

Much of our critique of the hypothesis of extended cognition has, of course, turned on recognizing the distinction that is implicit in the extended cognition literature. For one thing, the supporters of extended cognition have tried any number of ways of squeezing a constitutional relation between cognitive processes and brain–body–world processes from observations of causal relations between cognitive processes and brain–body–world relations. As we detailed at length in Chapters 6 and 7, the coupling-constitution arguments are centrally concerned with trying to find a path from a causal premise of one form or another to a constitution conclusion of one form or another. The complementarity argument from Chapter 8 draws attention to the benefits of using tools. These benefits accrue to us because of our causal interactions with them and because tools have properties and undergo processes that are not found in the brain. In this regard, brain–tool systems are like any other sort of system. Finally, the evolutionary argument that Rowlands gave seems to be yet another effort to draw attention to important kinds of causal interactions that organisms have with their environment, interactions that in theory increase fitness, then draw a constitutional conclusion from this.

But why, we ask, should we be at all interested in pursuing the radical idea that cognition depends constitutively on the body and environment? In Chapter 6, we proposed that the constitution claim enabled the advocates of extended cognition to advance a radical break from orthodoxy, which is apparently what they want. But let us reconsider this idea. Why make a radical break from orthodoxy? Why seek a revolutionary scientific approach, one that overthrows the orthodox view of what cognition is and where it is to be found? Why not aim for a scientific and philosophical contribution that is empirically plausible and interesting? Sticking with the claim that cognitive processes are causally dependent on bodily and environmental processes is, of course, an orthodox view in early twenty-first century cognitive science. This is just the familiar rejection of Leibnizian monadology. That hypothesis alone is not an advance. But one might take positive steps forward in cognitive science by spelling out the kinds and scope of causal dependencies between cognition, body, and environment. Indeed, there is a much more conservative segment of the embodied and embedded cognitive science literature that does just this. We have mentioned some of this in previous chapters, but we might view this here again in a new light as an *alternative* to research on extended cognition. Perhaps rather than pursuing the hypothesis of extended cognition, one ought to explore some of the related hypotheses that occur in much of the same literature.[2]

In a work that shares the bold and provocative spirit of much of the extended cognition literature, George Lakoff and Mark Johnson develop a theory of the embodiment of mind and its challenge to Western thought.[3] They draw attention to what they believe are some underappreciated causal influences on cognition. They claim that the human mind is inherently embodied and that reason is shaped by the body. By this, they mean two principal things. In the first place, they mean *neural embodiment*. This is the claim that the structure of the neural networks making up the brain shapes the concepts and categories we use. As an example, they cite the fact that the human retina has about 100 million photoreceptors, but only about one

---

[2]   This methodological suggestion is one of the morals of Rupert (2004).
[3]   Lakoff and Johnson (1999).

million retinal ganglion cells leading out of the eye. This, they maintain, forces the nervous system to impose categories on the light information impinging on the retina. Further, what happens in the earliest stages of visual processing is characteristic of the brain as a whole. As another example of neural embodiment, they cite the role of our neural apparatus in the creation of color concepts. Without the particular combination of cones and other neural apparatus for processing electromagnetic radiation of a given frequency, humans would not have color concepts, or not the color concepts that they have. In addition to neural embodiment, they draw attention to *phenomenological embodiment*. This is the idea that the concepts we have are acquired and shaped through contingent features of our bodies. As an example of this, they cite the concepts of *front-of* and *back-of*. These are concepts that we have and use because human bodies have fronts and backs that mediate our interactions with the world. In our normal daily lives, we move in the direction our front faces and interact with others via our front side. We then project these concepts derived from our bodies onto other objects. Cars have a front in virtue of the direction in which they move. Televisions and stoves have a front because of the way in which one normally interacts with them. Following these principles, we can see that trees and rocks do not have fronts or backs.

Gallagher (2005) presents another study of the ways in which cognitive processes (and conscious experience) are causally influenced by – or, as he says, shaped by – being embodied in the way they are. In Gallagher's account, the notions of *body image* and *body schema* are the principal theoretical posits. A *body image* consists of a set of perceptions, attitudes, and beliefs pertaining to one's own body. A *body schema* is a system of sensory and motor capacities that function without perceptual monitoring or awareness. Here we do not propose to examine or critique Gallagher's approach or theories. Our only point is to draw attention to the existence of another scientific project that can be described as the study of embodied cognition, and that does not necessarily depend on a revolutionary conception of the cognitive or where in the world it can be found.[4]

---

[4]   Gallagher does, however, at one point argue for extended cognition. In the following passage, he appears to commit the coupling-constitution fallacy: "The body schema functions in an integrated way with its environment, even to the extent that it frequently incorporates into itself certain objects – the hammer in the carpenter's hand, the feather in the woman's hat, and so forth" (Gallagher, 2005, p. 37; cf., p. 38). This, however, does not appear to be a central thesis of Gallagher's work.

As one final example of a non-revolutionary approach to embodied cognition, we might draw attention to the studies that have interested Sutton (2004). Sutton proposes to bring theories of memory as treated in clinical neuropsychology, media theory, developmental psychology, Holocaust studies, molecular neurobiology, computational neuroscience, cognitive neuropsychology, social psychology, psychoanalysis, museumology, postcolonial studies, and literary theory not into a single science, but into "neighboring discursive universes." There is, he proposes, no single conception or theory of memory that unites these diverse academic projects. Instead, there might be "an integrated framework within which different memory-related phenomena might be understood" (Sutton, 2004, p. 188). Here is a project that can be undertaken while leaving much of the cognitive psychology of memory as the study of processes that take place, essentially without exception, within nervous systems. One does not have to insist that the hypothesis of intracranial processes of memory processing is a mere relic of an unexamined Cartesian prejudice. Instead, one can maintain, as we do, that there is a scientifically and philosophically motivated reason to believe that there are psychological processes that are found in brains that are unlike processes that span brains, bodies, and environments.

Bibliography

Adams, F. (1991). Causal contents. In B. McLaughlin (ed.), *Dretske and his Critics*. Oxford: Blackwell, pp. 131–56.

— and Aizawa, K. (1994). Fodorian semantics. In T. Warfield and S. Stich (eds.), *Mental Representation: A Reader*. Cambridge, MA: Blackwell, pp. 223–42.

— and — (2001). The bounds of cognition. *Philosophical Psychology*, 14, 43–64.

— and — (forthcoming a). Defending the bounds of cognition. In R. Menary (ed.), *The Extended Mind*. Aldershot, Hants: Ashgate.

— and — (forthcoming b). Why the mind is still in the head. In P. Robbins and M. Aydede (eds.), *Cambridge Handbook of Situated Cognition*. Cambridge: Cambridge University Press.

— and — (forthcoming c). Embodied cognition and the extended mind. In P. Garzon and J. Symons (eds.), *Routledge Companion to the Philosophy of Psychology*. London: Routledge.

Aizawa, K. (2003). *The Systematicity Arguments*. Boston, MA: Kluwer Academic.

— (2007a). The biochemistry of memory consolidation: A model system for the philosophy of mind. *Synthese*, 155, 65–98.

— (2007b). Understanding the embodiment of perception. *Journal of Philosophy*, 104, 5–25.

— and Adams, F., (2005). Defending non-derived content. *Philosophical Psychology*, 18, 661–9.

Anderson, J. R. (1974). Verbatim and propositional representation of sentences in immediate and long-term memory. *Journal of Verbal Learning and Verbal Behavior*, 13, 149–62.

— (1981). Interference: The relationship between response latency and response accuracy. *Journal of Experimental Psychology: Human Learning and Memory*, 7, 311–25.

— (1995). *Learning and Memory: An Integrated Approach*. New York: John Wiley.

Anderson, M. L. (2003). Embodied cognition: A field guide. *Artificial Intelligence*, 149, 91–130.

Anonymous (1979). On being aware. *British Journal of Anaesthesia*, 51, 711–12.

Atkinson, R. C., and Shiffrin, R. M. (1968). Human memory: A proposed system and its control processes. In K. W. Spence and J. T. Spence (eds.), *The Psychology of Learning and Motivation*, vol. 2. New York: Academic Press, pp. 89–195.

Bahrick, H. P. (1984). Semantic memory content in permastore: Fifty years of memory for Spanish learned in school. *Journal of Experimental Psychology: General*, 113, 1–24.

Beer, R. D. (2003). The dynamics of active categorical perception in an evolved model agent. *Adaptive Behavior*, 11, 209–43.

Biederman, I. (1987). Recognition-by-components: A theory of human image understanding, *Psychological Review*, 94, 115–47.

Birch, E. E., Stager, D., Leffler, J., and Weakley, D. (1998). Early treatment of congenital unilateral cataract minimizes unequal competition. *Investigative Ophthalmology and Visual Science*, 39, 1560–6.

Block, N. (2005). Review of Alva Noë, *Action in Perception*. *Journal of Philosophy*, 102, 259–72.

Bowering, E. R., Maurer, D., Lewis, T. L., and Brent, H. P. (1993). Sensitivity in the nasal and temporal hemifields in children treated for cataract. *Investigative Ophthalmology and Visual Science*, 34, 3501–9.

Brooks, R. (1999). Intelligence without representation. In R. Brooks (ed.), *Cambrian Intelligence: The Early History of the New AI*. Cambridge, MA: The MIT Press, pp. 79–101.

Campbell, E. J., Freedman, S., Clark, T. J., Robson, J. G., and Norman, J. (1967). The effect of muscular paralysis induced by tubocurarine on the duration and sensation of breath-holding. *Clinical Sciences*, 32, 425–32.

—, Godfrey, S., Clark, T. J., Freedman, S., and Norman, J. (1969). The effect of muscular paralysis induced by tubocurarine on the duration and sensation of breath-holding during hypercapnia. *Clinical Sciences*, 36, 323–8.

Chemero, A. (2000). Anti-representationalism and the dynamical stance. *Philosophy of Science*, 67, 625–47.

Clark, A. (1997). *Being There*. Cambridge, MA: The MIT Press.

— (1998). Author's response: review symposium on *Being There*. *Metascience*, 7, 95–103.

— (2001). Reasons, robots, and the extended mind. *Mind & Language*, 16, 121–45.

— (2002). Towards a science of the bio-technological mind. *International Journal of Cognition and Technology*, 1, 21–33.

— (2003). *Natural-Born Cyborgs*. Oxford: Oxford University Press.

— (2005). Intrinsic content, active memory, and the extended mind. *Analysis*, 65, 1–11.

— (forthcoming a). Active externalism and the extended mind. In P. Robbins and M. Aydede (eds.), *Cambridge Handbook of Situated Cognition*. Cambridge: Cambridge University Press.

— (forthcoming b). Coupling, constitution and the cognitive kind: A reply to Adams and Aizawa. In R. Menary, *The Extended Mind*. Aldershot, Hants: Ashgate.

— and Chalmers, D. (1998). The extended mind. *Analysis*, 58, 7–19.

— and Grush, R. (1999). Towards a cognitive robotics. *Adaptive Behavior*, 7, 5–16.

Craik, F. I. M., and Tulving, E. (1975). Depth of processing and the retention of words in episodic memory. *Journal of Experimental Psychology: General*, 104, 268–94.

Cummins, R. (1996). *Representations, Targets, and Attitudes*. Cambridge, MA: The MIT Press.

Dawkins, R. (1999). *The Extended Phenotype: The Long Reach of the Gene*. Oxford: Oxford University Press.

— (2004). Extended phenotype – But not *too* extended. A reply to Laland, Turner, and Jablonka. *Biology and Philosophy*, 19, 377–96.

Dennett, D. C. (1981). *Brainstorms: Philosophical Essays on Mind and Psychology*. A Bradford book. Cambridge, MA: The MIT Press.

— (1987a). Evolution, error, and intentionality. In *The Intentional Stance*. A Bradford book. Cambridge, MA: The MIT Press, pp. 297–321.

— (1987b). Review of J. Fodor, *Psychosemantics*. *Journal of Philosophy*, 85, 384–9.

— (1990). The myth of original intentionality. In Mohyeldin Said, K. A., Newton-Smith, W. H., Viale, R., and Wilkes, K. V. (eds.), *Modeling the Mind*. Oxford: Oxford University Press, pp. 43–62.

— (1996). *Kinds of Minds*. New York: Basic Books.

Descartes, R. (1641). Meditations. In J. Cottingham, R. Stoothoff, and D. Murdoch (trans.) (1984). *The Philosophical Writings of Descartes*, vol. 2. Cambridge: Cambridge University Press.

Di Pellegrino, G., Fadiga, L., Fogassi, L., Gallese, V., and Rizzolatti, G. (1992). Understanding motor events: A neurophysiological study. *Experimental Brain Research*, 91, 176–80.

Ditchburn, R. W., and Ginsborg, B. L. (1952). Vision with a stabilized retinal image. *Nature*, 170, 36–7.

Donald, M. (1991). *Origins of the Modern Mind*. Cambridge, MA: Harvard University Press.

Dretske, F. (1981). *Knowledge and the Flow of Information*. Cambridge, MA: The MIT Press.

— (1988). *Explaining Behavior*. Cambridge, MA: The MIT Press.

Ellemberg, D., Lewis, T. L., Maurer, D., and Brent, H. P. (2000). Influence of monocular deprivation during infancy on the later development of spatial and temporal vision. *Vision Research*, 40, 3283–95.

—, Maurer, D., Brar, S., and Brent, H. P. (2002). Better perception of global motion after monocular than after binocular deprivation. *Vision Research*, 42, 169–79.

—, Lewis, T. L., Maurer, D., Liu, C. H., and Brent, H. P. (1999). Spatial and temporal vision in patients treated for bilateral congenital cataracts. *Vision Research*, 39, 3480–9.

Emery, N. J., and Clayton, N. S. (2004). The mentality of crows: Convergent evolution of intelligence in corvids and apes. *Science*, 306, 1903–7.

Fendrich, R., Wessinger, C. M., and Gazzaniga, M. (1992). Residual vision in a scotoma: Implications for blindsight. *Science*, 258, 1489–91.

Fine, I., Smallman, H. S., Doyle, P., and Macleod, D. I. A. (2002). Visual function before and after the removal of bilateral congenital cataracts in adulthood. *Vision Research*, 42, 191–201.

Fodor, J. (1987). *Psychosemantics*. Cambridge, MA: The MIT Press.

— (1990). *A Theory of Content and Other Essays*. Cambridge, MA: The MIT Press.

Froese, A. B., and Bryan, A. C. (1974). Effects of amnesia and paralysis on diaphragmatic mechanics in man. *Anesthesiology*, 41, 242–54.

Gallagher, S. (2005). *How the Body Shapes the Mind*. Oxford: Clarendon Press.

Gibbs, R. W. (2001). Intentions as emergent products of social interactions. In B. F. Malle, L. J. Moses, and D. A. Baldwin (eds.), *Intentions and Intentionality*. Cambridge, MA: The MIT Press, pp. 105–22.

— (2006). *Embodiment and Cognitive Science*. Cambridge: Cambridge University Press.

Gibson, J. J. (1979). *The Ecological Approach to Visual Perception*. Hillsdale, NJ: Lawrence Erlbaum.

Giunti, M. (1995). Dynamical models of cognition. In R. Port and T. van Gelder (eds.), *Mind as Motion: Explorations in the Dynamics of Cognition*. Cambridge, MA: The MIT Press, pp. 549–71.

Glenberg, A., and Adams, F. (1978). Type I rehearsal and recognition. *Journal of Verbal Learning and Verbal Behavior*, 17, 455–63.

Gregory, R. L., and Wallace, J. G., (1963). *Recovery from Early Blindness: A Case Study*. Monograph no. 2. Cambridge: Experimental Psychology Society.

Gross, C. G., Rocha-Miranda, C. E., and Bender, D. B. (1972). Visual properties of neurons in inferotemporal cortex of the macaque. *Journal of Neurophysiology*, 35, 96–111.

Grush, R. (2003). In defense of some "Cartesian" assumptions concerning the brain and its operation. *Biology and Philosophy*, 18, 53–93.

Haugeland, J. (1998). Mind embodied and embedded. In Haugeland, J. (ed.), *Having Thought*. Cambridge, MA: Harvard University Press, pp. 207–37.

Hubel, D., and Wiesel, T. (1963). Receptive fields of cells in striate cortex of very young, visually inexperienced kittens. *Journal of Neurophysiology*, 26, 994–1002.

— and — (1965). Comparison of effects of unilateral and bilateral eye closure on cortical unit responses in kittens. *Journal of Neurophysiology*, 28, 1029–40.

— and — (2005). *Brain and Visual Perception*. Oxford: Oxford University Press.

Hurley, S. (1998a). Vehicles, contents, conceptual structure, and externalism. *Analysis*, 58, 1–6.

— (forthcoming). Varieties of externalism. In R. Menary (ed.), *The Extended Mind*. Aldershot, Hants: Ashgate.

Hutchins, E. (1995a). *Cognition in the Wild*. Cambridge, MA: The MIT Press.

— (1995b). How a cockpit remembers its speeds. *Cognitive Science*, 19, 265–88.

Kandel, E. R., Schwartz, J. H., and Jessell, T. M. (2000). *Principles of Neural Science*, 4th edn. New York: McGraw-Hill.

Kohler, I. (1964). Formation and transformation of the perceptual world. *Psychological Issues*, 3, 1–173.

Lakoff, G., and Johnson, M. (1999). *Philosophy in the Flesh: The Embodied Mind and its Challenge to Western Thought*. New York: Basic Books.

Leibniz, W. (1979). Monadology. In G. R. Montgomery (trans.), *Leibniz: Discourse on Metaphysics/Correspondence with Arnaud/Monadology*. Lasalle, IL: Open Court.

Lettvin, J. Y., Maturana, H. R., McCulloch, W. S., and Pitts, W. H. (1959). What the frog's eye tells the frog's brain. *Proceedings of the Institute of Radio Engineers*, 47, 1940–50.

Lewis, D. (1969). *Convention*. Cambridge, MA: Harvard University Press.

Lewis, T. L., Maurer, D., and Brent, H. P. (1995). The development of grating acuity in children treated for unilateral or bilateral congenital cataract. *Investigative Ophthalmology and Visual Science*, 36, 2080–95.

—, Ellemberg, D., Maurer, D., Wilkinson, F., Wilson, H. R., Dirks, M., and Brent, H. P. (2002). Sensitivity to global form in glass patterns after early visual deprivation in humans. *Vision Research*, 42, 939–48.

Machamer, P., Darden, L., and Craver, C. (2000). Thinking about mechanisms. *Philosophy of Science*, 67, 1–25.

Macaulay, D. (1998). *The New Ways Things Work*. Boston, MA: Houghton Mifflin.

Menary, R. (2006). Attacking the bounds of cognition. *Philosophical Psychology*, 19, 329–44.

Miller, G. A. (1956). The magical number seven, plus or minus two: Some limits on our capacity for processing information. *Psychological Review*, 63, 81–97.

Milner, D. A., and Goodale, M. A. (1995). *The Visual Brain in Action*. Oxford: Oxford University Press.

Mioche, L., and Perenin, M. (1986). Central and peripheral residual vision in humans with bilateral deprivation amblyopia. *Experimental Brain Research*, 62, 259–72.

Miura, S., Kashimoto, S., Yamaguchi, T., and Matsukawa, T. (2001). A case of awareness with sevoflurane and epidural anesthesia in overian tumorectomy. *Journal of Clinical Anesthesia*, 13(3), 227–9.

Newell, A., and Rosenbloom, P. S. (1981). Mechanisms of skill acquisition and the law of practice. In Anderson, J. R. (ed.), *Cognitive Skills and Their Acquisition*. Hillsdale, NJ: Lawrence Erlbaum, pp. 1–51.

Noë, A. (2004). *Action in Perception*. Cambridge, MA: The MIT Press.

O'Regan, J. K., and Noë, A. (2001). What it is like to see: A sensorimotor theory of perceptual experience. *Synthese*, 129, 79–103.

Prinz, J. (2006). Putting the brakes on enactive perception. *Psyche*, 12(1), 1–19.

Riggs, L. A., and Ratliff, F. (1952). The effects of counteracting the normal movements of the eye. *Journal of the Optical Society of America*, 42, 872–3.

Rizzolatti G., and Craighero, L. (2004). The mirror-neuron system. *Annual Review of Neuroscience*, 27, 169–92.

Rockwell, T. (2005). *Neither Brain Nor Ghost*. Cambridge, MA: The MIT Press.

Rowlands, M. (1999). *The Body in Mind*. Cambridge: Cambridge University Press.

— (2003). *Externalism: Putting Mind and World Back Together Again*. Montreal: McGill-Queen's University Press.

Rupert, R. (2004). Challenges to the hypothesis of extended cognition. *Journal of Philosophy*, 101, 389–428.

— (2006). Review of Raymond W. Gibbs, Jr., *Embodiment and Cognitive Science*. In *Notre Dame Philosophical Reviews*, August 20, 2006.

Rupert, R. (forthcoming a). Representation in extended cognitive systems: Does the scaffolding of language extend the mind? In R. Menary (ed.), *The Extended Mind*. Aldershot, Hants: Ashgate.

— (forthcoming b). Nativism and empiricism. In P. Robbins and M. Aydede (eds.), *Cambridge Handbook of Situated Cognition*. Cambridge: Cambridge University Press.

Sacks, O. (1995). *An Anthropologist on Mars: Seven Paradoxical Tales*. New York: Knopf.

Sandin, R., Enlund, G., Samuelson, P., and Lennemarken, C. (2000). Awareness during anaesthesia: A prospective case study. *The Lancet*, 355, 707–11.

Schwender, D., Kunze-Kronawitter, H., Dietrich, P., Klasing, S., Forst, H., and Madler, C. (1998). Conscious awareness during general anaesthesia: Patients' perceptions, emotions, cognition, and reactions. *British Journal of Anaesthesia*, 80, 133–9.

Searle, J. (1980). Minds, brains, and programs. *Behavioral and Brain Sciences*, 3, 417–58.

— (1984). *Minds, Brains, and Science*. Cambridge, MA: Harvard University Press.

Sekuler, R., and Blake, R. (2002). *Perception*, 4th edn. Boston, MA: McGraw-Hill.

Sellars, W. (1956). Empiricism and the philosophy of mind. In H. Feigl and M. Scriven (eds.), *The Foundations of Science and the Concepts of Psychology and Psychoanalysis*. Minnesota Studies in the Philosophy of Science, vol. I. Minneapolis, MN: University of Minnesota Press, pp. 253–329.

Shapiro, L. (2004). *The Mind Incarnate*. Cambridge, MA: The MIT Press.

Sherman, S. M., and Spear, P. D. (1982). Organization of visual pathways in normal and visually deprived cats. *Physiological Reviews*, 62, 738–855.

Slamecka, N. J., and Graf, P. (1978). The generation effect: Delineation of a phenomenon. *Journal of Experimental Psychology: Learning, Memory, and Language*, 4, 592–604.

Smith, S. M., Brown, H. O., Toman, J. E., and Goodman, L. S. (1947). The lack of cerebral effects of d-tubocurarine. *Anesthesiology*, 8, 1–14.

Speaks, J. (2006). Is mental content prior to linguistic meaning? *Nous*, 40, 428–67.

Stevens, J. K., Emerson, R. C., Gerstein, G. L., Kallos, T., Neufeld, G. R., Nichols, C. W., and Rosenquist, A. C. (1976). Paralysis of the awake human: Visual Perceptions. *Vision Research*, 16, 93–8.

Stich, S., and Warfield, T. (1994). *Mental Representation: A Reader*. Cambridge, MA: Blackwell.

Stratton, G. M. (1896). Some preliminary experiments on vision without inversion of the retinal image. *Psychological Review*, 3, 611–17.

— (1897a). Upright vision and the retinal image. *Psychological Review*, 4, 182–7.

— (1897b). Vision without inversion of the retinal image. *Psychological Review*, 4, 341–60, 463–81.

Susi, T., Lindblom, J., and Ziemke, T. (2003). Beyond the bounds of cognition. In K. Forbus, D. Gentner, and T. Regier (eds.), *Proceedings of the 25th Annual Conference of the Cognitive Science Society*. Mahwah, NJ: Lawrence Erlbaum, pp. 1305–10.

Sutton, J. (2004). Representation, reduction, and interdisciplinarity in the sciences of memory. In H. Clapin, P. Staines, and P. Slezak (eds.), *Representation in Mind: New Approaches to Mental Representation*. Amsterdam: Elsevier, pp. 187–216.

— (forthcoming). Exograms and interdisciplinarity: History, the extended mind, and the civilizing process. In Menary, R. (ed.), *The Extended Mind*. Aldershot, Hants: Ashgate.

Thelen, E., and Smith, L. (1994). *A Dynamical Systems Approach to the Development of Cognition and Action*. Cambridge, MA: The MIT Press.

Thompson, E., and Varela, F. J. (2001). Radical embodiment: neural dynamics and consciousness. *Trends in Cognitive Science*, 5, 418–25.

Thorndike, E. L. (1911). *Animal Intelligence*. New York: Macmillan.

Topulos, G. P., Lansing, R. W., and Banzett, R. B. (1993). The experience of complete neuromuscular blockade in awake humans. *Journal of Clinical Anesthesiology*, 5, 369–74.

Tytla, M. E., Lewis, T. L., Maurer, D., and Brent, H. P. (1993). Stereopsis after congenital cataract deprivation in the monkey. III. Reversal of anatomical effects in the visual cortex. *Investigative Ophthalmology and Visual Science*, 34, 1767–73.

—, Maurer, D., Lewis, T. L., and Brent, H. P. (1988). Contrast sensitivity in children treated for congenital cataract. *Clinical Vision Sciences*, 2, 251–64.

Ungerleider, L. G., and Mishkin, M. (1982). Two cortical visual systems. In J. J. Ingle, M. A. Goodale, and R. J. W. Mansfield (eds.), *Analysis of Visual Behavior*. Cambridge, MA: The MIT Press, pp. 549–86.

van Gelder, T. (1995). What might cognition be, if not computation? *Journal of Philosophy*, 91, 345–81.

— (1998). The dynamical hypothesis in cognitive science. *Behavioral and Brain Sciences*, 21, 615–65.

— and Port, R. (1995a). It's about time: An overview of the dynamical approach to cognition. In R. Port and T. van Gelder (eds.), *Mind as Motion: Explorations in the Dynamics of Cognition*. Cambridge, MA: The MIT Press, pp. 1–43.

— and — (1995b). Preface. In *Mind as Motion: Explorations in the Dynamics of Cognition*. Cambridge, MA: The MIT Press, pp. vii–x.

Weiskopf, D. (unpublished). Patrolling the boundaries: A reply to Clark and Chalmers.

Wilson, M. (2002). Six views of embodied cognition. *Psychonomic Bulletin and Review*, 9, 625–36.

Wilson, R. (2000). The mind beyond itself. In Sperber, D. (ed.), *Misrepresentations: A Multidisciplinary Perspective*. New York: Oxford University Press.

— (2004). *Boundaries of the Mind: The Individual in the Fragile Sciences*. Cambridge: Cambridge University Press.

— and Clark, A. (forthcoming). How to situate cognition: Letting nature take its course. In M. Aydede and P. Robbins (eds.), *The Cambridge Handbook on Situated Cognition*. Cambridge: Cambridge University Press.

Zeki, S. (1974). Functional organization of a visual area in the posterior bank of the superior temporal sulcus of the rhesus monkey. *Journal of Physiology*, 236, 549–73.

Index

"A-not-B" error   135
achromotopsia   162, 164
active externalism   90, 95
Adams, F.   10, 15, 21, 24, 35, 37, 46–8,
    50, 58, 67, 91, 99, 101–4, 126, 129
adaptability   85
agnosia   162, 167
air conditioning system   91, 117–18,
    131, 146
airliner (landing process)   77, 111
Aizawa, K.   10, 15, 21, 24, 35, 36,
    47–8, 50, 58, 91–2, 99, 101–4, 126,
    129
akinetopsia   162, 164
aluminum cans, search for   32, 52–3,
    54
Alzheimer's disease   3, 4, 74, 102–3
analogous structures   59
Anderson, J. R.   63, 65, 138
animal cognition   32–4, 52, 59, 71–2,
    73
antagonistic muscles   115
anti-representationalism   35, 51–4, 79
artifacts   40, 41, 44, 103–4, 147
"as if" intentionality   41
assigned meaning   42
asymmetric causal dependency   37,
    40

Atkinson, R. C.   68
atomism   9
attention/attentional processing   62,
    75

backward causation   98
Bacon, F.   58, 73
Bahrick, H. P.   67
bandwidth (narrow/high)   113, 114
behaviorism   136
"belief boxes"   44
beliefs   24, 44, 45–6, 135
    dispositional   28, 121, 122, 123, 136
best explanation, inference to   14,
    152–73
Biedermann, I.   62
biochemical apparatus (cells)   49
biology (research projects)   86–7
Birch, E. E.   160
bit-mapped images   48
Blake, R.   33
blindsight   121, 123–4
Block, N.   89, 99, 157
bodily manipulation   5, 6, 90
body   10
    environment and   2, 4–8, 25, 27,
        31, 88
    image   88, 178

body (*cont'd*)
  role   3–4, 5
  schema   88, 178
  see also embodied cognition;
    embodiment
Body in Mind, The (Rowlands)   150
boundaries/bounds
  of cognition   16–25, 29
  definitions   16–22
  of skin and skull   48, 126, 142
  see also cognition
Bowering, E. R.   160
brain
  -bound cognition   8–10, 70
  states (of Martians)   48–9
  see also cognitive processes/
    processing; extracranial cognition;
    intracranial cognition; minds;
    transcranial cognition
British Journal of Anaesthesia   171
Brooks, R.   32, 51, 53–4, 79–80, 85,
  86
Bryan, A. C.   169

Campbell, E. J.   169
Cartesian prejudice   9, 22, 141, 179
Cartesian tradition   146
causal dependency   88–9, 91, 92, 175,
  177
  asymmetric   37, 40
causal power   36
causal systems/interactions   1, 7, 10,
  20, 44, 74, 126, 176–7
causation
  backwards   98
  constitution and   89, 91, 94, 100–5,
    175
central nervous system   18, 20, 22, 70,
  89, 107, 113–14
Chalmers, D.   2, 6, 9, 83, 142
  coupling theory   89–90, 92, 95,
    119–20, 125, 129

extended cognitive systems   106–7,
  119–30
  Inga–Otto thought experiment
    see main entry
  parity principle   7, 27–8, 134, 145
Chemero, A.   52
circulatory system/processes   10–11
Clark, A.   2, 6, 9, 14, 26, 70, 142
  coupling theory   89–90, 92, 95–6,
    119–30
  critique of original content   34,
    46–50
  extended cognition style   76–7,
    80–1, 83
  extended cognitive systems   106–7,
    119–30
  Inga–Otto thought experiment
    see main entry
  parity principle   7, 27–8, 134, 145
Clayton, N. S.   32
CLT example   123–4
cognition
  animal   32–4, 52, 59, 71–2, 73
  bounds of   16–25, 29
  brain-bound   8–10, 70
  broader category of   70–4
  as computation   76–8, 80
  definitions/theory   22–5, 29
  embedded   6, 8–9, 112, 177
  embodied   6, 8–9, 12, 20, 57, 89,
    107, 112, 177, 178–9
  extended *see* extended cognition
  family resemblances   72–3, 91, 140
  general   73–4, 141, 147
  human   24–5, 30, 57, 141
  information processing   76–8
  non-human   30, 31, 32
  rules and representations   47, 60–1,
    174
cognitive agents   11, 21, 32, 54, 85–6,
  102–3, 124–5, 146
  operational definition   79, 82

cognitive apparatus 4, 8, 103, 123
cognitive capacities 20, 147
cognitive equivalence 14, 28, 74–5,
  78, 120, 133–4, 175
  complementarity argument 7–8,
    143–7
  evolutionary arguments 147–50
  importance of mark of cognitive
    150–1
  Inga–Otto example 135–41
  Tetris example 141–3
cognitive integration 21, 102, 103–4
cognitive mechanisms 4, 53–4, 57,
  67, 84, 137–8, 141, 143
cognitive objects 92, 126
cognitive processes/processing 1, 12,
  20–2, 24, 26–8, 31, 50, 55
  broader category of cognition
    70–4
  coupling-constitution fallacy
    88–105
  definitions 16–24
  dynamical systems and 51–4
  extended see extended cognitive
    systems/processes
  future directions 174–9
  individuating processes 58–70
  non-cognitive processes and 4, 10,
    23, 57, 107
  non-derived representations 9, 10,
    13, 32–9
cognitive psychology 2, 9–12, 18, 19,
  22, 32–3, 86, 127–8, 132
  cognitive equivalence 138–41, 143,
    146–7
  future directions 174, 176, 179
  individuating processes in 60–70
cognitive resources 120–3
cognitive science 17, 83, 128
  orthodoxy 1–2, 4, 8, 174, 177
cognitive systems 6, 11, 23, 102,
  145–6, 150–1

Clark's approach 125–30
  coupled system as 7, 89–90, 92–3
  extended see extended cognitive
    systems/processes
cognitive tasks 21, 80–2, 102, 175
color blindness 162, 164
color concepts 178
color illusions 123
color vision 71, 123, 162, 164, 178
complementarity 20
  arguments 7–8, 12, 14, 24, 74,
    143–7, 151, 176
  cognitive equivalence and 133–51
  principle 145
  components 130–1, 146, 175
  coupling of 7, 112–19
  definition 113
computation 6, 50, 51–2, 61
  cognition as 76–8, 80
  pencil and paper 2–3, 4, 5, 8, 10,
    24–5, 88, 93, 94
Computational Promiscuity 128, 129
computers/computing 116–17, 118,
  146
cone system 18, 69, 71, 114, 165
congenital cataracts 2, 152–3,
  157–63, 173
constitution
  causation and 89, 91, 94, 100–5,
    175
  see also coupling-constitution fallacy
constitutive dependency 5, 89, 175,
  176
content
  derived 13, 32, 35–42, 44, 46–7, 50,
    143
  intrinsic 35, 47–50
  non-derived 9, 10, 13, 31, 32–41,
    44, 46–50, 143, 146
  semantic 34, 36–7, 42, 43, 44
coordination 85
corporeal environment 26

coupled system   7, 89–90, 119–20
coupling   28–9
   arguments   5–8
   Clark's view   89–90, 92, 95–6,
      119–30
   of components   7, 112–19
   dynamical systems theory   107–12
coupling-constitution fallacy   10–11,
   27, 74–5, 88–92, 175, 176
   Clark's theory   125–30
   examples   14, 93–9
   extended cognitive systems   108,
      112, 117, 119, 126–30
   replies to   99–105
Craighero, L.   33
Craik, F. I. M.   65, 138
Creatures (cognitive agents)   79, 85
Cummins, R.   37, 39, 40

Darwin, C.   58
Dawkins, R.   22
Dennett, D. C.   20–1, 34–5, 38, 47, 48
   critique of original content   39–46
dependence
   constitutive   5, 89, 175, 176
   nomological   81–2
   see also causal dependency
depth of processing   65, 66–7, 138–9
derived content   13, 32, 35–42, 44,
   46–7, 50, 143
derived intentionality   39–41, 42–3,
   44–5
derivations
   ontogenetic   42, 43, 44
   phylogenetic   42, 43, 44
Descartes, R.   8, 16
design stance   45
desires   45–6, 135
Di Pellegrino, G.   33
dispositional beliefs   28, 121, 122,
   123, 136
distance (of objects)   3–4

distorting lenses   163–5
distractor paradigm   67
Ditchburn, R. W.   165
DNA   42, 44, 45, 49
Doctrine of Intrinsic Unsuitability
   128–9
Donald, M.   143–4, 175
Dotto example   121–3
Dretske, F.   36, 39, 40
ducks thought experiment   49
dynamical processes   23, 107–12
dynamical systems   35, 135
   anti-representationalism in   51–4
   chaotic   76, 87, 109
   coupling and   107–12
   processes   23, 107–12
   theory   2, 106, 107–12, 130

effect, law of   61
electric garage door opener   82
Ellemberg, D.   160
embedded cognition   6, 8–9, 112, 177
embodied cognition   6, 8–9, 12, 20,
   57, 89, 107, 112, 177, 178–9
embodiment   92, 99
   neural   107, 169, 177–8
   of perception   20, 155
   phenomenological   178
Emery, N. J.   32
enactive perception   14
   case against   166–72
   Noë's case (evidence)   152–3,
      156–66
   theory of   153–6
endocrine system   115–16, 125
engrams   144
environmentalism   125
environments   21
   body and   2, 4–8, 25, 27–8, 31,
      88–9
   extracorporeal   17, 25–6, 76
epistemology   9

evolution 8, 12
  cognitive equivalence and
    133–51
  theory 12, 58–9
  see also natural selection
evolutionary arguments 14, 147–50,
  177
exograms 144–5, 175
experiential blindness 158, 161–3,
  164, 169
extended cognition 3, 4, 14–15,
  18–21, 31
  cognitive equivalence 134, 137,
    140, 145–7, 150
  coupling-constitution fallacy 92–4,
    95, 98–100, 102–4
  debate/terminological dispute
    83–5
  dynamical systems 2, 23, 35, 51–4,
    107–12
  enactive perception 152–73
  family resemblances 72–3
  future directions 174–9
  general cognition 73–4
  hypothesis (arguments) 5–10, 12
  Inga–Otto thought experiment
    see main entry
  operationalism 79–83
  possibility of 25–9, 30
  principal weaknesses 10–12
  style 76–87
extended cognitive systems/processes
  6, 106, 145–6
  Clark's theories 119–30
  dynamical systems theory and
    107–12
  Haugeland's theory 112–19
extended mind 50, 125, 145
external symbol storage 144
external vehicles 91, 102, 104
externalism
  active 90, 95

locational 125
  vehicle 125
extracorporeal environment 17,
  25–6, 76
extracranial cognition 8, 14, 60
eyes 101, 177–8
  cone system 18, 69, 71, 114, 165
  congenital cataracts 2, 152–3,
    157–63, 173
  electric 82–3
  human 82–3
  retinal ganglion cells 18–19, 69–70
  rod system 18, 69, 71, 114, 165
  see also vision; visual processing

face agnosia 162, 167
false memories 172
false tokening 43, 44
family resemblances 47, 72–3, 91,
  140
Fendrich, R. 123
Fine, I. 161
flywheel 51
Fodor, J. 37, 39, 40
"folk psychology" 13
food (obtaining) 33, 34, 52
form agnosia 162
free recall memory 63, 64–5, 137–9
Freon™ 91, 131
Froese, A. B. 169
functional isomorphism argument
  134
functional poise 134–5, 150–1
functional roles 134, 135–6
functionalism 4, 25, 30, 69, 136
"functions as" 104–5

Gallagher, S. 117, 178
Garson, J. 99
general cognition 73–4, 141, 147
generation effect (memory) 66, 139
geons 62

Gibbs, R. W.   2, 5, 6, 14, 20, 88, 96–8, 147, 174
Gibson, J. J.   4
Ginsborg, B. L.   165
Giunti, M.   51
Glenberg, A.   67
glial cells   17
Goodale, M. A.   73
Graf, P.   66
Gregory, R. L.   157, 159, 161
Gross, C. G.   33
Grush, R.   46–7

Haugeland, J.   6, 8, 78, 80, 85, 96, 111
   coupling   89, 90, 92, 112–19, 125, 130
   systems theory   14, 106, 146
heat   58, 73
Herbert (robot)   32, 54, 86
Hering illusion   159
homology/homologous structures   59
"how" explanations   100
Hubel, D.   33, 160
human cognition   24–5, 30, 57, 141
human genome   44
human muscular system   115
Hurley, S.   3, 7, 92, 99, 100–1, 125
Hutchins, E.   77, 111

indicator function account   40
individualism   125
individuating process/processes   58–70
infection   59
inference to the best explanation   14, 152–73
information processing   11, 17–19, 21, 23, 31, 60, 68–9, 76–8, 81, 107, 146, 174
information processor   11, 77
Inga–Otto thought experiment   3, 4–5, 7–8, 11, 20, 23–5, 28–9, 50,

74, 102–5, 107, 110, 118, 120, 125–6, 129, 131, 134, 135–41, 150–1
inheritance   59
integration   89, 91, 162
   cognitive   21, 102, 103–4
integrationism/integrationists   91, 102–4
intelligence   51, 54, 78, 80–1, 85, 112, 129
intelligibility (of systems)   116–17, 126
intentional stance   45–6
intentionality
   as if   41
   derived   39–41, 42–3, 44–5
   original   39–40, 41–2, 44–5, 46
intentions   6, 32, 36, 96–8
interactionism   8
interactions, causal   1, 7, 10, 20, 44, 74, 126, 176–7
interfaces   113–14, 115–16, 130–1
internal vehicles   102
internalism/internalists   91, 102, 104–5
intimacy   90, 96
intracranial cognition   8, 9–10, 12, 14, 17, 28, 60–2, 74, 78, 84, 93–4, 96, 98, 101, 107, 135, 140, 146–8, 150, 175, 179
intrinsic content   35, 47–50
intrinsic unsuitability   128, 129
ion transport   62
isomorphism   37, 134

Johnson, M.   88, 177

Kandel, E. R.   17
knowledge   85
   sensorimotor   153–4, 155, 166–8
Kohler, I.   163

Lakoff, G.   88, 177
Lamarckian theories   59
Lashley, K.   144
lateral geniculate nucleus (LGN)   70
law of effect   61
laws   61–2
learning   4, 61
Leibniz, W. G.   1, 5, 177
Lettvin, J. Y.   32, 33
Lewis, D.   38
Lewis, T. L.   160
light   69, 71–2, 82
    distance and   3, 4
linguistic processing   71, 75
linguistic usage (terminology)   83–5
locational externalism   125

Macaulay, D.   131
McGurk effect   127–8
Machamer, P.   62
"magic number five"   140
"magic number seven"   62, 68, 70
making (causal production)   43–4
manipulation   89, 103
    bodily   5, 6, 90
    of external vehicles   91, 104–5
    physical   5, 6
mark of the cognitive   10, 22–4, 29,
    74–5, 127, 129
    extended cognition style   76–87
    importance of   150–1
    non-derived content   32–5
Martians thought experiment   48–9
Maturana, H. R.   32
meaningful
    cognition in the   76–8
    making an object   43–4
meanings
    assigned   42
    derived   38–9, 42, 43
    intrinsic   35, 47–50
    semantic   34, 36–7, 42, 43, 44

mechanisms
    attentional   62, 75
    cognitive see cognitive mechanisms
    stimulus-driven   61
    taxonomy-by-   58–70
memory   28, 61, 150–1, 179
    depth of processing   65, 66–7,
        138–9
    episodic   73
    formation   63–5, 138
    free recall   63, 64–5, 137–9
    long-term   4, 62, 68, 73
    normal internal   23–4
    procedural   73
    scientific study of   122–3, 175
    short-term   3, 4, 9–10, 62–3, 68, 70,
        73
    see also Alzheimer's disease
Menary, R.   6, 13, 21, 26, 89, 91–2,
    101–5, 110
mental content/states   34, 46, 100,
    136
mental representations   9, 48, 61,
    142–3
mental rotation   119, 121, 142–3
Miller, G. A.   9–10, 63
    magic number   62, 68, 70, 140
Milner, D. A.   73
minds
    embodied   6, 8–9
    extended   50, 125, 145
    monadology   1, 5, 177
    see also brain
Mioche, L.   160
mirror neurons   33
Mishkin, M.   73
MIT   32, 54
Miura, S.   171
mobile robotics   2, 35, 51–4, 79, 80
monads/monadology   1, 5, 177
Mother Nature   45
motion blindness   162, 164

motion parallax   3–4, 5
movement (role)   3–4, 5
Müller–Lyer illusion   159
muscles   19, 68–9, 115
    see also neuromuscular blockade;
    neuromuscular junction
muscular cognition   19
muscular system, human   115
Museum of Modern Art (MOMA)   3,
    102, 105

natural selection   8, 27, 36–7, 41,
    42–3, 58–9, 149
naturalistic conditions   9, 35, 37, 55
naturalized semantics   31, 55
nerves   18–19
neural embodiment   107, 169, 177–8
neuromuscular blockade   169–72,
    173
neuromuscular junction   19, 149,
    169–70, 173
neurons   17, 18, 19, 36, 68–9, 84, 85,
    144
neuroscience   32, 36, 62, 70
New Way Things Work, The (Macaulay)
    131
Newell, A.   61
Noë, A.   3, 6, 20, 25–6, 27
    coupling-constitution fallacy   89,
    90, 94–5, 100, 104
    enactive perception   14, 152–69,
    171
nomological dependence   81–2
non-cognitive links   11, 85
    basics on   35–9
    Dennett's critique   39–46
    non-derived content   31, 32–5
    processes/mechanisms   4, 10, 23,
    57, 107
non-derived content   13, 31, 32–4,
    143, 146
    basics on   35–9

Clark's challenge   46–50
Dennett's critique   39–46
mental representations   9, 10, 55–6,
    60–1, 130
non-human cognition   30, 31, 32
nuclear fission   27, 94, 99, 101, 125

off-loading/offload   6, 21
ontogenic derivation   42, 43, 44
ontogeny   22, 42–3, 44
ontology (of the cognitive)   62
operationalism   79–83
optic ataxia   167–8
O'Regan, J. K.   154
original content see non-derived
    content
original intentionality   39–40, 41–2,
    44–6
orthodox view
    cognitive psychology   8, 12, 18, 31,
    141, 146
    cognitive science   1–2, 4, 8, 177
oscillator   59–60

paralysis   153, 166–72, 173
parathyroid hormone (PTH)   115–16,
    125
parentheses, cognitive   50, 55
parity principle   7, 27–8, 134, 145
pendulum example   108–11, 112
perceiving/perceptual processing   4, 5
perception   26, 27, 81, 94
    embodiment of   20, 155
    enactive see enactive perception
    perceptual abilities/experience   155–6
Perenin, M.   160
phenomenological embodiment   178
phenomenology   2, 59, 178
phenotypes   22
philosophy   2
photoreceptors   18–19, 69, 114
phylogenetic derivation   42, 43, 44

phylogeny   42, 43, 44
physical manipulation   5, 6
physical stance   45
physical substrate (of cognition)   16,
   25–6, 27, 89–90, 94, 99, 174, 176
physicalism   8, 16
picture theory of representation   37,
   40
plants   72, 79, 85
Poggendorf illusion   159
Port, R.   5, 20, 107
power
   causal   36
   law of learning   61
practice, memory formation and
   63–5, 138
prejudice   8, 85, 140
   Cartesian   9, 22, 141, 179
   skin-and-skull based   48
primacy effect   63, 68, 137–8, 139
principled basis/reason   12, 13, 22,
   140
principled difference   142
Prinz, J.   89, 99, 157
process types, individuating   58–60
processes
   attentional   62, 75
   biological   16
   chemical   16
   cognitive see
      cognitive processes/processing
   dynamical   23, 107–12
   extended cognitive see extended
      cognitive systems/processes
   meaning conferring   42
   muscular   19
   neuronal   17, 18, 19
   physical   16
promiscuity, computational   128,
   129
promiscuous theory   11, 24, 76, 86
punctuation marks, cognitive   50, 55

quadriplegia   169
quasi-syllogism   133

Ratliff, F.   165
real-values processes   61
realization   2, 6, 70, 89, 176
recency effect   63, 68, 137–8
receptor binding   62
recognition memory   63, 64–5,
   137–9
remembering, capacity for   4
representationalism   47
   challenges   35, 51–4
representations   78
   mental   9, 10, 55–6, 60–1,
      130, 142–3
   picture theory   37, 40
   rules and   47, 60–1, 174
retinal ganglion cells   18–19,
   69–70
retinally stabilized images   165–6
retinotopic map   70
rhymes (memory test)   66
Riggs, L. A.   165
Rizzolatti, G.   33
robot cognition   57
robot thought experiment   41, 42,
   44–5
robotics, mobile   2, 35, 51–4, 79,
   80
Rockwell, T.   1, 5, 6, 9, 18–19, 89, 90,
   92, 99, 101
rod system   18, 69, 71, 114, 165
Rosenbloom, P. S.   61
Rowlands, M.   3, 5–6, 8, 9, 14, 20,
   76–7, 81–3, 89, 90, 111, 125,
   147–50, 177
rules and representations   47, 60–1,
   174
Rupert, R.   10, 13, 24, 57, 89, 174,
   177
Rush Hour game   93

Sacks, O.   157, 159, 161
same functional role   134
San Jose task   80, 85, 96
Sandin, R.   172
satisfaction of conditions   38–9, 48
Schwender, D.   171
science
    individuating process types in
        58–60
    see also cognitive science
Searle, J.   34, 35–6, 40
Sekuler, R.   33
selection
    for   43
    natural   8, 27, 36–7, 41, 42–3, 58–9
Sellars, W.   123
semantic content/meanings   34, 36–7,
    42, 43, 44
semantically evaluable triggers   134
semantics, naturalized   31, 55
sense-datum theory   9
sensorimotor knowledge   153–4, 155,
    166–8
sensorimotor skills   8, 95, 100, 152,
    154–60, 162–70, 172
sensory nerves   18–19
sensory transduction   18–19, 69
Shapiro, L.   22
Sherman, S. M.   160
Shiffrin, R. M.   68
ship navigation   77
Simon, H.   116
single-cell recordings   32–3
skills, sensorimotor   8, 95, 100, 152,
    154–60, 162–70, 172
skin-and-skull boundaries   48, 126,
    142
Slamecka, N. J.   66
Smith, L.   135
Smith, S. M.   169
spacing effect (memory)   67, 139
Speaks, J.   34

Spear, P. D.   160
spinal cord   18, 19
stance
    design   45
    intentional   45–6
    physical   45
state-space   51–2
Stevens, J. K.   169
Stich, S.   33, 35
stimulus–response connection   61
Stratton, G. M.   163
"supermind"   77
supervenience   92, 99, 176
supervenience base   16, 68, 89, 112
survivorship argument   40, 41–6, 48
Susi, T.   21
Sutton, J.   70, 134, 145, 179
symbols   38–9, 42, 43, 44, 144
synonyms (memory test)   66
systems   14
    causal   1, 7, 10, 20, 44, 74, 126,
        176–7
    central nervous   18, 20, 22, 70, 89,
        107, 113–14
    circulatory   10–11
    cognitive see cognitive systems
    cooling   91, 117–18, 131, 146
    coupled   7, 89–90, 119–20
    definition   113
    heating   58, 73
    intelligibility   116–17, 126

taste   26, 27, 90, 94
taxonomy
    by-mechanisms   58–60
    in cognitive psychology   60–70
    in science   58–60
Tenet of Computational Promiscuity
    128, 129
test-study cycles   67
Tetris (game)   119, 135, 141–3
Thelen, E.   135

Thorndike, E. L.   61
thought experiments   25, 26, 123
    ducks   49
    Martians   48–9
    robot   41, 42, 44–5
    Tetris   119, 135, 141–3
    see also Inga–Otto thought
        experiment
tokening   43, 44
Topulos, G. P.   169, 170, 172
training   4
transcorporeal process   28
transcranial cognition   12, 14, 28, 60,
    62, 78, 94, 96, 98, 134, 135
transduction   18–19, 69
trust and glue, conditions of   121
trust conditions   120–5
Tulving, E.   65, 138
Turing-equivalent computations   61
"two visual systems" hypotheses   73
Tytla, M. E.   160

underived content see non-derived
    content
underived intentionality   39–40,
    41–2, 44–5, 46
Ungerleider, L. G.   73

van Gelder, T.   5, 14, 20, 51–2, 85–6,
    89, 92, 106, 107–8, 110, 112
vehicle externalism   125

Venn diagrams   48
Venus flytrap   52
Virgil (patient)   157, 159–60, 161
vision   57, 62, 68–70
    blindsight   121, 123–4
    color   71, 123, 162, 164, 178
    experiential blindness   158, 161–3,
        164, 169
    see also eyes
visual equivalence   75
visual fading   165–6, 173
visual processing   2, 62, 73, 75, 124,
    127, 156, 177–8
visual system   18–19, 32–3, 73,
    82–3
voltage-gated ion channels   62

Wallace, J. G.   157, 159, 161
Warfield, T.   33, 35
Weber's law   61
Weiskopf, D.   134
Wiesel, T.   33, 160
Wiles, A.   145
will/willing   38
Wilson, M.   10, 57
Wilson, R.   5, 6, 20, 26, 28, 89, 90,
    93–4, 125–9

Yerkes–Dodson law   61

Zölner illusion   159